The Archaeology of
Medieval England

The Archaeology of Medieval England

HELEN CLARKE

A COLONNADE BOOK

PUBLISHED BY BRITISH MUSEUM PUBLICATIONS

Colonnade Books
are published by British Museum Publications Ltd
and are offered as contributions to the enjoyment, study
and understanding of art, archaeology and history

The same publishers also produce the official
publications of the British Museum

Published by British Museum Publications Ltd,
46 Bloomsbury Street, London WC1B 3QQ.

British Library Cataloguing in Publication Data

  Clarke, Helen
    The archaeology of medieval England.—
    (A Colonnade book)
    1. England—Antiquities
    I. Title
    942   DA175
    ISBN 0–7141–8058–0

Designed by Sebastian Carter

Filmset in Monophoto Lasercomp Sabon by
Northumberland Press Ltd, Gateshead
and printed in Great Britain by
Fletcher & Son Ltd, Norwich

Contents

TO GILES AND ELLIS

Foreword

Firstly I should like to thank my family, colleagues and students for their patience and forbearance while this book was in preparation and for their encouragement which finally spurred me on to its completion. I should also like to express my gratitude to David Wilson who read the text while in manuscript, made many invaluable comments and criticisms and bore no ill-will when not all were adopted; to Celia Clear and her staff, particularly Jenny Chattington, who had the unenviable task of seeing the book through the press; to Peter E. Leach who drew the figures; and to Sheila Shaw and Anne Tafler who typed the manuscript with speed and accuracy.

Sutton, Surrey, June 1983.   HELEN CLARKE

1. The late fourteenth-century castle of Bodiam, Sussex, with its strongly defended gatehouse, round corner towers and access across the moat.

Introduction

Compared with many other branches of archaeology, the archaeological study of the Middle Ages in England is in its infancy. The foundation of the Society for Medieval Archaeology in 1956 first acknowledged its existence as a recognised subject in its own right, but it is only since the early 1970s that it has been taught as an academic discipline in British universities. In common with all 'new' subjects, the early years have been devoted to amassing information rather than to interpreting the evidence, and most of the many archaeological publications on medieval topics take the form of straightforward excavation reports which present excavated data, rather than synthetic analyses of the data as a whole. This book is offered as an attempt at a synthesis of at least some aspects of a subject whose complexity has increased with increasing knowledge. It does not set out to pile detail upon detail, but rather to present broad outlines of topics, to summarise what we know now and to suggest lines for future research.

The aim of the book is to present what we know about medieval England from archaeological, that is mainly excavated, evidence, not from the historical sources. As we are dealing with an historical period it would obviously be ridiculous to disregard the documentary evidence entirely, and it is brought into the discussion as a necessary background, but the emphasis throughout will fall on the material evidence for the period. The emphasis is also on those centuries which are variously called the Late Middle Ages or the High Middle Ages, roughly the period stretching from the Norman Conquest of 1066 to c. 1500 – the post-Conquest period. The years before the Conquest are not totally disregarded, though, for it is impossible to treat our main period of interest in a chronological vacuum. In the same way, although the theme of the work is the Middle Ages in England reference is occasionally made to other areas of the British Isles and Europe. Influences from all parts of the known world reached medieval England at one time or another and the country stood no more in a geographical vacuum than the period did in a chronological one.

Most of the evidence used in this book comes from recent archaeological excavations in this country. Many of these excavations have been briefly reported in the 'Medieval Britain' section of *Medieval Archaeology* and they are presented here in the form of maps which show the distribution of excavations in England over the past twenty-five years. The maps show that the distribution is by no means equal over the whole country, and there are biases in the information that has been retrieved for different areas and topics. The charts (figs 10, 37, 38, 56, 70, 84) have been compiled from the same source and show how the fashion in excavation has changed over the past decades. Clearly some topics have been favoured at the expense of others, and this is mentioned more than once in the body of the text. The changing fashion in excavation objectives has largely been the result of personal preferences on the part of individual excavators, and not of national policy. This has led to a number of obvious gaps and glaring omissions in our knowledge of medieval England from archaeological sources. The desirability of a national policy towards archaeological research and excavation is mentioned more than once in the following pages; it is a personal opinion with which many archaeologists would disagree, but it could hardly be more unsatisfactory than the piecemeal approach to excavation over the past couple of decades which has been forced upon the study of archaeology in general through the exigencies of 'rescue' excavation.

By far the vast majority of excavated sites described in this book have been dug as 'rescue' excavations (fig. 2), that is, in response to threatened redevelopment of areas mainly through house- and road-building or the employment of new agricultural techniques which are likely to destroy ground containing valuable archaeological information. Finance for most archaeological excavation comes from the public purse through the agency of the Ancient Monuments section of the Department of the Environment. For many years the distribution of funds has been confined to those sites threatened in the ways mentioned above, and in so far as there has been a national policy it has been one of financial constraints. For a heady period at the beginning of the 1970s virtually any 'rescue' site was given funds and the number of excavations increased in proportion (see figs 10, 37, 38, 56, 70, 84). But there appears to have been little co-ordination in the choice of sites to be dug and the result has been the proliferation of some types of site and the almost total disregard of others. The charts in this book show this all too clearly. There have been excavations on innumerable pottery kilns, almost none on total pottery-making complexes; other medieval industries have hardly been touched on. Medieval towns have profited from 'rescue' excavations; churches are only now being recognised as worthy of attention. The list is endless, and the consequences regrettable. In some fields we have so much recently excavated information that it is impossible to digest it; in others we have no information at all. The chapters in this book inevitably reflect this however much one might wish that they did not.

The time has surely now come for us to look dispassionately at the archaeological evidence for the Middle Ages, to discover where the gaps are and decide

2. A 'rescue' excavation on an urban site: Palace Plain, Norwich.

on methods of filling them. This leads to a problem-orientated approach which, although accepted by many archaeologists as the only rational means of capitalising on the information already to hand, remains a contentious subject. Some will follow the principle set out by Philip Barker[1] that 'the only valid questions to ask of a site are "What is there?" and "What is the whole sequence of events on this site from the beginnings of human activity to the present day?"' Others will maintain that we should erect hypotheses and test them through a strategy of sampling sites.[2] Before we can hope to achieve a national policy of research priorities in medieval archaeology we must try to resolve these fundamental differences.

Another method which is beginning to insinuate its way into medieval archaeology is that of the 'New Archaeology'. This theme and method of approach to the interpretation of archaeological data has been developed by prehistorians over the past couple of decades and has achieved some remarkable results through the comparative use of ethnographic and archaeological evidence. Its highly theoretical base has not so far been much favoured by medievalists largely, one suspects, because the written evidence for the period can be used in much the same way as ethnographic parallels are used to help in the interpretation of information about preliterate societies. Several recent articles have suggested ways in which 'New Archaeology' could be used in the interpretation of the medieval period,[3] and more than ten years ago Jope[4] set out his views on model-building in medieval studies, but despite these attempts medieval archaeology remains set in a 'traditional' mould. Certainly it is the traditional approach that is presented in this book.

The aim of the archaeologist studying the medieval period should be to present as complete a picture as possible of the life of the people at that time, drawing his information from the material remains that those people left behind them. Such remains may take many forms, from castles and abbeys to boots and shoes, and the sheer quantity of evidence of medieval man's activity preserved both above and below ground makes the assessment and synthesis of it a daunting task. The only way in which this mass of information can be assimilated and presented in an intelligible form is to break it down into topics, and this has been done here. It has also been done by archaeologists themselves in an attempt to further the study of the subject as a whole, for in addition to the Society for Medieval Archaeology there are now smaller individual 'topic' societies devoted to one particular aspect of medieval archaeology: villages, moated sites or ceramics, for example; and the Council for British Archaeology has set up working parties to deal with towns, churches and industry. The fragmentation of the subject has both advantages and disadvantages. It has certainly focused attention on particular aspects of medieval life and by doing so encouraged research and increased knowledge, but there is a danger that the individual topics may grow more important in the eyes of their enthusiasts than the subject as a whole and that the view of life in medieval England be biased too much in favour of one or other facet. It cannot be emphasised too strongly that the archaeology of medieval England should be treated as a whole and that the essentially interdependent nature of all the topics be constantly borne in mind. So although this book is divided into chapters under a number of different heads which broadly correspond to the interests of the topic societies mentioned above, the unitary nature of medieval archaeology should never be forgotten. More than once in the following pages the detailed study of a specific region is mentioned as the ideal method of approach to a particular problem, and there would be much to recommend this approach for the study of the archaeology of medieval England as a whole. Regional studies of all features of a medieval landscape have been attempted for a couple of areas (for example, Northamptonshire and West Yorkshire)[5] and stand as models of what can be achieved by such a method. Any future national policy of research into medieval archaeology could do worse than follow these examples.

Regional studies, though, do not figure significantly in the present work, which attempts to cover the country as a whole along the traditional lines. It has proved impossible to cover all aspects of medieval life which have been illuminated by archaeological excavation in recent years and the selection presented here is inevitably a personal one. Towns are discussed, but not the results of modern work by scientists into their environment;[6] there is a chapter on parish churches, but not on cathedrals;[7] the subject of rubbish disposal, perennially fascinating to archaeologists, has only been touched on. Many readers will find their favourite topic treated with scant regard. For this I make no apology. At this stage in the history of medieval archaeology one must be selective, and it is a personal selection that is offered here. The opportunities for research into individual aspects of medieval archaeology remain endless, the gaps in our knowledge are waiting to be filled. I hope that this book will serve to highlight those gaps as well as to illustrate that part of medieval life which we think we know already.

3. Castle Combe, Wiltshire: a late medieval cloth-making centre.

1. The Countryside

VILLAGES

The rural landscape of modern England preserves many features of its medieval past. These can most clearly be seen in what seem to be 'natural' features (parks, woodlands or field systems), in roads and bridges, in standing buildings such as castles or parish churches and in villages which today, as in the Middle Ages, form the centres of population in large areas of the country (fig. 3). Although the villages often preserve their basic medieval street pattern, with buildings grouped around a village green or strung out along either side of the main street for example, normally the only truly medieval building to survive is the parish church. Dwellings have been built, rebuilt and modified over the centuries and it is difficult to reconstruct the way of life of our medieval ancestors from a study of the standing remains alone. As we shall see, it is even difficult to be certain that village plans as we see them today are a true reflection of the village in medieval times, as buildings have often been rearranged quite drastically and whole villages removed and re-established elsewhere in the intervening years. Study of surviving villages and their architecture, therefore, can only give us partial information about the medieval countryside and, however contradictory it seems, the picture can only be filled out by the investigation of those villages which are no longer inhabited and which survive only as earthworks or even as crop-marks or soil-marks invisible except on photographs taken from the air.

These sites are the remains of villages which were occupied in the Middle Ages but which were abandoned and allowed to fall into decay before their medieval features were modified or obliterated by modern developments. Their importance as sources of information for medieval rural life was first realised at the end of the 1940s by W. G. Hoskins, whose publications such as *The Making of the English Landscape* (1955) were to be so influential on the historians', geographers' and archaeologists' view of the development of the English countryside, and by M. W. Beresford, who has remained the driving force behind research into deserted medieval villages and, with John Hurst, the Deserted Medieval Village Research

15

Group, founded in 1952. Although neither Hoskins nor Beresford was trained as an archaeologist, they realised that the sites which they were discovering could only yield information through a combination of historical study and archaeological investigation, and so they set in train a line of research which has become one of the major preoccupations of medieval archaeologists over the past thirty years. The archaeological excavation of deserted village sites has proved to be one of the most rewarding aspects of medieval archaeology, producing information about life in rural England in the Middle Ages which could not be extracted from surviving historical documentation alone. But at the same time the study of deserted medieval villages has provided a meeting point for archaeologists, historians and historical geographers, who have combined their individual and specific skills in a cross-disciplinary approach to a subject which is of common interest to all.

In 1971 the word 'Deserted' was dropped from the title of the Medieval Village Research Group. The group felt that by doing this it would emphasise its 'interest in all aspects of medieval settlement'[1] and would not rule out research into those villages that have medieval roots but are still inhabited today. Study of such villages involves topics such as vernacular architecture and post-medieval demography which cannot be included here, so this chapter will concentrate on *deserted* medieval villages which have been so well illustrated by archaeological investigation. Although it is certainly true that the thousands of villages still extant and flourishing can tell us something about medieval rural life, the roughly three thousand which survive only as earthworks can tell us more. After the village populations disappeared the villages remained, decayed, desolate and with their buildings often razed to the ground and surviving only as overgrown foundations at best, but essentially unchanged for generations. Each deserted village has fossilised its little part of the medieval landscape as it was when it was abandoned and can show us a part of the countryside unaffected by later modifications.

A number of general questions immediately come to mind about deserted villages. What constitutes a deserted village? Why were villages deserted and why are deserted villages common in some parts of the country and rare in others? These questions can best be answered from historical sources, so the documentary evidence and the views of historians will form most of the first part of this chapter. Then we shall move on to the more specific questions that can be asked of villages and which can, at least in part, be answered through archaeological excavation.

The answer to the first question is fairly straightforward. Deserted medieval villages are nucleated settlements which were founded, occupied or recorded in documents during the medieval period but which no longer exist. The Medieval Village Research Group and others have made a somewhat arbitrary distinction between two types of village. The first are sites which are totally deserted, that is those with no standing remains apart from perhaps a church, farm, manor house or fewer than three houses (fig. 4). The second are those which are 'shrunken', so that there is still an inhabited village nucleus which is surrounded by earthworks that indicate the remains of buildings long since abandoned and decayed. There is

4. Aerial view of the deserted medieval village of Goltho, Lincolnshire, from the east.
Although this site lies in an area of clay sub-soil it shows well-preserved traces of crofts,
roadways and a manor.

no fundamental difference between the two types and they will be dealt with here
under the general heading 'deserted'. About three thousand such sites have been
discovered through intensive fieldwork and other methods (pp. 24–6) and the
most recent distribution map to be published (of sites known up to 1977)[2] shows
them to be concentrated in the central Midlands, in parts of north-east England
and in Lincolnshire. To some extent their distribution reflects the amount of
fieldwork, which has been intensive in certain areas of the country and less so in
others. This is clearly shown by comparing the map of sites known up to 1966[3]
with the more recent publication. In 1966, for example, only one site was shown
in Shropshire and two in Cheshire, whereas fifteen and eleven respectively are
known today. In 1966 Staffordshire boasted only fifteen sites, in 1977 there were
over seventy, and Somerset shows a similar picture. The most spectacular increases
have occurred in the north-west, however, with Lancashire displaying no sites on
the 1966 map yet having thirty-one in 1977 and Cumberland with eight in 1966 and

fifty-one today. Despite these modifications which are clearly the result of the Research Group's efforts, the pattern of distribution remains essentially unchanged, with the heaviest concentrations of known deserted village sites still in the same areas as before. This goes a long way towards substantiating the initial theory put forward as early as 1954[4] that the most dense concentrations of deserted settlements lay in the areas of heavier clay-lands which were densely populated in the Middle Ages and where nucleated settlements and arable farming were the norm. It must be emphasised and always borne in mind that what we are looking at and dealing with here are *deserted* villages which for one reason or another failed to remain viable throughout the centuries; for a more accurate idea of the density of population in the medieval countryside their distribution must be supplemented by that of the many thousands of villages which succeeded in maintaining themselves as living units not only through the Middle Ages but up to the present day.[5] The study of deserted sites can be seen perhaps as the study of failure, and it may not give us a truer picture of the vitality of medieval rural England than would a study confined to surviving villages. The Medieval Village Research Group acknowledged this when it changed its name.

The areas which appear as blanks on the distribution map are not necessarily places without population or settlements in the Middle Ages. Rather, they are areas where circumstances enabled settlements to survive. They may be regions such as the Fenland, where a mixed farming economy allowed the villages to escape the worst effects of medieval depopulation, or moorland and forest areas, where isolated farmsteads rather than nucleated villages were the usual settlement-pattern and so where village desertion could not, in the nature of things, be a problem to be reflected in modern distribution maps.

The reasons why villages were deserted in the Middle Ages have fascinated archaeologists, historians and historical geographers since deserted villages were first discussed by modern scholars and they are still the subject of controversy today. Historical rather than archaeological research has done more to produce explanations for village failure and it is mainly the historical factors which will be discussed in the following pages, although those excavations which have indicated reasons for the desertion of individual villages will also be mentioned.

The depopulation and abandonment of villages in the Middle Ages was not confined to England, and many examples of deserted villages are known from the Continent, where the phenomenon has been particularly studied in Germany.[6] Continental desertions are generally considered to be the result of overall population decrease or declining grain prices and consequent lack of profits from arable farming at the beginning of the fourteenth century,[7] or the deliberate regrouping of populations by the great landowners, who sometimes forced wholesale migrations into neighbouring towns.[8] Research has shown that village desertions in England cannot always be explained in such black-and-white terms, and a number of complex and interacting reasons have been discovered in addition to those which superficially appear straightforward and simple. One of the complicating factors in the English desertions is that villages were seldom depopulated totally at any given time, but rather went into a period of decline which only culminated in total desertion after perhaps two centuries of steadily decreasing size.

In England there appear to have been several main periods in the Middle Ages which saw village desertion. The first of these (in the eleventh and twelfth centuries) quite closely parallels the Continental model, and one can argue for abrupt and total desertion, but the second (fourteenth and fifteenth centuries) displays much more complex features than those of the earlier phase.

At the end of the eleventh century and the beginning of the twelfth the newly arrived Norman kings established their rights over the country by building castles (either in their own name or through their nobles) and founding royal forests. Most of the larger and royal castles were founded in existing urban centres and there are examples of mottes being erected on land previously occupied by burgage plots (for example Oxford or Lincoln), but there is some slight evidence of this also happening in the countryside, at Eaton Socon, for example, where late Saxon buildings have been discovered and excavated beneath the bank of the castle built by Hugh de Beauchamp in the early twelfth century.[9] The establishment of royal forests demanded large areas of unpopulated land which would be subject to 'forest law'; in the New Forest, for example, villages were depopulated for this reason and never reinstated.[10]

King William's infamous 'Harrying of the North' in 1069 – 71 in response to an abortive uprising against Norman domination must also have been responsible for the desertion of innumerable villages as far south as the Humber. Judging from historical sources,[11] the peasant population of northern England was virtually wiped out by William's brutal reprisals and had hardly replaced itself by the end of the Middle Ages. Many villages destroyed by the Norman troops, therefore, remain only as earthworks in the fields of the north-east.

In the twelfth century the foundation of monastic houses also led to depopulation. The rule of the Cistercian order (p. 99) demanded that their monastic houses and granges should be founded in depopulated places, and in some cases this led to village populations being transported wholesale to other areas. At Pipewell, Northamptonshire, for instance, the foundation of a Cistercian house in 1143 led to the destruction of a village,[12] and the village of Osmerley, Worcestershire was removed by the Cistercians of Bordesley Abbey, about 1140.[13]

Well-attested desertions such as these give a firm final date for the abandonment of the village and as such would be an ideal excavation objective, where the excavated evidence could be dated independently by documentation. Unfortunately, the sites which have been excavated so far seldom fall into this category but generally seem to belong to periods of desertion where no precise final date can be given. It will be seen below that the villages which have been excavated seem mainly to have been depopulated sometime during the late thirteenth to fifteenth centuries and that there is seldom sufficient evidence to suggest that there was ever a total desertion at any given time. As mentioned above, desertion very often seems to have been a piecemeal affair, with individual buildings and plots being abandoned at different times so that the village underwent a period of 'shrinkage' before the entire settlement was depopulated and left to decay. Declining population, climatic deterioration, natural disasters and wars are some of the explanations put forward for the desertion of villages from the late thirteenth century until the end of the Middle Ages, and it is to those that we must turn.

In England, as on the Continent, the thirteenth century saw the medieval population at its peak with an estimated five to six million people in the country before the end of that century.[14] Calculations of the size of the population are notoriously difficult, based as they must be on records which have either survived only partially or contain insufficient data (e.g. Domesday Book, poll tax returns), but it seems probable that by the second half of the fourteenth century the population stood at roughly three million. This drastic and rapid decline was due to economic pressures at the turn of the thirteenth century, exacerbated by agricultural failures early in the fourteenth century and, of course, culminating in the Black Death of 1348 – 9 and its recurrences in 1360 – 2, 1369 and 1375.

The rapid increase in population during the thirteenth century led to the foundation of many new settlements, very often on so-called 'marginal land', that is, land which could be cultivated to yield an arable crop sufficient to keep the cultivators above subsistence level as long as climatic conditions were right, the soil was kept well fertilised and there was a sufficient labour force to work it. Once any of these essential conditions were removed the land could no longer be persuaded to yield even subsistence crops to support the population. Famine and dearth would be the result, with consequent disastrous effects on a peasant people already living close to the bread-line and often unable to move to better-favoured areas because of the nature of their tenancy. Decreasing life-expectancy and increasing infant mortality are recorded from the end of the thirteenth century, when crop yields already seem to have been falling, and the well-attested failure of harvests and fatal animal diseases of the second decade of the fourteenth century further debilitated an already failing population.

The crop failure and animal diseases of the time may be attributed at least in part to the progressive deterioration of the climate which is described both in contemporary records and in modern scientific research.[15] We read of floods and droughts, fluctuating mild and severe winters, torrential rain at harvest time, and so on, all symptoms of a move away from the climatic optimum of AD 1000 – 1200. Such conditions need not in themselves be disastrous to an economy or population, but taken together with an already hard-pressed peasantry living at the edge of subsistence on land which needed optimum conditions and much attention, and where the technological improvements in arable farming and animal husbandry which might have saved the situation were beyond the skill or resources of the rural population, they proved too much for a large proportion of the population, which by the time of the Black Death was ready to be decimated by a much less potent epidemic.

The marginal lands which suffered most from the declining conditions and which were the most densely populated were largely the heavy clay-lands of the Midlands, whose soils could be reduced to impermeable clay under a regime of alternating drought and flood. These were the areas where the agricultural economy was based on crop-raising in extensive open fields (p. 44) and where the population lived in nucleated villages surrounded by their fields, each village on average no more than a mile from its neighbour. With the onset of unfavourable conditions the village populations began to decline and the smaller villages on the poorer land suffered accentuated population loss through the voluntary migration of peasants to larger and more flourishing villages nearby. By 1341 the tax record *Nonarum Inquisitiones*[16] noted soil infertility and bad weather as the main reasons for so many villages failing to pay their taxes. This shows that even before the Black Death many villages were finding themselves in dire straits and some had by then become depopulated.

Such were the causes leading to some village desertions in the fourteenth century, but the same factors also had much longer-term effects which did not truly show themselves until a century later. A survey of eighty-two known deserted settlements in Northamptonshire published in 1966 shows that although 17% were abandoned in the late fourteenth or early fifteenth centuries, the majority (60%) were not depopulated until the second half of the fifteenth century.[17] The causes of these desertions at the end of the Middle Ages can be traced back to the events mentioned above, the large-scale desertions of the later period probably being the culmination of a decline which had already set in by the beginning of the fourteenth century. This decline may have been accentuated by the 'enclosure movement' of the late fifteenth century, when what had previously been arable land was converted into sheep-runs for economic reasons. A declining population led to a decrease in the labour force and a consequent rise in wages. This, together with the low prices paid for grain and an increasing demand for wool, led landlords to turn from labour-intensive arable production to sheep-farming, where the financial returns were better and the number of labourers needed was small. Until recently the argument has been that landowners (usually the local lords of the manor who owned both village and surrounding fields) turned the arable fields into pasture and deliberately depopulated the villages, forcing the peasant population whom, as tenants, they controlled absolutely, to migrate, normally to neighbouring towns, where they swelled the numbers of the urban poor.[18] But this explanation seems to be an over-simplification of the desertions which undoubtedly did occur in the latter half of the fifteenth century. Evidence is now coming forward from both historical and archaeological sources to show that even if a village were deserted, its population did not necessarily migrate wholesale, but may have become dispersed into isolated farmsteads in the surrounding countryside, each farming the land immediately surrounding them, using it for animal pasture rather than crop-raising. This seems to have happened in the fifteenth and sixteenth centuries at the excavated village of Caldecote, Hertfordshire.[19] The numbers of peasants with freehold land in villages also increased in the later Middle Ages, so the local lords would have found it difficult to eject entire populations in a single action. In Northumberland, for example, many villages were controlled by a single landlord and as a result suffered drastic changes;[20] elsewhere the system was different and the pattern of depopulation consequently took more diverse forms.

Why then did the late medieval village suffer from the decline which it undoubtedly did? There can be no simple and single answer to this. Recent work in the West Midlands[21] has led to the conclusion that a number of factors were at work which led to widespread desertions during the period 1320 – 1520. These included the nationwide decline in population, the tendency of peasant families to move (voluntarily) from one village to another, a breakdown in the authority of landlords who could have prevented migration (as they often did at the beginning of the fifteenth century, for instance, by rebuilding or repairing village houses which had fallen into decay) and a change in land-use, mainly from arable to pasture. The attribution of late fifteenth-century desertions solely to the change from arable to pasture, therefore, can no longer be maintained for the West Midlands, and similar studies in other regions of England would be invaluable for elucidating this problem elsewhere.

The causes which led to the desertion of villages, therefore, are complex and largely the preserve of the historian, but although archaeological evidence for the desertion is less easy to discover, one of the possible causes mentioned above can be reflected in the excavated evidence and has consequently been emphasised by archaeologists: that is the influence of climatic change on village development and eventual desertion. The subject is a contentious one, and many words have been expended on it, not only in discussions about medieval villages but also about the origin and development of moated sites, where increased rainfall and the need for improved drainage have often been held to be the dominant motives for their construction (below p. 56). The question in relation to villages has come particularly to the fore in recent years with Guy Beresford's excavations at Goltho and Barton Blount, but is by no means new and has been discussed by archaeologists since the earliest years of medieval village excavation. There is by now quite a formidable body of evidence from excavated sites to support the view that their plans were modified and in some cases they were totally deserted as a result of increasing precipitation and declining temperatures in the fourteenth and fifteenth centuries. Very often this has been put forward as the sole reason why a particular settlement was deserted, and it is worth bearing in mind that historians consider such a view to be much too simple. A most salutary warning to this effect was sounded by Susan Wright[22] in her discussion of the desertion of Barton Blount. She contests the excavator's suggestion that deteriorating climate was the single main reason for the depopulation of the village and convincingly argues for a much more subtle approach to the problem.

Nevertheless, there seems little doubt that some medieval villages did accommodate themselves to a deteriorating climate towards the end of their existence.

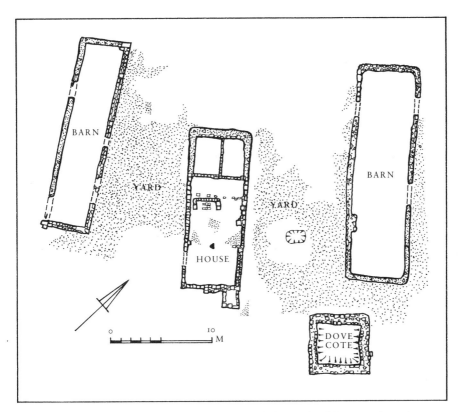

5. Croft C, Caldecote, Hertfordshire. Chalk foundations of a late medieval farm complex with cobbled yards.   After *Med. Archaeol.* 1974

Peasant houses seem to have been adapted to deal with a wetter climate by increasing the amount of paving around them (as at Caldecote, Hertfordshire; fig. 5), by deepening the ditches which surrounded the crofts and even in some cases constructing elaborate drains within the houses themselves. In the south-west of England the construction of raised earth platforms on which the houses were built (so-called 'platform houses', as at Garrow Tor, Cornwall)[23] is attributed to progressive waterlogging of the settlement and surrounding fields which eventually led to the abandonment of the village in the fifteenth century; and similar reasons are put forward for the desertion of settlements on Dartmoor (where, however, 'platform houses' are not known).

One of the problems about drawing direct connections between climatic deterioration and village desertion is that the precise dating of both phenomena is difficult and therefore the relationship must remain uncertain. Another point which is often brought up in discussion about the effects of climate is that one must in some way explain away the fact that neighbouring villages show differential patterns, with one village deserted by the end of the Middle Ages and the other still flourishing today. Guy Beresford, the most forceful propagandist for the climatic deterioration school of thought, maintains that differing qualities of soil could account for this; clay soils in particular may vary from field to field let alone village to village and therefore one village may well have suffered from adverse weather conditions considerably more than did others in the vicinity.[24] Furthermore, it has often been noted that it was generally the smaller and poorer villages that were deserted in the Middle Ages, so a combination of the two factors could quite easily explain apparent differential desertion within regions. It is most probable, though, that climatic deterioration was only one of the factors which finally tipped the balance in favour of desertion and abandonment. It is one factor which can be established archaeologically; the other reasons, based largely on historical evidence and summarised above (pp. 19–22) must also be taken into account before a convincing explanation for the desertion of any specific site can be advanced.

It is not only in finding evidence for the causes of village desertion in the Middle Ages that the historian has a crucial role to play, but also in the discovery of the villages themselves, for it is mainly by painstaking research into documentary sources that the sites of deserted villages have been traced. For the past thirty years the Medieval Village Research Group has co-ordinated this research, and there have been a number of archaeological publications dealing with the discovery of sites through documentary sources[25] or through early maps such as the 1444 map of Boarstall, Buckinghamshire (fig. 6)[26] or late sixteenth-century estate maps.[27] The rewards can be great, but there are many difficulties inherent in the interpretation of historical documents of which any archaeologist making use of them needs to be aware. Similar cautionary words occur elsewhere in this book: co-operation between archaeologist and historian is the ideal way of studying subjects where both disciplines meet, and the study of deserted medieval villages is one area of research which illustrates the advantages of a cross-disciplinary approach. As we shall see, many specialists have been and still are involved in this work. Certainly, archaeological excavation is but one method of approach to a fascinating subject.

Archaeological methods of locating the sites of deserted villages include the study of aerial photographs, which can show either earthworks which may also be seen as slight undulations in the ground surface (fig. 7) or the traces of settlement remains in the form of crop- or soil-marks, which often are not visible from ground level. A ruined church standing apparently isolated in the fields can also pin-point the presence of a settlement of which it once formed a part, and even a church still in use can indicate areas of settlement which were inhabited in the Middle Ages but are now no more than open spaces. The intensive study of Launditch Hundred, Norfolk, for example, has shown that some of the churches in that Hundred which lie today a little apart from the modern centre of population were actually in the middle of their respective villages in the Middle Ages.[28] So a deserted medieval village may lie cheek-by-jowl with its modern successor; in this instance the village

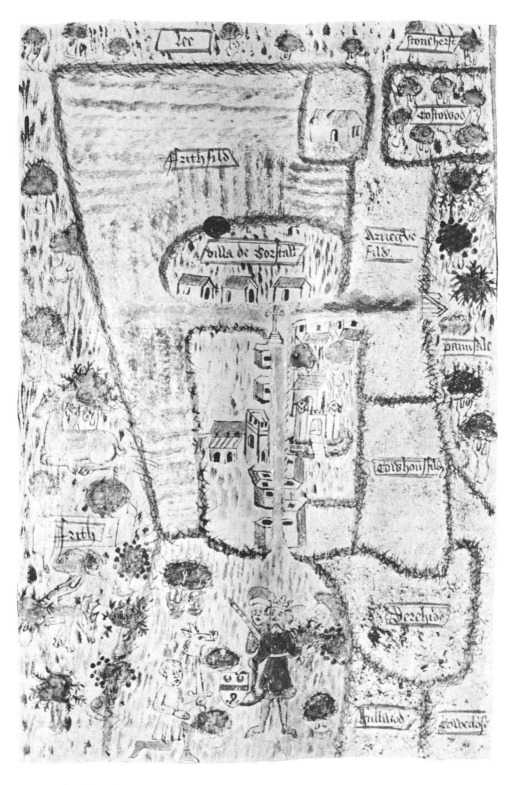

6. The village of Boarstall, Buckinghamshire, as portrayed in a map of 1444, bound in the Boarstall Cartulary. The church, moated manor, peasant houses and fields are all clearly depicted.

7. Aerial view of the deserted medieval village of Olney Grounds, Buckinghamshire, showing the earthworks of the village lying in the midst of its fields.

has not been depopulated during the Middle Ages, it has moved its position. There are instances of villages changing their sites as many as three times during the late Saxon and medieval periods;[29] with each move they left behind them traces which can be discovered today by methods such as fieldwalking (which was the way in which Wade-Martins made his important discoveries in Norfolk) and the examination of maps and aerial photographs. Excavation is a late stage in the investigation of medieval villages, the culmination of the methods of discovery mentioned above.

Even without excavation the earthworks of a well-preserved deserted village can give a good idea of its lay-out at the time of its desertion. As over three thousand deserted medieval villages are known, it will always be impossible to excavate more than a very small proportion of them, and even sites threatened by total destruction through modern development can at best be excavated in a very small way. Many such sites cannot even be sampled archaeologically on a small scale, and the best that can be hoped for is that a detailed survey of the earthworks can be carried out before they are destroyed. In some parts of the country, notably those regions with easily accessible building-stone for use in the construction of dwellings, field walls and so on, a detailed survey can be most revealing. The plan of the village with its streets, building plots and even its houses can easily be seen (as, for example, at Upton, Gloucestershire, fig. 8) and often the boundaries between village and surrounding fields and the trackways leading into them are also visible. The plans produced by the surveys can be extremely vivid and one may well wonder whether any more information could be produced by excavation. It is worth bearing in mind, therefore, that, however detailed, a surveyor's plan can only record what is visible on the ground at the time of the survey, and so can only indicate what the village may have looked like in its final phase of occupation. Excavations have shown that the plans of villages often changed quite radically during the course of their existence and that the final arrangement of streets and

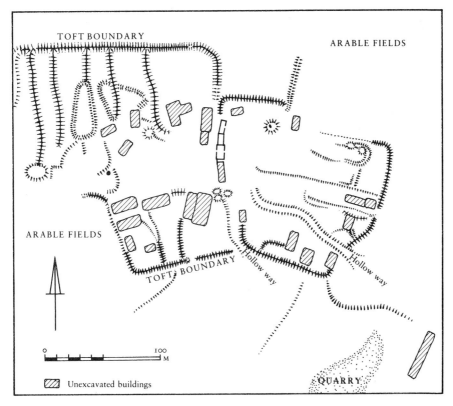

8. Field survey of the deserted medieval village of Upton, Gloucestershire. The plan of this stone subsoil settlement can clearly be seen even without excavation.   After Hilton and Rahtz 1966

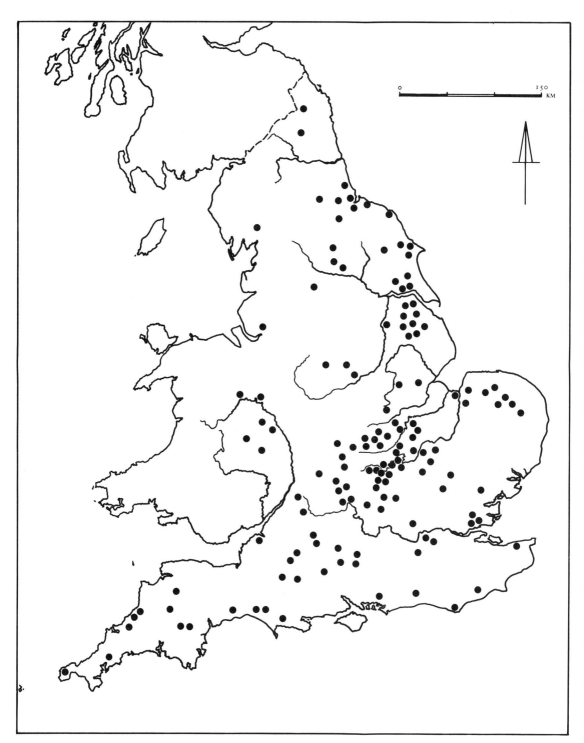

9. Distribution map of excavations of deserted medieval villages 1956–80. Compiled from the 'Medieval Britain' section of *Med. Archaeol.*

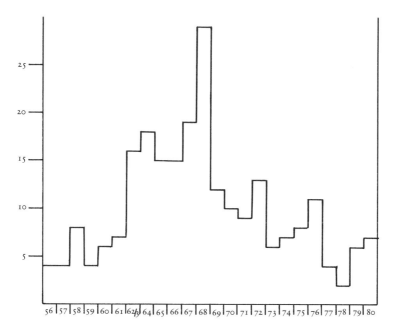

10. Chart showing the number of excavations per year on deserted medieval village sites 1956–80. Compiled from the 'Medieval Britain' section of *Med. Archaeol.*

buildings may bear little if any resemblance to that of earlier years. Field surveys, therefore, are useful but by no means an alternative to excavation for discovering the total history of a village.

Deserted medieval villages have been one of the most popular excavation objectives in the past decades. About 150 different excavations have been recorded in the 'Medieval Britain' section of *Medieval Archaeology* 1956 – 80, and in the Reports of the *Medieval Village Research Group* (fig. 9). The 1960s was the decade with the greatest number of excavations with a maximum of 29 sites being reported in 1968 (fig. 10). The number of excavations dropped radically from 1970, largely as a result of the increasing emphasis on urban excavation during the 1970s (p. 169). Most of the excavations have been of a 'rescue' nature and many of them were of very limited scope and short duration. In many cases the information which was obtained was of only marginal interest, but the larger-scale excavations (for example at Hangleton, Sussex; Gomeldon, Wiltshire; West Whelpington, North-

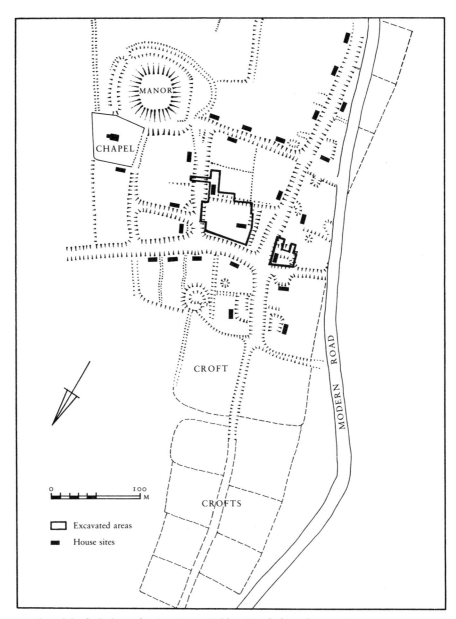

11. Plan of the final phase of occupation at Goltho, Lincolnshire, showing the arrangement of peasant houses within the crofts and the lay-out of crofts in relation to the streets. The excavated areas are denoted by heavy outlines.   After G. Beresford 1975

umberland; Goltho, Lincolnshire; and Barton Blount, Derbyshire) have shed much light on the history of the medieval village and most examples here will be drawn from these. But by far the most important contribution to this subject has been made by the excavations at Wharram Percy, Yorkshire, begun by Maurice Beresford on a small scale in 1950 and still continuing under his and John Hurst's direction. Excavation there is entirely research-orientated and the site is the only one funded by the Department of the Environment on that basis. Work at Wharram Percy has been the inspiration for all other medieval village excavations over the past three decades and will undoubtedly remain so in the forseeable future. It pioneered the 'open-area' method of excavation which was unknown in England in the 1950s, although practised on the Continent,[30] and has also been instrumental in changing the emphasis of village excavation from a detailed but myopic obsession with house-types to a much more wide-ranging attempt to fit the village into its context and to regard it as just one manifestation of a constantly changing pattern of land-use and occupation throughout the ages. As Taylor says: 'The work at Wharram is now conceptually far removed from the collection of low earthworks which first attracted scholars to the site.'[31] By setting a lead in this respect, the excavators of Wharram Percy have influenced the whole of medieval village research throughout the country.

Before this recent change in attitude towards the place of the deserted medieval village in the English landscape, excavation objectives tended to favour the elucidation of a certain specific aspect of the medieval village, notably the individual house and the enclosure in which it stood. The acquisition of information rather than its application to wider issues is inevitable during the initial stages of any subject, and this was certainly true when the study of the medieval village was in its infancy during the 1950s and 1960s. Concentration on the excavation of the peasant house, often to the exclusion of even its immediate surroundings, led to a much better understanding of this form of dwelling, none of which has survived to the present day as a standing structure, but did not contribute very much to the subjects which are likely to preoccupy the archaeologist of today. A growing interest in social, economic and environmental questions, for example, has left its mark on medieval village studies in the form of discussions of changing village plans (and even their sites), village economy, climatic influences on village development and so on. The remaining pages of this section will be devoted to some of these problems.

A 'typical' medieval village such as that illustrated in fig. 11 consisted of a street or green around which were arranged, usually in quite an orderly fashion, the tofts and crofts of the medieval peasants. The same type of arrangement but with modifications can often still be traced in modern villages. The toft was a small rectilinear enclosure which contained a dwelling and associated outbuildings; the croft was the continuation of the enclosure, usually extending as far as a boundary bank which cut the village off from the surrounding fields. Each croft was encircled by bank, ditch, fence or wall which may sometimes still be seen as an earthwork, depending on the building materials used and the state of preservation of the site.

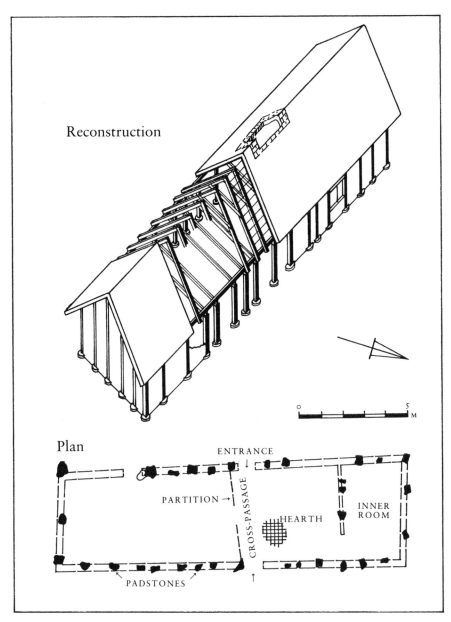

Reconstruction

Plan

ENTRANCE

PARTITION →

CROSS-PASSAGE

HEARTH

INNER ROOM

PADSTONES

12. Plan and reconstruction of House 18, Croft C, Goltho, showing the division into rooms and the use of timber framing for the walls with padstones supporting the uprights.　After G. Beresford 1975

The interior of the toft may be slightly raised above its surroundings, either deliberately or as a result of debris from ditch-cleaning being spread over it. In stone-subsoil sites the remains of buildings can often be distinguished quite clearly even before excavation; they show up as usually rectangular earthworks often lying beside the front or street-side of the toft. In addition there may be the earthworks of a manor house (sometimes moated, p. 49), a parsonage and perhaps the still upstanding ruins of a church. In some cases, as mentioned above, the church may be intact and still in use. Examples of all these buildings have been excavated at one site or another (in the case of Wharram Percy all the features mentioned, plus additional structures such as a water-mill and the boundary banks and streets, have been investigated), but by far the most work has been expended on the excavation of the peasant house in its toft.

As early as 1961 John Hurst gave a seminal lecture on the types of houses found on deserted medieval villages in which he distinguished three basic forms: the cot, the long-house and the farm.[32] The cot was the dwelling of the poorest members of the peasant community, the cottars or bordars, who seldom had rights of cultivation of strips in the open fields and who owned no draught animals. Their livelihood was largely based on what they could raise in their crofts and the wages which they might earn by working as agricultural labourers for wealthier peasants or, more frequently, for the lords of the manor, who owned the fields and the villages themselves. Such poor peasants formed a high proportion of village populations in the Middle Ages, particularly in the thirteenth century, when the population increase over the country as a whole led to a shortage of land and a consequent increase in landless families.[33]

A number of peasant cots have been excavated in deserted medieval villages, for example at Goltho and Barton Blount.[34] In common with the other peasant dwellings from medieval villages they were rectangular in shape with a maximum width of 5m. They were no longer than 10m, though, and had either one or two rooms. Unlike the long-houses described below, there was no space for keeping cattle or agricultural produce. Study of documents relating to peasant houses in Worcestershire[35] has shown that the smallest, one-bay, houses belonging to the poorest class of society were commonplace, and can be equated with the excavated cots found in deserted villages.

Richer peasants or villeins occupied slightly larger buildings, known to us as long-houses, which were rectangular in ground-plan, but divided by a cross-passage running between opposing doorways in the long walls into dwelling-quarters and byre or store-room (fig. 12). Byres for cattle are found in those areas of the country (the south-west or the north) where mixed farming was the basis of the medieval economy. In places where arable farming was the rule (the Midlands and East Anglia, for instance) the byre was replaced by a store-room, probably for keeping crops and seed corn, or was even used for some type of industrial process, as at Upton, Gloucestershire, where the lower room in one excavated long-house may have been used for fulling and finishing cloth.[36] Long-houses could be anything up to 30m in length, but still maintained a maximum width of about 5m because of the method of roofing and the availability of suitable timber for it. Across the passage from the byre or store-room there was a living-room with a hearth and beyond that, beside the gable, a small 'inner room', which may have been intended to give a modicum of privacy to the elders in an otherwise essentially communal existence.

The villeins who occupied these three-roomed houses had rights of cultivation of strips in the common fields and either owned or had access to draught animals and ploughs. They were seldom free men, however, and both land and buildings belonged to the lord, who often exacted compulsory labour from them on the manorial fields. Technically they, like the cottars, were bound to the land and could not move from their village without the lord's consent but, as mentioned earlier, migrations from villages did become more common in the later Middle Ages. It was also possible for a villein to buy his freedom if he wished, but this does not seem to have been a common occurrence. After the disasters of the fourteenth century and the steep drop in population free tenants became more common, and the resultant increase in mobility of the rural population has been cited as one of the causes of village desertions towards the end of the Middle Ages (pp. 21–2).

The events of the fourteenth century were also partly responsible for the development of the third type of peasant dwelling known from excavation: the farm. This was the property of the richest peasants who cultivated the greatest number of strips in the open fields and had acquired the largest areas of living space in the villages. In the farms the dwelling-quarters and byre or store-room became separated into two distinct buildings, which were usually arranged at right-angles around two sides of a yard. This development seems to have been the result either of the growing prosperity of individual families or of declining population, with the consequent increase in the number of unoccupied properties, whereby the tofts and crofts originally occupied by a number of families could be absorbed into a single property and the farm buildings spread over them. The clearest example of the development of a farm complex out of what was originally a long-house arrangement can be seen at Gomeldon, Wiltshire,[37] where by the fourteenth century there was a single farm standing on ground occupied by long-houses in the twelfth and thirteenth centuries (fig. 13), and at Hangleton, Sussex,[38] where a single farm was laid out in the fifteenth century on land which had previously been split up into several different tofts (fig. 16). The change from long-house to farm cannot be taken as a chronological indicator, as some farms had developed by the fourteenth century, whereas in many cases long-houses remained in occupation throughout the lifetime of the village. The transformation is more likely to indicate growing prosperity and perhaps enhanced social status, although a change in agricultural practice rather than prosperity is argued for at Goltho and Barton Blount. The peasant farms in medieval villages may in some instance have been the homes of those peasants who were rich enough to buy their freedom from their lords and become both freemen and freeholders.

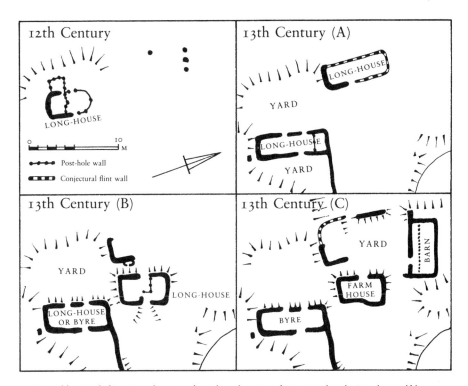

12th Century	13th Century (A)
LONG-HOUSE	LONG-HOUSE
0 ... 10 M	YARD
•••• Post-hole wall	LONG-HOUSE
▪▪▪ Conjectural flint wall	YARD
13th Century (B)	13th Century (C)
YARD	YARD
LONG-HOUSE	BARN
LONG-HOUSE OR BYRE	FARM HOUSE
	BYRE

13. Gomeldon, Wiltshire. Development from long-house to farm complex during the twelfth and thirteenth centuries.   After *Med. Archaeol.* 1966

As none of the peasant house-types described above have survived intact and unmodified as standing buildings into modern times[39] our knowledge of their forms, construction and appearance has to depend on what can be culled from contemporary descriptions and from excavation. Written evidence for the peasant house is slight, but Field's work on manorial court rolls for Worcestershire of the second half of the fourteenth and the fifteenth centuries shows that a good deal of information can be extracted from those documents which do survive.[40] The peasant houses are not described in detail, but the agreements between landlords and tenants for the building or rebuilding of dwellings allow inferences to be made about the methods of construction and the materials used. In Worcestershire most fourteenth- and fifteenth-century rural buildings seem to have been constructed of timber, largely of oak for the load-bearing posts and rafters, and wattle-and-daub for the infilling panels. Cruck construction (fig. 14)[41] seems to have been favoured in that part of England at that time, but box-framed buildings (fig. 12) were also built. All the buildings discussed by Field seem generally to have been of a single

35

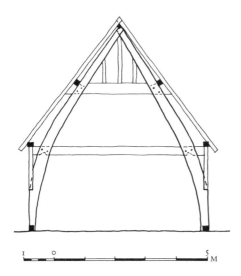

14. Cross-section of a house built in cruck construction.

storey, open to a roof which was thatched with straw. They varied greatly in size from one to five bays in length (a bay being the distance between two principal load-bearing wall-posts); the single-bay houses must have been the equivalent of the peasant cot, those between three and five bays in length probably being the dwellings of richer tenants, or even in some cases the houses of manorial officials. The houses were often divided into rooms, and it was not uncommon for one end of the house to be used for livestock (that is, a long-house as described above from archaeological evidence; see pp. 33–4). The farm complex also occurs, where dwelling and byre are separated as in the classic archaeological definition (p. 34). Field's study is a regional one and differences may emerge elsewhere when similar studies are applied to other areas, but it is reassuring to note the close similarities between the historical and archaeological picture of the medieval peasant house as illustrated by the Worcestershire examples. Unfortunately, other parts of England have not yet been as well served by historical research, and we must turn to purely archaeological evidence for knowledge of the medieval peasant house in England as a whole.

The map in fig. 9 shows that there have been excavations in medieval villages over most of the country, although there are concentrations in the East Midlands, Lincolnshire and East Anglia. One of the interesting facts to emerge from these excavations is that the long-house, with or without byre, was a ubiquitous type and may well be regarded as the 'normal' peasant house of the Middle Ages. Until this was discovered by medieval village excavation the long-house was regarded as an essentially 'Celtic' type of house,[42] as buildings with division into dwelling and animal quarters have been preserved in the western areas of the British Isles up to the present day. Extant examples are not of medieval date, being largely of nineteenth-century construction, but they are of a long-lived form which probably has its roots in the Middle Ages, and the tradition of such buildings has lived on in those areas where the pastoral farming economy encouraged it to do so. In the rest of the country the form died out by the middle of the sixteenth century with the changing economy of the post-medieval period and is now unknown except from excavated evidence. The methods and materials used in the construction of these buildings in the Middle Ages have also been revealed by archaeological excavation and, apart from some slight regional differences resulting from the availability of local building materials, show a surprisingly uniform pattern.

Throughout England until the thirteenth century the medieval peasant house was built mainly of timber, with no stone incorporated into its structure. Stout timber uprights were embedded in the subsoil (in 'post-holes') to support both walls and roof. Either the spaces between the posts were filled with panels of wattle-and-daub, or the posts themselves may, as at Goltho, have been encased in clay, which formed the walls and also protected the timbers from rotting. In many excavated examples the alignment of the wall-posts is somewhat irregular and the walls that they supported may have been straightened up by the thick clay that surrounded the posts. This would enable a straight line to be achieved at the top of the posts where the ends of the rafters could lie. In the south-west of England turf was used to build walls which did not need reinforcing with posts and which were sturdy enough to support the rafters. The inner faces of turf walls were often lined with wattle, which leaves traces in the form of rows of small stake-holes, as at Hound Tor and Hutholes, Devon.[43] As we shall see later, this type of construction had a long history, extending in some cases as far back as the seventh or eighth century, but in common with most of the rest of England the tradition was abandoned in the thirteenth century when stone began to be used in the construction of peasant houses.

During the thirteenth century stone began to be used as a building material in many parts of England, both in villages and in towns. In the areas where stone was abundant (the south-west, and the chalk and limestone belt from central southern England to Yorkshire) peasant houses began to be built with usually unmortared stone walls, sometimes to their full height of probably about 1.7m as at Hangleton, Sussex, where flint was used (fig. 15), at the Dartmoor site of Hound Tor or in the Northamptonshire village of Wythemail, where a thirteenth-century building with low stone foundations was replaced in the first half of the fourteenth century by a substantial and totally stone-walled building constructed of limestone blocks.[44] Alternatively, the houses may have been built with stone dwarf walls, never more than a few courses high, which would then carry either timber-framed or cob walls to eaves height. At Wharram Percy, Building 1 in Area 6 had dwarf walls with deliberately levelled and even surfaces to carry timber beams into which wall-posts could have been jointed.[45] It is salutary to note, though, that Building 4 in Area 10 at Wharram Percy was built at the same time as Building 1, Area 6, but with stone walls reaching to full height, so different building techniques were obviously used at the same time in the same village. This is not only true of Wharram Percy.

There are many examples of a mixture of building methods being employed simultaneously in a village and it is dangerous to draw hard and fast rules or give precise dates for changes of practice or materials. At West Hartburn, Co. Durham, wattle-and-daub, clay with stone facings and heavy rubble footings carrying wooden superstructures were all used as walling in separate but contemporaneous buildings[46] and the houses at Draycott, Derbyshire, were built in all manner of ways, including crucks with bases supported by padstones, stone walls, and timber-framed walls with earth-fast posts set in individual post-holes or in trenches.[47]

Nevertheless, the generalisation about the adoption of stone in the thirteenth century remains broadly true, even though there are exceptions such as Deane, Hampshire, where the discovery of a number of superimposed timber buildings showed that stone was never used at all,[48] and Field's documentary work in Worcestershire also illustrates the perpetuation of a timber-building tradition.

The adoption of stone as a building material can be seen less clearly in the clay-lands of the Midlands and eastern England, but even there stone was being used to some extent by the thirteenth century. At that date buildings with wall-posts embedded in the earth were replaced at Goltho and Barton Blount by houses with walls carried by timber uprights resting on padstones (fig. 12), and at Faxton, Northamptonshire a post-hole building of *c*. 1200 was replaced about fifty years later by a house with stone footings which carried a mud or clay superstructure.[49]

The emphasis on stone in the later medieval centuries may have been the result of a decrease in the amount of suitable building timber available to the peasants, through either natural causes or tighter restrictions on their access to woodlands owned by their lords. But it may equally be a reflection of a change in the standard of living, showing itself in the construction of buildings which, by having their timbers resting on stone foundations or padstones, would last longer than houses with earth-fast posts. As different methods of construction could be in use at the same time, though, the change to stone probably did not happen at one time and for any one reason. It is quite possible that the new fashion would be adopted at different stages by a village community, where some families were more prosperous, or just more adventurous, than others. If peasant houses were demolished and rebuilt not merely when they were beyond repair but on inheritance by the next generation, as some people believe, then the adoption of new building methods could well have been spread over a long period until all the members of the 'new' generation had inherited.

Whatever wall construction was used, the other features of the peasant houses remained fairly constant. The floors were usually of clay or trodden earth with only occasional use of stones or cobbles for areas of heavy wear, such as thresholds. It is unusual to find much occupation debris on the floor surfaces, which seem to have been kept remarkably clean, presumably by frequent sweeping. The actual top surface of a floor often appears to have been swept away completely, leaving the interior of the house slightly below the level of its surrounding yard. This means that even where no traces of walls remain the dimensions of a house can be

15. Reconstruction of a peasant house at the Weald and Downland Museum near Chichester, Sussex. Using evidence from remains excavated at Hangleton, Sussex, the walls have been built with flint to eaves height and the roof thatched with straw.

established from the slightly sunken area denoting the floor. Objects lost or discarded by the medieval inhabitants are more likely to be found by excavating outside the houses, where they were swept by the tidy householder.

An open hearth usually lay roughly in the centre of the living-area and there must have been a smoke-hole in the roof for ventilation. There is no evidence for chimneys but there are sometimes traces, as at Hound Tor, of a wattle-and-daub canopy above the fire to help create a draught and channel the smoke towards the smoke-hole in the roof, which would have been clad with turf, thatch or occasionally stone slates. Hearths were sources of heat and light, and also used for cooking, although there was often an oven in one corner of the living-area, or occasionally in a separate building. Very little evidence remains of other furnishings; they must have been sparse and mostly made of wood with few metal parts which might have survived to the present day.[50] Iron latches, keys and hinges found on many sites suggest that the houses had solid wooden doors but the lack of window-glass indicates that they had unglazed, perhaps shuttered, windows.

Although most peasant houses seem to have been single storeyed and open to the roof, traces of a possible staircase were found at Seacourt, Berkshire,[51] and a line of stones and signs of wear in one of the buildings at Caldecote, Hertfordshire, have been interpreted as the remains of a stair.[52] Such evidence is, however, unusual.

A number of attempts have been made to reconstruct peasant houses from their excavated plans, either in the form of experimental buildings (such as that at the Weald and Downland Museum near Chichester, Sussex, where a house based on the ground-plan of a building excavated at Hangleton (fig. 15) is open to the public) or, more often, on paper. The reconstruction of buildings with cruck construction does not present many problems, but unfortunately few cruck buildings have been excavated in medieval villages; the twelfth-century House 2 from Gomeldon is a rare example, where the positioning of posts against the walls suggests the use of crucks. Suggested reconstructions of timber-framed and stone-walled houses have been published for Wharram Percy, Great Beere, Devon, and Goltho and Barton Blount among other places,[53] and the simplest methods of construction have been the most favoured (fig. 12). But the subject of architectural reconstructions from archaeological evidence is a contentious one, as shown by two recent articles in the journal *Vernacular Architecture*[54] and much must inevitably remain conjectural. There is no doubt, though, that without the excavations in deserted medieval villages over the past thirty years even conjectural reconstructions of the buildings and the way of life of the medieval peasant would be almost impossible.

Important though this concentration on the medieval peasant house has been, there are many other questions about medieval villages which are equally significant. Archaeology can answer some of the questions by extending the scope of its investigations away from concentration on any one specific and detailed aspect of the medieval village towards a more generalised view of the village as a whole. The variability of street and plot patterns in medieval villages, the peasant economy and the causes of village desertion have recently taken a more important place in archaeological research and in some cases are still hotly debated. There is still much work to be done on these and other topics, but some of the conclusions proposed so far will be discussed in the remaining pages of this chapter.

Both archaeological excavation and fieldwork which does not entail excavation have thrown new light on the changing pattern of village life in the Middle Ages. In particular, they have shown that the medieval village was not a static unit which, once established, changed little throughout its lifetime.[55] On the contrary, it has been proved that most villages were undergoing quite drastic changes at all periods and that their lay-outs, far from fossilising the plan initially laid down when they were established or reflecting the shapes illustrated by preserved earthworks or the few early cartographic illustrations which we have, were in a constant state of flux. Positions of churches and great houses within a village may have remained static, the street pattern may not have changed radically, but there seems little else within that basic framework which did not alter.

Firstly, the individual houses may have been realigned a number of times during the lifetime of the village. Their frequent replacement has been mentioned above (p. 38) and connected with either construction material and methods, or inheritance. The buildings at Goltho, for example, probably had a life of about twenty years when they were built of timbers embedded in clay walls, of more than fifty years when they incorporated padstones in their construction. The turf houses of Hound Tor village are believed to have been replaced at roughly thirty-year intervals and it is on this basis that the settlement is thought to have originated in the seventh or eighth century. It is difficult, however, to establish the longevity of a peasant house by archaeological means (the artifacts found on medieval village sites are few and difficult to date within close limits) and peasant buildings may have been much older than the suggested twenty or thirty years when they were finally demolished to make way for new ones.[56] Regular repair and maintenance of thatch or wall-posts must have extended their life, and evidence for this might be difficult to find by archaeological means (for example, when a post is replaced in an original post-hole there is not necessarily any recutting of the post-hole, and replacement beams on dwarf walls would leave no trace). The written references to landlords repairing ruined buildings[57] in an attempt to prevent their tenants from migrating show that repair rather than rebuilding was not unusual.

Whatever the life-span of peasant houses, we can be certain that they were replaced from time to time and be equally certain that they were not necessarily replaced on precisely the same spot as before. At Hound Tor, for example, a sequence of buildings with sunken floors, turf-walled houses and finally a thirteenth-century stone long-house showed that the buildings were replaced throughout on the same north-south orientation, but in a slightly different position each time, so that the final house lay farthest south. At Wythemail, Northampton-shire, excavation of a single croft revealed three periods of building spanning the thirteenth and fourteenth centuries. The earliest structure was a timber building standing within a property which was bounded by shallow ditches. In the second period, still within the thirteenth century, a much more substantial stone building was placed above and at right angles both to the timber structure and to the slope of the land. It also lay across the original property boundary ditch which was recut elsewhere. Finally, in the fourteenth century, the Period 2 house was replaced by yet another stone long-house which reverted to the original orientation. At this time a cobbled village street was laid diagonally across the whole property and may account for the repositioning of the building. As the cobbled street appears to have been used as a main thoroughfare and not merely for access to the property in question some major realignment of the village street-plan may have been taking place. Evidence for such sweeping changes in village plan has also been shown by excavations elsewhere and it is clear that the realignment of individual buildings was not the only change which took place during the lifetime of the medieval village.

Rearrangements of buildings within tofts as at Wythemail can be seen at many other excavated sites such as Wharram Percy, where the excavation of Area 10 has shown that after the abandonment of the twelfth century manor house the land on which it had stood was used initially for chalk quarries and then from the thirteenth to fifteenth centuries as a peasant croft which carried buildings of widely differing alignments. All the peasant buildings in Area 10, whatever their alignment, lay at the edge of the croft and beside the village street. This was not the case in all excavated examples, for it can be shown that in the early years of occupation of many villages the peasant buildings lay towards the back of the crofts, away from the street, and that they were gradually moved forward over the course of time, so that in their last phase they were situated on the street frontage near to the croft entrance. Building 9 at Hangleton, Sussex, for instance, shows just such a move over a couple of centuries (fig. 16); the houses of Periods 1 and 2

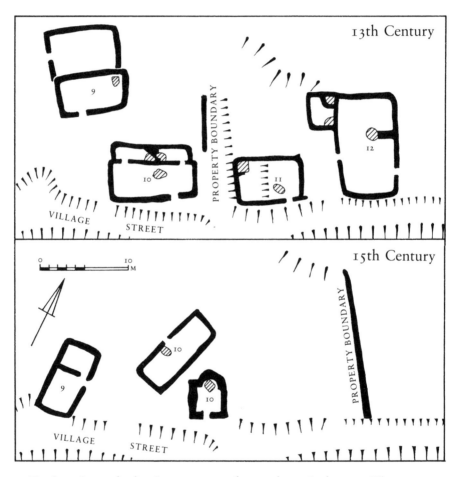

16. Hangleton, Sussex: the changing arrangement of peasant houses in plots 9–12. What were originally four separate properties in the thirteenth century were amalgamated into a single farm by the fifteenth century. After Holden 1963

(eleventh – thirteenth centuries) in Croft A at Goltho lay in the centre of the croft, but by Period 3 (late thirteenth and early fourteenth centuries) the buildings stood beside the road. By that time the long-houses at Goltho had developed into the farm type mentioned above (p. 34), with separate buildings used as dwelling and animal-quarters and a cobbled farmyard (crew-yard) in which cattle could be kept. The positioning of the buildings may be associated with the need to drive animals in and out of the croft and to provide sufficient unimpeded space for them once they were there. The same development can also be seen at Barton Blount, Derbyshire, but there is as yet insufficient evidence from excavations elsewhere to suggest that this was a common phenomenon.

Excavated evidence also shows that individual crofts were sometimes amalgamated to form a single large property. By the fifteenth century, for example, four of the crofts at Hangleton had been merged to form one large single croft housing a farm of the classic type. Similar amalgamations are not unknown elsewhere, and they probably reflect conditions in the later Middle Ages, when shrinking village populations allowed the surviving villagers to take over properties which were no longer occupied.

There were even more drastic changes which affected the plan of the entire village rather than the arrangement of buildings within individual crofts or the absorption of many crofts into a single property. At Wharram Percy the settlement began in the Anglo-Saxon period with several settlement nuclei lying in the valley near to the church (which has been proved by excavation to have been founded in the Anglo-Saxon period) and further north. In the twelfth century the manor was built to form the northern boundary of the village and then in the thirteenth century a new manor house was founded even further north and a row of tofts built in a regular pattern to join the southern and northern parts of the village together.[58] At the same time the site of the original manor house was adapted to form a peasant croft. In this instance the change of position of the manor house can be seen as influential on the village plan, and this is associated with a transfer of ownership of the manor and its lands. In other cases where the village pattern shifted dramatically such a clear-cut reason cannot be given, although the siting of moated manors on land once occupied by peasant crofts is a well-known phenomenon (p. 59). The building of a church in a village might also lead to a radical rearrangement of a village plan, as at Broadfield, Hertfordshire,[59] where the village church was founded on the site of several peasant crofts and the lay-out of streets was modified accordingly.

The most sweeping changes in the overall plans of villages now deserted seem to have occurred by the fourteenth century. This suggests that they were instigated by the local lords whose stranglehold on the village population began to decline after that date. By the fifteenth century village populations were less likely to acquiesce without protest to a total rearrangement of their way of life, and wholesale replanning of villages ceased.

The changing position of buildings within a croft and the development of farms was mentioned earlier (p. 34) as a result of an increased emphasis on pastoral farming, at least at sites such as Goltho and Barton Blount. This brings us to the question of the economy of the medieval village and the archaeological evidence that we have for the subsistence of the villagers. It is beyond question that the economic basis of village life was agriculture and many works have been published on the rural economy of medieval England based on historical documentation.[69] Archaeological evidence for the economy of the medieval village, however, is not so prolific and there has so far been no adequate synthesis of the economic evidence produced by excavation other than that published in *Deserted Medieval Villages*.[61] It is beyond the scope of the present work to assemble all the evidence which is scattered in excavation reports of individual villages and in unpublished excavation records; that is a subject crying out for intensive research. All that can be done here is to extract a little of that evidence and to point to lines which could profitably be pursued in the future.

The growing population of England up to the end of the thirteenth century led to the reclamation of land from waste and its transformation into arable fields. The fossilised remains of these fields can be seen today, particularly in the Midlands, in the form of land now under permanent grass but displaying the characteristic ridge-and-furrow of medieval ploughing (fig. 17). Many deserted medieval villages lie in the midst of such field systems with their characteristic reversed s-shaped ridges thrown up by medieval plough-teams. These fields formed the open-field system so typical of the clay-lands of central England, where the villagers could cultivate scattered strips of land, producing little more than subsistence crops of grain. The development and organisation of medieval field systems have been subjects of historical and geographical research for many generations[62] and archaeologists have more recently turned their attention to them.[63] Most of the archaeological work has been confined to surveying the fields, and there have been very few excavations which have revealed traces of the fields themselves. One of these few is the excavation at Hen Domen, Montgomery, which showed that a pattern of ridge-and-furrow lay beneath the eleventh-century castle, proving that here at any rate this type of field system was of pre-Conquest date;[64] the same has been shown to be the case at Sandal castle, Yorkshire.[65] It is uncertain what proportion of the ridge-and-furrow fields in the rest of England is of such an early date; unless their traces can be found beneath later structures of known date, fields are very difficult to place chronologically. Some of the earthworks of medieval villages overlie previously cultivated fields, and in some other cases the fields themselves encroached upon villages once the outlying buildings had been abandoned; in this way their relative chronology can be built up.

The crops which were cultivated in such fields seem to have been predominantly wheat, barley and oats. They have left their traces in the archaeological record either by the remains of the grains themselves, as at Wharram Percy, by the presence of drying kilns (Hound Tor, for example), or by the fragments of grind-stones used for grinding grain. The lava grind-stones which are found on many medieval village

17. Aerial view of the medieval ridge-and-furrow field system at Padbury, Buckinghamshire.

sites show that the villagers must have ground their own grain and not taken the whole of their crops to the manorial mill as laid down by law. This is an interesting insight into the character of the medieval peasant who in such ways as this must have striven to maintain his independence in the face of the strictures of his landlord.

Pastoral farming must always have played some part in the medieval economy, although it does not seem to have become dominant until the end of the Middle Ages when soil exhaustion and other factors (p. 21) led to its adoption at the expense of crop-raising. At Goltho and Barton Blount, for instance, cattle were kept in crew-yards associated with farmsteads from the fourteenth century, although arable farming predominated before that date, and the finds of animal bones on other sites show that sheep, cattle and pigs were kept throughout the lifetime of the villages. Surprisingly little work has been done on the animal bones from medieval village sites, and we need to know much more about the sizes of medieval domesticated animals, selective breeding and so on before we can build up a generalised picture of medieval pastoralism, although the animal bones from some excavations have been studied with interesting results. At Wythemail, for example, osteology suggests that the sheep were kept mainly for their wool and were generally not slaughtered before their sixth or seventh year, when their wool yield was declining, and at Wharram Percy cattle were the most important source of meat. It is important to bear in mind that the bones recovered from excavated sites are indicative of the diet of the inhabitants rather than of their rearing policies, but with that proviso, there is still no doubt that much more could be learned about medieval pastoral farming from osteological research.

The non-agricultural aspects of village economy have also been poorly served by the medieval archaeologist. Few sites have produced evidence for industrial processes, for example, although one of the crofts in the village of Lyveden, Northampton, showed that ironworking and the production of pottery and tiles had been carried on there at different periods of its occupation (pp. 148, 161). Pottery and tile production is unusual on a village site, but the almost ubiquitous presence of iron slag indicates ironworking at virtually every site so far investigated. The slag is probably the debris from smithing rather than smelting, although there is a possibility that iron ore was being smelted at Wharram Percy during the thirteenth century. The smithy found at Goltho is more likely to be typical of an ironworking centre in a medieval village. It is interesting that the knives discovered at Goltho which were investigated metallographically were made in a number of different ways, of varying sophistication, and some had cutlers' marks. It is unlikely, therefore, that any of them were made in the village, so the smithy at Goltho must have been used for the repair and refurbishing of tools rather than for their manufacture.

There is sufficient evidence to show that medieval villages were not isolated, self-sufficient units with little contact with the outside world but that they traded fairly extensively to obtain goods such as the knives mentioned above, small artifacts such as jewellery and buckles, and, particularly, pottery. The diverse sources of the pottery found at Wharram Percy, for example, show that that village was able both to afford and to obtain goods from outside. The immediate source of these commodities was probably the local market town (Malton in this instance) and most villages must have been within reach of markets of equivalent rank. The villagers must, therefore, have been able to produce sufficient surplus by their labours to obtain other goods in exchange, and excavated evidence from village sites suggests that the villagers enjoyed a surprisingly high standard of living, certainly one considerably better than one might expect from the documentary sources for the late Middle Ages.

18. Aerial view of the clearly discernable earthworks of the moated site of Quarrendon, Buckinghamshire.

MOATED SITES

Another aspect of the medieval countryside which has been much discussed with reference to climatic questions is moated sites, whose characteristic features – square, rectangular, circular or D-shaped enclosures surrounded by a ditch – show up with varying degrees of clarity on the ground (fig. 18). Some moats may have survived in their original shape and be filled with water and surround medieval buildings, as at Lower Brockhampton, Herefordshire (fig. 23); others may be partially destroyed and appear as no more than a pond or ponds with no associated buildings. Their variability in shape, state of survival and their frequent association with either buildings of medieval date or the earthworks of deserted villages contribute to the fascination of this type of field monument.

Although not all moats date from the Middle Ages, and the most recently

47

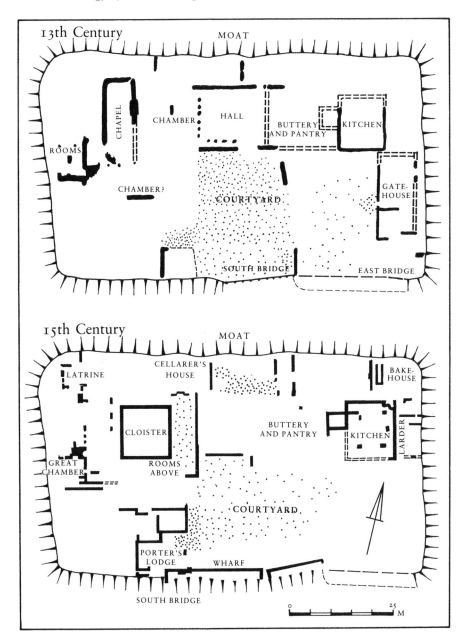

19. The royal hunting lodge at Writtle, Essex. Plan of the lay-out of buildings in the thirteenth century (above) and fifteenth century (below).   After Rahtz 1969

compiled distribution map shows over five thousand known sites which span all periods from the twelfth to the eighteenth centuries,[66] study of documentary sources including maps[67] and over 150 excavations have shown that by far the greater number of them are medieval in origin. Their main significance for the archaeologist is that they indicate places of medieval settlement; this is obviously true when the moats form part of a village complex or encircle buildings, either still surviving or destroyed to foundation level, but is also the case when the enclosures seem never to have contained features of any kind. These 'empty' moated islands could have been used for stock-yards, orchards, gardens or for a hundred other purposes which did not demand structures substantial enough to have left behind features which can be discovered by archaeological excavation. Where medieval buildings are present in one form or another they do not appear to be significantly different from buildings known from non-moated sites; they typify certain aspects of medieval society, ranging from royal or aristocratic rural retreats (King John's Hunting Lodge, Writtle, Essex, fig. 19),[68] through monastic granges and manor houses to the simple homestead of the yeoman farmer. Moats were, of course, also used in an entirely different context as part of castle defences, but this aspect of the moat will not be touched on here as it is more appropriately discussed in Chapter 4.

In common with some other branches of medieval archaeology, the study of moated sites has recently been defined as a specialised topic by the formation in 1972 of the Moated Sites Research Group,[69] the members of which concentrate on the documentary investigation and archaeological excavation of moats of all, but mainly medieval, periods. The formation of the Group was not the beginning, but rather the crystallisation, of interest in this particular type of site which had already been present from the earliest days of archaeological activity[70] and been manifested by at least one historical geographer.[71] The 'Medieval Britain' section of *Medieval Archaeology* illustrates continuing interest from 1956. The following statistics have been compiled from that source.

In 1978 5,140 moated sites of all periods were known in England;[72] reports in *Medieval Archaeology* suggest that up to 1980 only 164 sites had been excavated to a greater or lesser degree (fig. 20), little more than 3% of the known total. The excavated sample is therefore small and not necessarily representative of the group as a whole. In common with almost all excavations in the past decades, most moated sites have been excavated under hurried rescue conditions in response to threatened destruction, and not in the course of research projects. The choice of site, therefore, has usually been forced upon the archaeologist through external pressures and is not necessarily the same choice as that which might have been made if a research- and problem-orientated approach had been possible. The constraints of 'rescue' excavation have also made themselves felt in the size of the areas which have been dug. Most investigations have been on a very small scale and the ideal of digging the whole enclosure has seldom been realised (Wintringham, Huntingdonshire and Chalgrove, Oxfordshire, are two of the few good

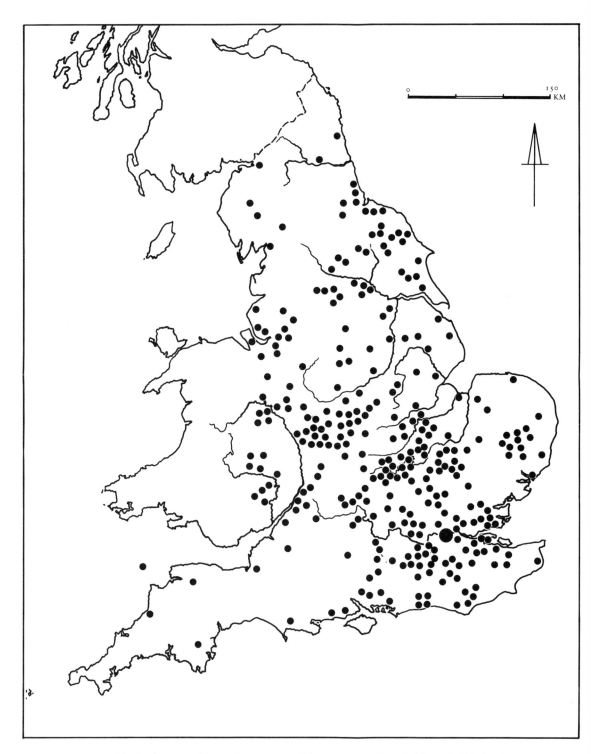

20. Distribution map of excavations on moated sites 1956–80.   Compiled from the 'Medieval Britain' section of *Med. Archaeol.*

examples of total excavation). The broad conclusions and generalisations drawn
from the excavated sites may, therefore, be biased and our picture of moated sites
to some extent erroneous, but these excavations give us the only information that
we have and must therefore be used as our data base. With this proviso, the
following section attempts to summarise the general characteristics which emerge
from recent archaeological work.

A number of questions arise when dealing with the subject of moats, some of
which can be answered with reasonable certainty by archaeological means; others
cannot, and lead to further questions in their turn.

The first question is, what qualifies as a moated site? A number of definitions
have been suggested including: 'one or more islands surrounded by ditches which
in antiquity were generally, though not invariably, filled with water';[73] '... the

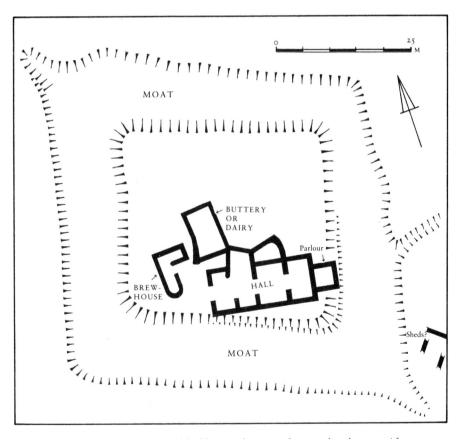

21. Hambleton, Lincolnshire. Manorial buildings within a simple moated enclosure.　After
L. A. S. Butler 1963

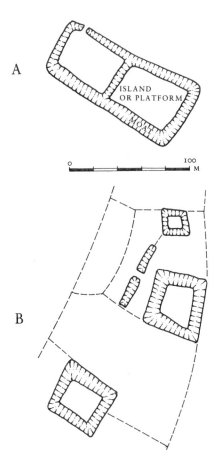

22. Plans of interlocking moats defining two connecting islands (A) and several independent but closely associated islands surrounded by moats (B). After C. C. Taylor 1978

moat is a broad, flat-bottomed ditch not less than 5m wide, which may completely, or partially, isolate a platform that is devoid of any defensive bank';[74] 'an area of ground, often occupied by a dwelling or associated structure, bounded or partly bounded by a wide ditch, which in most cases was intended to be filled with water'.[75] The common feature in these definitions is the moat or ditch; most excavated examples have been u-shaped in section, about 2m deep and 5m wide and this seems to have been the normal form. Today the moat may often be partially or totally silted, showing only as a crop-mark, or it may be partly destroyed with one or more arms preserved in the guise of ponds or dry hollows in the ground surface. The ditch may enclose a single island or platform (as at Hambleton, Lincolnshire, fig. 21), or consist of a number of interlocking ditches which together isolate several connecting islands (fig. 22a). There may also be a number of independent but closely associated islands, each surrounded by its own moat (fig. 22b). The moated platform may have the same ground level as the surrounding countryside or it may be slightly higher, apparently through the upcast from the moat being spread evenly over the platform during the course of construction. A low bank may also encircle the island. This may be the remains of some form of boundary, the residue from cleaning out the moat, or perhaps a measure to prevent children and animals from falling into the ditch. The island may contain a building or buildings sometimes extant,[76] or may have no visible traces of structures even when excavated archaeologically (p. 59).

The diversity of moated sites, in shape, size and the buildings they contain, has led to attempts at classification, using either shape and size[77] or topographical situation[78] as criteria. The former is the most widely used, although it is questionable how helpful such an exercise is, for what we really want to know is when a moat was dug and what was the status of its owner. This information is most likely to come from a combination of excavated and documentary evidence, but while this is missing, as it is in the majority of cases, classification based on remains on the ground must be relied on to give us some insight into the people who constructed and occupied moated sites in the Middle Ages. The connections between the size and complexity of moated sites and social status have so far been little researched, although it is natural to assume that there must be some correlation between size of moated area and social status and wealth. Much more excavation and documentary research is needed before such an assumption can be transformed into anything more concrete.

The second question to be asked is, where do moated sites lie? The table overleaf shows the number of moats (by pre-1974 counties) known in 1978 and fig. 20 shows the sites which have been excavated and reported in *Medieval Archaeology* between 1956 and 1980. Essex has the highest number of moats with 548 (also in first place by density), followed by Suffolk with 507. Yorkshire (320) and Lincolnshire (297) both score high totals numerically but are less well represented when density is taken into account; Cambridgeshire (270), Worcester (232). Bedfordshire (206) and Norfolk (206) all possess many moated sites. When plotted on a distribution map[79] it is quite clear that there are more moats per square kilometre in the south-east Midlands and East Anglia than elsewhere in England, these two areas being closely followed by the West Midlands. The common feature among all the high-density regions is the clay subsoil, apparently the most important prerequisite for digging moats, although in some instances there seems to be a connection between the distribution of moated sites and the destruction of woodland in the twelfth and thirteenth centuries when an expanding population led to the clearance of previously uncultivated land. Even where moats occur in prime agricultural, rather than marginal, land their concentration is on clay subsoils, ground which is fairly easy to dig, which is waterproof and needs little maintenance after construction. It is tempting, therefore, to assume that the construction of moats was dependent as much on the subsoil as on other factors.

Their distribution is also indicative of settlement patterns and land tenure in England in the Middle Ages. Many moated sites lie within or on the edges of villages, were closely associated with the medieval manorial system of rural

Numbers of known and excavated moats per (pre-1974) county

	known [*]	excavated [**]		known [*]	excavated [**]
Bedfordshire	206	5	Lincolnshire	297	5
Berkshire	50	2	Middlesex	30	3
Buckinghamshire	164	6	Norfolk	206	5
Cambridgeshire	270	1	Northamptonshire	49	4
Cheshire	98	6	Northumberland	1	0
Cornwall	2	0	Nottinghamshire	86	0
Cumberland	13	0	Oxfordshire	100	4
Derbyshire	45	1	Rutland	6	0
Devon	6	0	Shropshire	117	5
Dorset	21	1	Somerset	23	1
Durham	30	2	Staffordshire	177	5
Essex	548	12	Suffolk	507	11
Gloucestershire	79	1	Surrey	123	8
Hampshire	49	2	Sussex	190	9
Herefordshire	98	5	Warwickshire	154	13
Hertfordshire	187	4	Westmoreland	2	1
Huntingdonshire	134	9	Wiltshire	53	1
Kent	93	10	Worcestershire	232	3
Lancashire	127	3	Yorkshire	320	13
Leicestershire	120	3	Total	5,140	164

* After Aberg 1978   ** Compiled from *Med. Archaeol.* 1956–80

administration and often form an integral part of the deserted medieval village. Others are dispersed, lying as farmsteads amid fields which were reclaimed from woodland in the Middle Ages. The distribution of such sites, therefore, cannot simply be attributed to the physical characteristics of soil type; it is much more subtle than that. The same type of variability is evidenced elsewhere, for example in Ireland,[80] where a dispersed pattern of distribution, away from nucleated rural settlements, is more common.

But when were they constructed and occupied? This question can best be answered by excavation as no direct documentary evidence survives for the vast majority of moats, although where it does exist it can be used to very good effect.[81] In rare instances architectural evidence may be used (fig. 23), but it must always be borne in mind that surviving buildings are not necessarily contemporary with the moated enclosures within which they stand and they are therefore likely to tell us more about the date of more recent occupation of the enclosure than about the date when the moat was originally constructed. Reports published in *Medieval Archaeology* 1956–80 suggest that of 120 moated sites with datable remains, about half may have originated in the thirteenth century, a proportion which conflicts somewhat with the figures produced by Le Patourel and Roberts,[82] where about

23. The medieval gatehouse and hall at Lower Brockhampton, Herefordshire.

70% of dated moats are given a construction date of between *c.* 1200 and 1325. The dating of excavated moats, as of other excavated features, relies very heavily on the chronology of medieval pottery and so is not necessarily accurate to within closely defined limits, but the range given by both the *Medieval Archaeology* and the Le Patourel and Roberts information seems sufficient to suggest that many moated sites were constructed in the thirteenth century and occupied up to the end of the Middle Ages. A thirteenth-century date for the establishment of such sites fits in with the increasing population and occupation of marginal land discussed earlier in relation to the foundation and desertion of medieval villages (p. 20). As many moats lie on heavy clay soils of 'marginal' character they may be taken as representative of a general thirteenth-century phenomenon in England. A detailed survey of all available dating evidence for excavated moats and, if possible, more precise dating within more strictly defined limits is badly needed if the presently accepted hypothesis concerning the date of construction is to be tested.

The question of the date of origin of moated sites is inextricably bound up with the next problem of why and for whom they were constructed, and why they became so fashionable, both in England and on the Continent in the central and late Middle Ages. The immediate assumption is that moats must have been dug for defensive purposes, but were they? And for defence against what or whom? Some moats, of course, were defensive in character and integral to castles or other fortifications (Chapter 4), but many of them are hardly more than ditches surrounding a small area with neither need nor potentiality for defence.

Most of the moated sites which have been excavated and shown to have structural remains on their moated islands have had buildings made of timber or cob (Wintringham, Huntingdonshire, for example)[83] not unusual in clay-land situations of course, where good building-stone was not easily available, but similarly, not very suitable in a fortified site. In addition, few sites showed signs of being encircled by any feature more defensive than a hedge, the low banks running around the inner lip of some moats having so far produced no evidence to indicate that they supported a palisade or other defensive feature.

Bridges across moats could be either fixed or of the drawbridge type, the latter suggesting a degree of defensibility, but the inflammable nature of the enclosed buildings does not indicate that they were designed to withstand anything like a full-scale attack. Water-filled moats would, of course, reduce fire risk, but fire was a common domestic hazard in the Middle Ages and need not be associated with anything more threatening than an overstocked hearth or badly-fired oven. Attack from outside, then, cannot have played any great part in the construction of moats, although protection from intransigent troops or peasants in a period of lawlessness may sometimes have been necessary. Protection of stock against rustlers, of produce against predators or of portable wealth against casual thieves is likely to have been as important as the protection of the household against outright attack.

Other reasons for the construction of moats are of a more domestic nature. They may, for example, have been needed as fire-breaks in the wooded countryside in which many of them lay; they may have acted as cisterns for water storage; been used as fish-ponds; or been used to drain the islands which they enclose. The last possibility is an attractive one as so many of the sites lie in heavy clay-land where surface water could have been a problem, but the fact that many moats were deliberately sited near a source of water and filled by springs or streams does not support this suggestion. Another theory is based on the question of climatic change in the Middle Ages, a problem already discussed above in connection with the desertion of medieval villages. As mentioned there, this question is contentious, with much print being expended on each side in the controversy. Some medieval villages in marginal land are said to have been deserted because of the deteriorating climate; the same reason has been put forward for the digging of moats. This conclusion is based both on the occurrence of raised platforms on moat-encircled islands whereby the level of the island was raised above that of the surrounding countryside, and on the fact that some moated sites display an initial, pre-moat, occupation with buildings surrounded by shallow drainage ditches, and that they were subsequently converted into proper moated sites by the digging of much more substantial ditches, as, for example, at Brome, Suffolk.[84] There are objections to both these points. The raised island is by no means universal, and the digging of

24. The late thirteenth-century hall of Stokesay Castle, Shropshire, a good example of a moated site constructed by a great and wealthy family.

most moats seems to be a thirteenth-century phenomenon, when the climate of medieval England was still favourable. Deterioration was not apparent until towards the end of the century, so it is unlikely that climatic deterioration was a significant factor in moat-construction.

This leaves us with one other explanation for the construction of moats, and one that cannot easily be illustrated by archaeological evidence. It is that moated sites were status symbols, first becoming fashionable with the wealthier members of society (fig. 24) and subsequently being adopted by those of less wealth and social standing. It may be possible to test this archaeologically, by examining the structures on moated islands of differing sizes and evaluating the status implicit in the size of buildings, methods of construction, etc. The question of who lived on moated sites is closely associated with this suggestion of status. It is generally assumed that the term 'moated site' may be equated with 'manor' (as, for example, in 'Moats and Manors', in the 'Medieval Britain' section of *Medieval Archaeology*); this presupposes that the occupiers were the main landholders in a given area and those with positions of authority whose responsibilities demanded not only dwellings, but ancillary buildings indicative of wealth and power. Some evidence for this may emerge from archaeological excavation but more may be culled from documentary sources which suggest that moated sites and manors of the higher classes of society would comprise house, garden, orchard, chapel, farm buildings, forester's lodge, park lodge and windmill, whereas the moats of free tenants would simply enclose a dwelling.[85] This could be tested by the excavation of well-documented sites of considerable size or complexity and comparative excavation of smaller moats without historical documentation. The classification of moats according to size and shape could also be tested in this way.

Recent work on moated sites on the Continent has helped to elucidate certain aspects of English moats, particularly questions of why the moats were constructed, when and for whom. In Denmark most moated sites are thought to have been built by the powerful nobility and to date from the late Middle Ages. They are equated in some instances with motte-and-bailey castles (p. 109) and there is the implicit assumption that they are of a defensive nature. A few examples of moated farmsteads survive, particularly in southern Jutland near the German border, but as none has been excavated there is little information so far that can usefully be compared with the English evidence. The general impression is that Danish moated sites are a late medieval manifestation of the power and defensive needs of a landed class, in most cases aristocratic, but occasionally wealthy farmers.[86] A similar situation can be seen in the Netherlands,[87] but quite a different picture emerges from investigations in coastal Flanders where there is a very high density of moats dating mainly from the late thirteenth to the late fourteenth centuries. There are so many moats in coastal Flanders and the adjoining areas to the south that even the high-density counties in England, such as Essex and Suffolk, pale into insignificance by comparison. Verhaeghe believes that the Flemish moats were dug as status symbols by all social strata down to relatively poor free farmers.[88] These were to some extent aping their betters who had previously constructed and occupied mottes as symbols of wealth, power and freedom. By the second half of the thirteenth century, when the main period of Flemish moat-digging began, the construction and occupation of mottes had largely gone out of fashion, but their symbolic role was perpetuated in the moat which in Flanders (more often than in England) surrounds a slightly raised platform. In these countries, as in France,[89] the investigation of moated sites is still in its infancy; nevertheless, the similarities and differences between them and England are fascinating and await future work in both areas.

It has already been mentioned (p. 49) that most of the excavations on moated sites in England during the past twenty-five years have been fairly small-scale 'rescue' excavations and in no instance has it been possible to realise the ideal of total excavation of a moated island and its surrounding area. But there are some examples where the entire moated area has been uncovered, and some cases where a good part of it has been investigated. From these it is possible to see the structural history of moated sites, either those multi-period sites where there was occupation before the moat was dug, sites where the entire sequence of buildings on the moated platform has been revealed or even moated areas which never contained structures of any kind.

The spoil from the digging of moats seems very often to have been disposed of by being spread over the island. As a result, the remains of structures which had stood on the site previously have been preserved and we can see that the construction of a moat and its associated buildings was often only the culmination of a long history of settlement on the same site. In some instances the pre-moat structures were of peasant house type, surrounded by boundary ditches or drainage ditches as at Bradwell Bury, Buckinghamshire[90] where four timber buildings stood in crofts surrounded by ditches 1m wide and 1m deep. The area where they lay was subsequently occupied by a moated enclosure, dug in the thirteenth century, encompassing a dwelling, an aisled barn and a dovecote. At Milton, Hampshire, and Ashwell, Hertfordshire, there were remains of timber buildings on the ground surface prior to the construction of the moat[91] and at Brome, Suffolk, a large timber building occupied the site before the moat was cut.[92]

Boundary ditches, gullies and post-holes were discovered at Wickham Glebe, Hampshire,[93] where they were of eleventh- and twelfth-century date, and at Northolt, Middlesex, there was occupation from the late Saxon period, with domestic structures surrounded by shallow drainage ditches.[94] Chalgrove, Oxfordshire, contains one of the most elaborate sets of buildings so far excavated on a moated site. Its earliest period is of the pre-moat phase, and consists of a cob-walled structure of the late twelfth or early thirteenth century.[95] At Sapcote, Leicestershire, the remains of a ridge-and-furrow field system were discovered beneath later medieval fish-ponds.[96] These are but a few examples of the structures which are found beneath moated enclosures; they represent a continuity of settlement on the sites, at least from the twelfth century and in some cases from the late Saxon period.

Excavation has also shown that not all moated enclosures contained buildings. In some cases, such as Milton, Hampshire, and Ashwell, Hertfordshire, the moated areas contained paved yards or features which could be interpreted as stock-yards, animal pens or even gardens. In other instances (for example, at South Croxton, Leicestershire)[97] cobbled pathways were the only features found; these, again, must represent economic aspects of moated or manorial sites, although the dwellings have not been discovered. It is unfortunate that in these instances the areas outside the moat have not been excavated, as it is likely that the domestic accommodation may lie in the non-moated areas. A combination of non-moated dwelling and moated ancillary structures would be an interesting excavation objective, but one which has not yet been achieved.[98]

Perhaps the nearest thing there is to the realisation of that ideal is the excavation of Chalgrove, Oxfordshire,[99] where a site consisting of two moated islands has been extensively investigated. The smaller of the two contained no structures, but the larger island supported four periods of building spanning the twelfth to the fifteenth centuries. At least two twelfth-century buildings preceded the digging of the moat. Once the moat was dug hall, kitchen, farm buildings and other outbuildings were erected around an open yard roughly in the centre of the moated enclosure and forming a complex which illustrates a typical manorial lay-out of

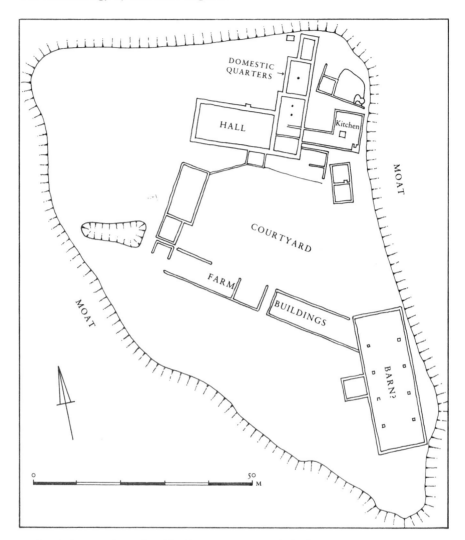

DOMESTIC
QUARTERS →

HALL

Kitchen

MOAT

COURTYARD

MOAT

FARM
BUILDINGS

BARN?

0   50
                                      M

25. A typical manorial complex of buildings set on a moated island: Chalgrove, Oxfordshire. After *Med. Archaeol.* 1972

the Middle Ages (fig. 25). Similar arrangements of manorial buildings within moated enclosures have been excavated elsewhere (Yorkshire, for example)[100] and moated sites with royal connotations are also known.[101]

The question of moated sites and climatic change has been pursued in a number of publications, notably that of the excavation at Wintringham, Huntingdonshire.[102] There, the first two periods of occupation dated from the twelfth and early thirteenth centuries, before the moat was dug, and were sealed by the upcast from the moat when it was constructed about AD 1250. The buildings of Periods 3 and 4 were erected on the slight eminence formed by the upcast, and cobbled pathways and thresholds were built for the first time (fig. 26). A combination of factors leads Beresford to infer a connection between moat-digging and climatic deterioration, an opinion which he has also expressed in relation to the desertion of medieval villages (p. 22).

This perfectly illustrates the close connection between the medieval moated site and the village. Both are part of the rural landscape of the Middle Ages and cannot

26. Reconstruction of the thirteenth-century manor house of Wintringham, Huntingdonshire. The uprights of the timber-framed building are set upon padstones and its thresholds are cobbled. After G. Beresford 1977a

be studied in isolation. Increasingly, the excavation of medieval village and medieval moat is being pursued as part of the same project. Guy Beresford, the main protagonist of the climatic change theory, is also an important figure in the dual excavation of moat and village; the sites of Goltho, Wintringham and Calde-cote have all been frequently quoted in this section, all display remains of moat and village and all have been investigated by Guy Beresford. Such integrated study should remind us that the fragmentation of research into the medieval period through the proliferation of 'research groups' is not altogether sensible. Life in medieval England did not seem to run along such well regulated lines!

2. Parish Churches

The parish church has long dominated the English landscape and is probably the best tangible reminder that we have of our medieval past. Even by the time of the Norman Conquest there were many hundred, if not several thousand, churches, not a few with lofty towers and nearly all built in stone, serving as focuses of worship for the Anglo-Saxon population. With the arrival of the Normans the rebuilding of old and the foundation of new churches increased enormously so that by the end of the Middle Ages there were at least eight thousand ecclesiastical buildings of all sizes and many architectural styles, most of which have been preserved in one form or another until the present day. Churches are undoubtedly the best-preserved medieval monuments in the country, richly redolent of the skills and aspirations of the people who built and worshipped in them and for whom they were the centre of much of everyday life. It is curious, then, that until the past decade they aroused little interest in the minds of most English medieval archaeologists who seem to have regarded the study of churches as the preserve of the architectural historian. Entries in the 'Medieval Britain' section of *Medieval Archaeology* show that there have indeed been some church excavations in each year since 1956 (fig. 27), but the bulk of these have taken place during the second half of those years, with eighty-seven reports for 1970–9 compared with sixty-four for 1960–9. The steady increase in interest[1] has been due both to personal initiative on the part of a few individuals, and to the creation in 1972 of the Churches Committee of the Council for British Archaeology[2] which stated that its aim was to 'encourage the rapid emergence of a rigorous tradition of church archaeology in Britain in which the highest standards of architectural and archaeological recording and of scholarly criticism are brought to bear on subjects so potent with historical information'.[3] This is, perhaps, the clearest instance of the deliberate fostering of a specific branch of archaeology, and it will be interesting to see how far the aim of the Council for British Archaeology has been realised during the past decade. The present section will attempt to do that.

63

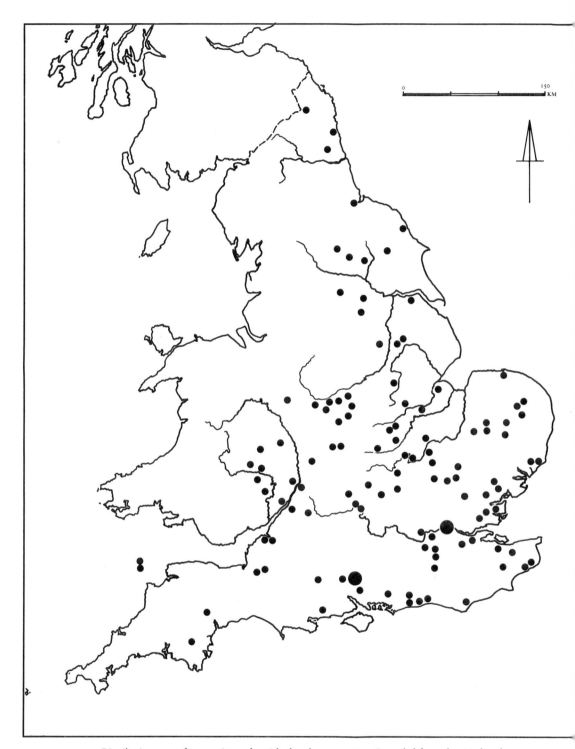

27. Distribution map of excavations of parish churches 1956–80.   Compiled from the 'Medieval Britain' section of *Med. Archaeol.*

One of the first responses to the CBA's foundation of a churches committee came from the Society of Antiquaries of London, which adopted the archaeological investigation of churches as one of its research projects.[4] Interest was largely concentrated on several well-known Anglo-Saxon churches, notably Deerhurst, Gloucestershire, and Repton, Derbyshire,[5] but investigation of apparently later foundations such as Asheldham, Hadstock and Rivenhall, all in Essex, was encouraged and the preliminary results published in *The Antiquaries Journal*.[6] At the same time the Brixworth Archaeological Research Committee was set up to analyse the earlier work on this outstanding Anglo-Saxon church and to co-ordinate a research programme of structural analysis of the fabric and excavation of below-ground features.[7] Mention of structural analysis and excavation brings us to the next point; what does the archaeological investigation of a church entail?

Church archaeology can take a number of different forms. Firstly, there is the excavation of churches without standing remains, the sites of which may be totally lost (for example St Mary Tanner Street and St Pancras, Winchester, below pp. 73–6), mistakenly located (St Helen-on-the-Walls, York, below p. 73) or known only from documentary sources (St Bride Fleet Street, London). Investigation of such sites is entirely dependent on field excavation techniques and hardly involves architectural study. Then there is the investigation of ruined or redundant churches, where excavation of the church and graveyard can be combined with structural analysis of the standing fabric. The church of St Martin in the deserted village of Wharram Percy (figs 28 and 30) is the most complete example of this form of church archaeology, where excavation and architectural study have complemented each other. In this instance study of the church itself has been integrated into a wider study of the church in a community, where parsonage, manor house and the dwellings of the villagers have all been investigated, and show how the development of a church may reflect the fluctuating fortunes of the parish and the parishioners it served.

Finally, there is the more difficult task of investigating a 'living' church, one still in use for services and where the graveyard may still be used for burial. Investigation of such churches is exemplified by the work at the Essex churches of Asheldham, Hadstock and Rivenhall mentioned above, and the problems involved in studying such churches have been described by their excavators.[8] Each different aspect of church archaeology brings its own results, each equally valid, but the aim of the archaeologist in most recent years has been to combine the field technique of excavation both within and outside the church with an analysis of the standing structure; in this way alone, it is argued, can a full picture of the history and development of a church be produced. Furthermore, the most recent work has also concentrated on placing the church in its topographical setting, regarding the church itself not merely as an architectural feature in its own right, but also as an expression of the society of which it was a product. This aim is integral to many church investigations of the past decade, such as that of Wharram Percy, and is perhaps best expressed by the investigators of Deerhurst church who are 'consider-

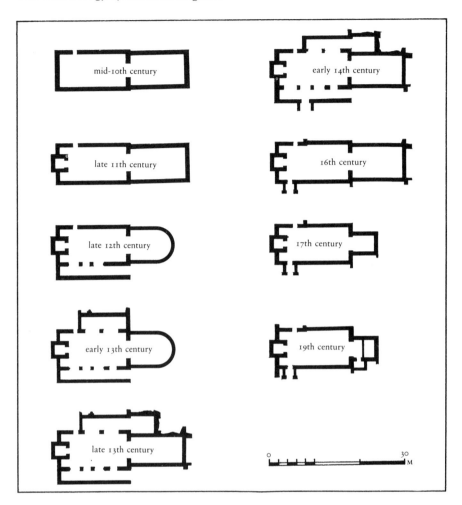

28. The changing plan of St Martin, Wharram Percy, Yorkshire, from the eleventh to the nineteenth century. After *Med. Archaeol.* 1973

ing not only its structure and use, but also its relationship to all aspects of the life of the district and community in which it is set'.[9] This objective naturally includes the investigation of churchyards, entailing the surveying of the headstones and the positions of what in most cases are relatively modern graves, and the excavation of earlier burials. Churchyard surveys are becoming fairly common, again largely as a result of the initiative of the Council for British Archaeology,[10] cemetery excavations rather less so because of the natural constraints placed on such activities when the church and churchyard in question are still in use, but Rodwell shows how much information can be gained by the excavation of a 'living' church, in this instance Rivenhall, Essex.[11] Excavation of cemeteries which have long been out of use can, on the other hand, be more extensive and thorough. The investigation of the churchyard of St Martin's church Wharram Percy, which had not been used for burial since the beginning of this century produced not only a large number of skeletons which can give a graphic picture of the life expectancy, physique and health of a medieval population[12] but also evidence for the expanding and contracting size of the cemetery, its boundaries, entrances, pathways and its relationship to its associated settlement.[13] The recent excavation of the cemetery of St Helen-on-the-Walls, Aldwark, York,[14] has shown the wealth of information that can be gained from an extensive investigation of a large number of medieval skeletons, in this case a minimum of 1,041 individuals, comprising the largest group of burials so far excavated from a medieval cemetery in this country. In addition to burials, the excavation of cemeteries can produce other unexpected results. In the case of Rivenhall, Essex, for example, although only roughly one twentieth of the churchyard area was excavated, the remains of twelve buildings were discovered. These ranged from a Romano-British villa to a seventeenth-century herring shed[15] and included both secular structures, such as priests' houses, and religious buildings like the hitherto unsuspected late Saxon timber church (fig. 29). It should be self-evident that the church and its churchyard are indivisible and need to be investigated as such. At the very least the chronology of a church and its surrounding burials must complement each other and the dating evidence for one will help in the dating of the other.

Archaeological investigation of the church itself, either through excavation or by structural analysis, can show the way that the church building developed during

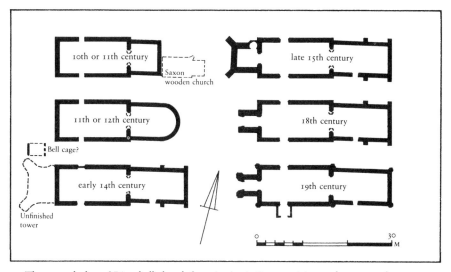

29. The ground plan of Rivenhall church from its Anglo-Saxon origins to the present day. After W. J. Rodwell and Rodwell 1973

the Middle Ages, increasing or diminishing in size in response to external factors. It supplements and expands the judgements of architectural historians who, until recently, have largely been responsible for all discussions on the development, expansion and contraction of church buildings.

The external pressures which were at work to influence church development can seldom be isolated through archaeological means alone, although an expanding or declining population can be seen to be instrumental in the changes of size of some churches when, as with St Martin, Wharram Percy, the church site can be excavated hand in hand with the excavation of its associated village. In this instance the addition of aisles, the shortening of the chancel and other alterations are attributed to the fluctuating size of the medieval population. In other cases, however, it is fairly clear that the church was increased or reduced in size because of the wealth of its owner or the enhanced status of its clergy.[16] Changes in liturgy also influenced the lay-out of a church; the need for more altars could lead to the addition of chapels, elaborate processions might demand aisles where formerly a nave was sufficient to serve the needs of the parishioners. A combination of excavated evidence and historical documentation, therefore, is necessary before the changing shape of church plans can be fully understood.

The aspects of church archaeology which have been touched upon above are, in the main, ideas which have been wholeheartedly accepted by medieval archaeologists in England only during the past couple of decades. There were, of course, many excavations in churches during the great period of church restoration in the nineteenth century,[17] some fewer in the first half of the twentieth century and some on ruined churches, in London for example,[18] after the bombing of the Second World War; but in almost all these cases the archaeological interest was focused on obtaining a church plan in much the same way as the monastic excavations of the nineteenth and early twentieth centuries were designed to elucidate the ground-plans of church and claustral buildings (p. 83). The concept of the church as an integral part of medieval settlement is new in this country, and it is with the acceptance of this new idea that church archaeology has really begun to blossom into a subject in its own right. In other European countries the excavation of churches has been an accepted discipline at least from the beginning of this century and, indeed, in most cases church archaeology became the foundation of medieval archaeology as it is known today. Sadly, this has not been the case in England, where the archaeological investigation of churches has remained a poor relation in the development of medieval archaeology; this, however, is changing.

England not only lags behind its European counterparts in the excavation of churches; it is regrettably in worse than second place when it comes to the planning and recording of the standing fabric and furnishings of those eight thousand or more churches which preserve their medieval origins either totally or in part. Nearly all these are described by Pevsner in his admirable *Buildings of England* series, many have plans published either in their local *Victoria Country History* or *Royal Commission on Ancient and Historic Monuments* volumes and a large number have a guide book in which a plan and description appears, but there is no systematic survey of the medieval churches of England (despite many popular general books), no attempt has ever been made to produce consistent plans of churches and there is not even a handlist of the medieval churches of England. This state of affairs is all the more regrettable when one looks at the situation on the Continent, in Scandinavia in particular, where churches have long been regarded not only as ecclesiastical buildings, but as expressions of social and cultural history. In Denmark the project *Danmarks Kirker* was set up in 1926 and in Sweden a similar project, *Sveriges Kyrkor*, was begun in the early 1900s, with its first publication as early as 1918.[19] These two projects have as their aim the publication of descriptions and inventories of every historic church in their respective countries; initially these were strictly confined to straightforward architectural descriptions, but more recently (at least from the 1940s) excavated results have been incorporated into the publications and in some instances research excavations have been carried out to answer specific problems. It is true that in both Sweden and Denmark the quantity of medieval churches is much smaller than the number in England, but bearing this in mind it is praiseworthy that by 1972 the project in Denmark was half-complete[20] and that by 1982 about 650 churches in Sweden had been published (pers. comm. E. Lagerlöf). The established churches in both these countries are the responsibility of central government, and funds for the projects come from their respective governmental sources; in England, of course, the responsibility for the upkeep of churches in use lies with the relevant ecclesiastical authority (the Church of England in the case of most medieval parish churches) and this system militates against any centralised, government-sponsored church-recording project. As more churches become redundant and fall out of use, however, the Department of the Environment is becoming increasingly involved with their preservation. Despite the present economic climate the time may now be ripe for the British government to give a more positive lead in the question of preparation of at least a summary survey of those medieval churches which remain to us, the numbers of which are declining drastically year by year.[21] Individual archaeologists and the Council for British Archaeology are attempting to do this, but a nationwide lead is desirable if a comprehensive coverage is to be achieved.

It can be said, quite fairly, that examination of historical documents and surveys of the standing fabric by architectural historians can tell us about the origin and development of the English medieval church. What then can archaeology contribute to a subject which can be covered so well by other disciplines? Here I shall indicate the aspects of the subject to which archaeology can make an independent contribution and mention some excavations which have added positively to our knowledge of the medieval church.

Historical documentation about the English parish church does not become common until the later Middle Ages, but there is sufficient early written evidence to suggest that the parochial system as we know it today was evolving during the century immediately before the Norman Conquest. Its origins are still far from clear and will probably remain so,[22] but it is evident that the first churches in England were founded by St Augustine and his followers in the seventh century as centres of missionary activity; these were to become known as 'minster churches', centres at which baptism or burial could take place and where religious services could be observed. They were essentially centres of a Christian mission whereby the religious message could be disseminated throughout the countryside. The more successful the mission became, the more necessary it was to establish churches other than the great central minsters, and so a network of smaller, dependent, churches began to emerge. These were often private foundations, the result of local initiative on the part of local lords or landowners, and are known as proprietary churches. They were probably not founded merely as acts of piety, for certainly by the tenth century the custom of paying tithes or taxes to the church was established and the secular founder of a church would expect to receive his share; in addition he would have the right of appointing clergy to his church (the 'avowdson') which could also be profitable. The increasing formalisation of administration during the last century of Saxon rule in England meant that by the end of the tenth century the country was divided into parishes and each householder was obliged to pay tithes. The parish system had come to stay.

Domesday Book of 1086 records the parish system as a well-known phenomenon, therefore implying that by that time England was organised ecclesiastically along parochial lines, each parish with its church. Only about two thousand churches are mentioned in Domesday Book, however, compared with its record of over thirteen thousand settlements,[23] so it is unlikely that all the churches in existence in England at that time are registered there. Many of the settlements recorded in Domesday must have possessed churches, so two thousand churches by 1086 is likely to be a conservative estimate.

From the eleventh century the number of documentary sources for the foundation or existence of parish churches increases dramatically, with most information coming from the late thirteenth century and later.[24] Historical documentation, therefore, is useful and demonstrably reliable when dealing with the later medieval church, but not so helpful in providing the date of initial foundation, particularly if this happens to be during the centuries before the Norman Conquest. In Winchester, for example, fifty-seven parish churches are known from the late thirteenth century, forty of these being in existence by 1141 when there are records of their having been burnt.[25] But excavation of six churches in recent years has shown that at least two of them, St Mary Tanner Street and St Pancras,[26] were of pre-Conquest origin, although no written records exist of their early foundation. Similar evidence has come from the excavation of other churches, notably Rivenhall (fig. 29) and Asheldham, Essex, where early timber structures have been seen to precede better-documented late medieval churches, St Michael, Thetford, Norfolk, where a simple post-built, two-cell building preceded an equally simple but larger stone church, and Wharram Percy, Yorkshire (fig. 30).[27]

As mentioned above, the archaeology of the church can take many different

30. The church of St Martin, Wharram Percy, from the south.

forms, and until recently the excavation of churches without standing remains has
been the most common. The most obvious result from such excavations is the
elucidation of the church plan although, as we shall see below, other, and perhaps
more significant, conclusions can sometimes be drawn. Excavation of churches
which no longer have any upstanding remains has one particular advantage; it is
often possible to excavate the entire church, whereas sites with standing structures,
more particularly 'living' churches, can often be excavated only on a selective basis.
It is becoming increasingly obvious that small-scale selective excavations within
churches do not always give a true picture of the church's development, so total
excavation is most desirable. But set against this advantage are several very
considerable disadvantages, the main one being the difficulty of dating the changes
in a church plan from excavated evidence alone. Most church sites in England
produce very few artifacts which can be used as dating evidence and so chronology
must depend largely on the excavated structure itself. This is in sharp contrast to
excavated churches in Denmark, for example, where literally thousands of coins
have been found in stratified contexts during church excavations,[28] or in Germany
where coins are commonly found in churches.[29]

The dating of English churches, then, is largely dependent on architectural
features such as the shape of windows, the tracery they enclose, mouldings on
carved stones and so on; it is unlikely that these will be discovered *in situ* on

archaeological sites and so the dating of excavated churches can often be very difficult. On the whole it is impossible to give precise dates to church plans and their development through excavation alone, but it is possible to establish the sequence in which changes to the plan occurred. Publications of church excavations invariably include figures illustrating the development of the church, in some cases they indicate major structural periods resulting from rebuilding or demolition of walls (as at St Pancras, Winchester) which are given approximate chronologies in the text; in other cases the figures indicate 'phases' in which both major and minor alterations are shown (St Mary, Tanner Street, Winchester).[30] There is no standardisation in the way such periods or phases are indicated, and although many illustrations of church development appear to use the same conventions the reader needs to take care to understand what precisely the illustrations are setting out to show.

The sequence of construction in a church of which only the ground-plan is known can be worked out by detailed examination of the surviving masonry, either foundations or the lowest course of the walls, with particular attention being paid to wall junctions, where the building sequence may be most clearly illustrated. It is also possible to establish the structural phases of a church when no masonry survives even in the foundation trenches. At the Old Minster, Winchester, for example, Martin Biddle was able to reconstruct the phases of its construction from a simple two-celled church of the seventh century to a highly elaborate late tenth-century monumental building largely on the basis of inter-cutting foundation trenches from which the masonry had been robbed.[31] The interpretation of structural development using as evidence either masonry foundations or trenches from which all masonry has been removed (robber trenches) demands scrupulous excavation and a keen eye; there is also a pitfall which even the most careful examination may find it difficult to avoid, that is, that the foundations may have carried walls of several different periods. In other words, a wall may have been demolished at some period and replaced, immediately or at a later date, by another wall incorporating different features but reusing the old foundations. This can be difficult to trace by excavation alone.

Comparisons of the plans of some recently excavated churches which had no remains visible before excavation show that the buildings must have had some features in common, although details of the plans naturally differ from site to site. Six of the churches which fall into this category are situated in towns (two each in Winchester and Lincoln, one in London and one in York) and were discovered and investigated as part of the large-scale programmes of urban archaeological research which became common in the 1960s and 1970s;[32] the remainder lie in the countryside and have been excavated either in isolation or as part of a medieval village excavation.

All six urban churches showed continuous expansion throughout the medieval period and all except St Helen-on-the-Walls, Aldwark, York began as small, two-celled buildings with rectangular nave and either an apsidal chancel (St Mary

Tanner Street, Winchester, and the seventh-century phase of St Paul-in-the-Bail, Lincoln) or a square east end (St Pancras, Winchester; St Nicholas-in-the-Shambles, London; St Mark, Lincoln).[33] Five of the six appear to have been founded in the Anglo-Saxon period, although only St Paul-in-the-Bail has documentary evidence which somewhat inconclusively suggests an early foundation date.[34] The two Winchester churches (fig. 31) and the churches of St Nicholas-in-the-Shambles in London and St Helen-on-the-Walls in York are not mentioned in historical records until long after the Norman Conquest although they were certainly in existence before then. Only at St Mark, Lincoln, does the first documentary mention conform to the archaeological evidence; the church of St Mark is recorded as being in existence by 1100–7[35] and the excavated foundations were attributed to the eleventh century.

Medieval additions in all the churches consisted either of side chapels, aisles and towers or of extended nave and chancel. In the case of St Helen-on-the-Walls the church was being extended even at a time when its parish was at its lowest ebb in terms of both wealth and population, and the church of St Pancras achieved its greatest extent when Winchester as a city was in decline. Such information raises speculation as to the reason for church expansion during financially unpropitious times.

Church furnishings and liturgical usage can also be inferred from some of these excavations. A probable font-base was discovered at St Mary Tanner Street, Winchester, where there was also evidence of a rood screen, in the form of postholes flanking the chancel arch, and sufficient wear in parts of the apse in certain phases to indicate the position of the altar (fig. 31a). At St Helen-on-the-Walls, York, on the other hand, there appears to have been no internal partition to separate nave from chancel, although differences in level in the floor suggest some form of division. The eleventh-century church of St Mark in Lincoln seems to have had a gallery at the west end of the nave. The best evidence for the internal arrangements within a church, though, comes not from a parish church but from that of the Cistercian monastery of Bordesley where an unusual depth of stratification preserved many early features.[36]

Burials within the churches were also discovered, but they seem to have been a late medieval phenomenon. At St Pancras there is written evidence of internal burials by 1360, and twenty late medieval graves were discovered there. Similarly, only late burials were found at St Mary Tanner Street. Research into medieval wills from Winchester suggests that burial inside churches in the city was not common until the fifteenth century, and the two excavations here seem to support this view.[37] Late burials are also recorded at St Helen-on-the-Walls, York.

Five of the six urban churches discussed here were in continuous use from the Anglo-Saxon period to the end of the Middle Ages or even later, so there is a clear case of continuity, pre- and post-Conquest. As we shall see below (p. 75) this is the case in many recently investigated churches, where undocumented Anglo-Saxon phases are now almost a commonplace. The arrival of the Normans in

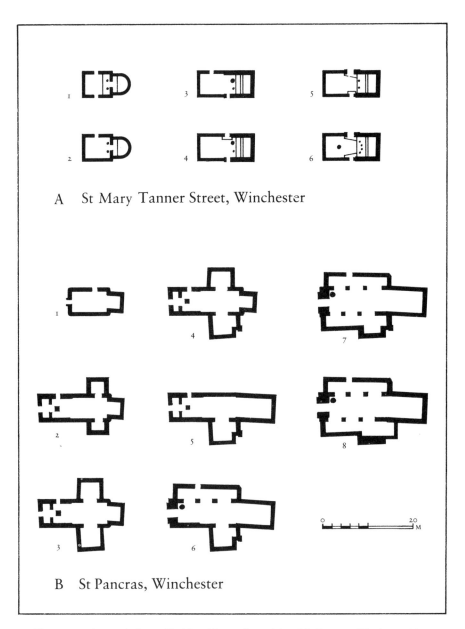

A   St Mary Tanner Street, Winchester

B   St Pancras, Winchester

31. The excavated ground plans of St Mary.Tanner Street (A) and St Pancras, Winchester (B). After Biddle 1972, 1975a

England seems certainly to have heralded a spate of new church-building, particularly in the greater churches,[38] but, at any rate in the smaller parish churches with which we are dealing here, it did not seem to have any marked effect. The Anglo-Saxon churches were extended, timber churches perhaps being converted into stone, but they were not moved to new positions. As more churches are being investigated it is becoming evermore obvious that they played a crucial role in the development of settlement in medieval England; this is well illustrated by recent work on rural sites in East Anglia where in almost all cases concentrations of middle Saxon pottery (of seventh- to ninth-century date) indicative of early settlement nuclei lie close to the present village church.[39] In towns with Romano-British origins it is even possible to suggest a continuity from the Roman period, although this is not necessarily an argument for continuity of Christian use.[40] Certainly, three of the churches described here lie above Roman buildings: St Paul-in-the-Bail is situated within the Forum at Lincoln, St Mark lies above Roman buildings which were derelict by the fourth century and St Helen-on-the-Walls, York, was constructed above a Roman town house of some substance. Many other examples may be cited and not only in urban contexts, for at Frocester, Gloucestershire, the church was found to be built on an underlying Roman building whose walls were used as the foundations of the first church.[41]

An interesting sidelight on the question of continuity emerges from the excavation of St Mary Tanner Street, where the first church (Phase I, tenth century) incorporated a stone building which originally had a secular function, perhaps as an aristocratic or 'thegnly' dwelling. This is an interesting change of use and underlines the likelihood of the church being founded as a private (proprietary) church. A fascinating reversal of this procedure is seen at Raunds, Northamptonshire[42] where a stone church originally built in the tenth century was first enlarged and then converted in the thirteenth century into part of a medieval manor complex. We need to bear in mind, therefore, that buildings may have changed from secular to ecclesiastical use or vice versa at any time within the Middle Ages.

St Mary Tanner Street has also provided evidence, from excavation alone, that it was a private church, probably one of many founded in Winchester in the tenth and eleventh centuries. It lay in an area which was to become populous but never particularly wealthy in the post-Conquest period, but at the time of its foundation as a church the neighbourhood was of some aristocratic significance. Its interpretation as being initially a private church relies on a number of factors: its small size, its conversion into a church from a secular building, the presence of two doorways into the nave, one leading from a lane but the other giving directly onto a private tenement plot. Many other churches in early medieval England were of private foundation, but it is usually difficult to establish this from archaeological evidence alone. St Mary Tanner Street seems to be a definite example of this type and Raunds must surely be another, for otherwise the conversion of church into manor house must have been impossible.

The excavation of both St Pancras and St Mary Tanner Street was part of the large-scale and far-reaching investigation of Winchester directed by Martin Biddle during the 1960s and early 1970s, the results of which figure in Chapter 6. The investigations were not only concerned with archaeological excavation; they also incorporated research into historical documentation, in particular into the Winton Domesday of AD 1148,[43] which contains, among other things, evidence for churches and parishes in Winchester at that date and slightly earlier. It is possible, therefore, to fit the excavated churches into their context, showing them both to be small churches serving parishes with relatively dense, but not particularly wealthy, populations.

Fifty-seven churches are recorded in Winchester by the middle of the twelfth century, six of which have been excavated; in addition to the two discussed here they are St Maurice, St Peter in Macellis, St Rumbold and St Mary in Brudenstret.[44] The size of parish and the number of tenements incorporating each parish has been worked out, and it can be seen that the churches along High Street each served on average eleven tenements, whereas in some of the side streets the number of tenements per parish was much higher. In Tanner Street, for example, which is particularly relevant here, the average number of tenements per church was 29.5. It is argued that the more tenements per church, the less wealthy the inhabitants, so this sets the two most recently excavated churches into their context, a context which is also filled out by the excavated evidence from their surrounding tenements which will be mentioned elsewhere (p. 180). Because of the amount of excavation in Winchester and its wealth of documentation the investigation of St Mary Tanner Street and St Pancras has provided us with probably more information about urban parish churches in their setting than have all the other excavated examples together.

The excavation of church sites in deserted medieval villages is another aspect of field techniques being applied to the archaeology of the church. Beresford and Hurst list twenty-two churches and chapels excavated by 1971[45] and others have been investigated more recently. The most comprehensively published example, however, remains that of Broadfield, Hertfordshire, excavated in the 1960s.[46] It was a simple, rectangular structure with no differentiation between nave and chancel which gradually grew from its original early thirteenth-century size of *c.* 13 × 4m to *c.* 15 × 4m by the mid-fifteenth century. Internal furnishings such as wall benches, a soakaway for a font and a tiled floor in the chancel were discovered, but its main interest lies in its situation, for when it was founded it was positioned above peasant crofts which must have been destroyed for its construction. The building of the church in this position led to the evolution of a new street plan in the village, aligned on the axis of the church itself, and similar instances are known from other medieval villages where, particularly in the twelfth century, churches were often founded on the site of houses previously occupied by the peasant population of the village. This is an interesting point, for as we have seen above, urban churches very often display continuity of site and usage from the Anglo-Saxon period, and the difference between them and many rural churches must reflect a social or economic

32. Watercolour of St Leonard, Heston, Middlesex, painted by John Wykeham Archer (1808–64) before its restoration in 1866. The painting shows many features such as inserted and blocked windows, patching of the stonework with brick and so on, which indicate many different phases in the life of the church.

difference of some kind. It may be that in rural sites more than in towns the church was the property of the lord of the manor throughout the Middle Ages and as he also owned the houses in the village, the church could be resited and rebuilt wherever and whenever he wished.

Excavation of ruined churches, therefore, can tell us about the evolution of individual plans, but also about a great deal more. Churches were integral parts of medieval society and therefore reflect much more than ecclesiastical considerations; excavations, indeed, may tell us more about socio-economic conditions than about the fabric itself or the building methods involved and for this we must turn to the second form of church archaeology to be discussed here – the integrated study of standing structure, historical documentation and below-ground evidence (fig. 32). The pioneer of this approach to the archaeology of the church in this country is H. M. Taylor, who has been the motive force behind the recent upsurge of interest. His personal research largely lies in the investigation of Anglo-Saxon churches (above p. 65) but he has inspired others to carry his methods through into

33. The excavated interior of St Peter, Barton-on-Humber, from the east.

the later medieval period. For example, Warwick Rodwell's recent (1981) publication *The Archaeology of the English Church* describes in detail the methods used in investigating churches and the results of his own study of churches, particularly in Essex, which have revolutionised our understanding of the evolution of the medieval parish church and its position in medieval society.

The method perfected by Dr Taylor for the investigation of Anglo-Saxon churches[47] and employed by all subsequent scholars studying churches of all periods involves the stone-by-stone drawing of the inner and outer faces of the walls and then the analysis of all the features discovered in this way. This 'above-ground archaeology' or 'structural analysis' of a building enables its constructional history to be evaluated and has resulted not only in a better understanding of the history of a church but even in the discovery of a number of hitherto unsuspected Anglo-Saxon or medieval churches. At Rivenhall, Essex, for example, the church was studied in this way once the rendering was removed from the outside of the north wall of the chancel; what had previously appeared to be a nineteenth-century Gothic revival structure proved to have Anglo-Saxon origins. By drawing each stone in the walls and differentially marking the various building materials used, features such as blocked Anglo-Saxon windows, medieval doorways, scars from earlier walls, and so on stand out clearly, enabling the building history to be reconstructed. This method is particularly well illustrated by Rivenhall,[48] – but an increasing number of investigations have been published showing similar results (for example, Hadstock, Essex, St Oswald's Priory, Gloucester, Wharram Percy, Yorkshire).[49] This method of study is, of course, dependent on there being large areas of unobscured masonry exposed, and this is not always possible to achieve. In particular, it is often difficult to carry out a structural analysis of the interior of a church where the walls have been plastered for generations, but there are some instances where the enthusiastic co-operation of clergy and laity has allowed internal wall plaster to be stripped off (usually during the course of renovation) so that the interior of the church can be subjected to scrupulous study. Deerhurst, Gloucestershire, and Brixworth, Northamptonshire, are but two examples where this helpful attitude on the part of the parishioners has led to invaluable results; many more instances could be cited[50] and the practice is becoming increasingly common.

Structural analysis of a church does not only make it possible to establish the stages by which it achieved its final form, a process covering perhaps many centuries, but it can even illustrate the day-to-day building methods that were employed. The recent study of St Peter, Barton-on-Humber (fig. 33),[51] included a close analysis of the mortar used in the standing structure which made it possible to work out the detailed methods involved in the church's construction virtually down to the amount of a day's work.[52] At Hadstock the investigators were able to establish the seasonal end to work on the tower by the extra thickness of mortar in one joint. Mortar can even be used for dating buildings, not only by the rough-and-ready methods based on colour and texture, but through scientific aids such as radiocarbon analysis of charcoal flecks incorporated into the mortar as a residue from lime-burning (as at Brixworth).[53]

In some instances it has been possible to complement structural analysis with archaeological excavation and thereby to increase the evidence of building methods, constructional history and liturgical arrangements. Post-holes lying within and immediately outside churches may have been used to support scaffolding; lime-kilns and masons' yards may have lain in the churchyard and bell-pits are not infrequently found within the churches themselves (for example at St Oswald's, Gloucester, and at Hadstock). The casting of bells actually within the standing structure may seem astonishingly hazardous to us, but the medieval masons seem to have indulged in the even more dangerous pursuit of melting-down the lead for roofs in the nave of Hadstock Church. Given such eccentricities, it is surprising that medieval churches were not burnt down even more often than they were, and when even pottery kilns are discovered in a church as at St Peter's, Bristol[54] one wonders even more at the resilience of medieval buildings.

The study of churches is by no means only ecclesiastical in its interest. Obviously it can tell us a good deal about building materials, methods of building and the adornment of churches (in the form of tiled floors, glazed windows and so on); it also illustrates the liturgy of the church throughout the Middle Ages, well exemplified by St Mary Tanner Street, Winchester (above p. 73), and contributes to secular history by its role as the centre of many a medieval settlement, urban or rural. The parish church has been a permanent feature of the English scene since its earliest beginnings before the Norman Conquest; the fabric of the church and the strata in its churchyard capture much of both the spiritual and secular sides of medieval life.

3. Monasteries

Remains of medieval monastic houses have attracted antiquarian interest for centuries[1] – and as early as the seventeenth century Dugdale (1655–73) published his *Monasticon Anglicanum*, listing and illustrating the structures of some one thousand monastic houses then known (fig. 34). Despite these early beginnings, it was not until the nineteenth century that the historical and architectural study of religious foundations really got into its stride, with the growing interest in medieval architecture, particularly that of English cathedrals and major parish churches. In the second half of the century, in particular, the restoration of nearly all our great medieval buildings encouraged antiquarian as well as architectural study of their fabric by at least the more reputable of the Victorian architect-restorers. Most of this work concentrated on those standing structures which had survived virtually intact from the Middle Ages,[2] but gradually interest also became focused on the remains of monastic buildings which had stood in ruins since the Dissolution.

By that time many of the monastic remains had decayed or been destroyed to such an extent that little survived above ground to illustrate their architectural features, and even their ground-plans were hidden beneath the turf. Digging was often the only way of exposing the foundations of monastic houses which had lain ruined since the sixteenth century and so from about the 1850s scholars and antiquarians began to reveal the plans of monastic buildings, particularly the churches and associated domestic quarters, by excavation. Excavation was usually combined with the study of surviving documents relating to specific religious houses and many histories of individual monasteries published in the nineteenth century are an amalgam of historical and archaeological evidence. The scholars most closely associated with works such as these are Lynam, St John Hope, Brakspear and Bilson, who might be said to be the 'fathers' of monastic studies in this country. In many ways, also, they were the first people to appreciate the importance of archaeological excavation as an important discipline in medieval studies. Medieval archaeology today owes them a great debt of gratitude. Their

34. Osney Abbey, Oxfordshire, by Wenceslaus Hollar (1607–77), showing this house of Augustinian canons as it would have been known to Dugdale.

particular interests, however, lay mainly in the recovery of the ground-plans of monastic churches and monks' dwelling-quarters rather than in the exploration of monastic sites in their entirety, with all the associated social, economic as well as religious aspects, so their archaeological work tended to consist of 'following the walls' rather than of exploring wider areas. It is no criticism to say that the early investigators of monastic sites were simply asking: 'What is there?' and were attempting to make sense of the plans revealed by their excavations. Their pioneer work has provided the medieval archaeologists of today with a secure basis on which to build; nowadays, the questions that we ask can and should be more subtle (despite Barker's well-known statement, p. 11) because we know, thanks to our predecessors, what actually is there. But, of course, their first tentative steps into the complexities of archaeological excavation led to occasional misunderstandings of their results, and their concentration on the central, 'most important', areas of monastic complexes resulted in an almost total disregard of the outer portions of the precincts where, far removed from the main masonry buildings, the economic life of the monastery was carried on.

The pioneer work of the nineteenth-century enthusiasts was continued during the first half of the twentieth century, largely by the Office of Works (now part of the Department of the Environment) as it became responsible for many monastic ruins. Much work was needed at that time to repair and make safe the mostly very dilapidated structures before they could be opened to the public, and excavation was also included as part of the restoration programme. Emphasis was still on the recovery of ground-plans and foundations so that intelligible plans could be drawn up for presentation to the public, who started to visit the sites in ever-increasing numbers. Many of these plans, measured and drawn in the early decades of this century, still illustrate the handbooks of those monastic sites in the care of the Ancient Monuments section of the Department of the Environment; they are admirable in many ways, and no doubt largely accurate, but (as will be shown below) they can only hope to illustrate one aspect of monastic life: that concentrated on the church and the domestic quarters situated around the cloister garth (see fig. 35 for plan and terminology). It may be argued that precisely these areas were indispensable to monastic houses in the Middle Ages (after all, monasteries were religious foundations, centred on the church and served by the monks as a religious body) and should therefore be concentrated on, to the relative exclusion of more mundane aspects; but the result of this concentration over a century or so has been that we now know the essentials of the ground-plans of very many monastic foundations, we can cite the standard arrangement of the claustral buildings belonging to the different religious orders, but we still know very little about the structures of medieval monasteries which were not directly associated with church or cloister.

The dominance and scale of church and cloister (figs 35 and 45) account to some extent for the lack of interest in the ancillary buildings which has been shown by archaeologists. The greatest wealth and skill were naturally lavished by the medi-

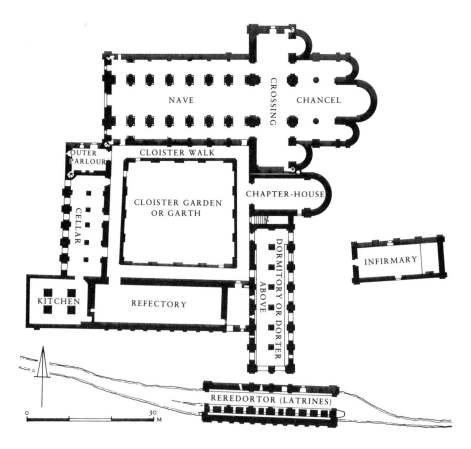

NAVE

CROSSING

CHANCEL

OUTER
PARLOUR

CLOISTER WALK

CHAPTER-HOUSE

CELLAR

CLOISTER GARDEN
OR GARTH

INFIRMARY

DORMITORY OR DORTER
ABOVE

KITCHEN

REFECTORY

REREDORTER (LATRINES)

0   30
                     M

35. Typical lay-out of a Benedictine monastery.

eval monks and masons on what they considered to be the most important
buildings in the complex whose remains will probably be of great beauty and
architectural interest. The more mundane buildings on the periphery of the precinct
are unlikely to have attracted so much architectural attention and may even have
been constructed in timber rather than masonry, and therefore be more difficult to
discover by the fairly primitive excavation techniques used by nineteenth- and early
twentieth-century archaeologists. It is natural, then, that interest should have
focused on structures the masonry walls of which could more easily be discovered
and which might produce finds of aesthetic worth. The recent swing of archaeological interest away from spectacular and outstanding sites to those of socio-
economic significance, however, should mean that the economic and industrial
buildings of the medieval monastery are more likely now to attract the attention

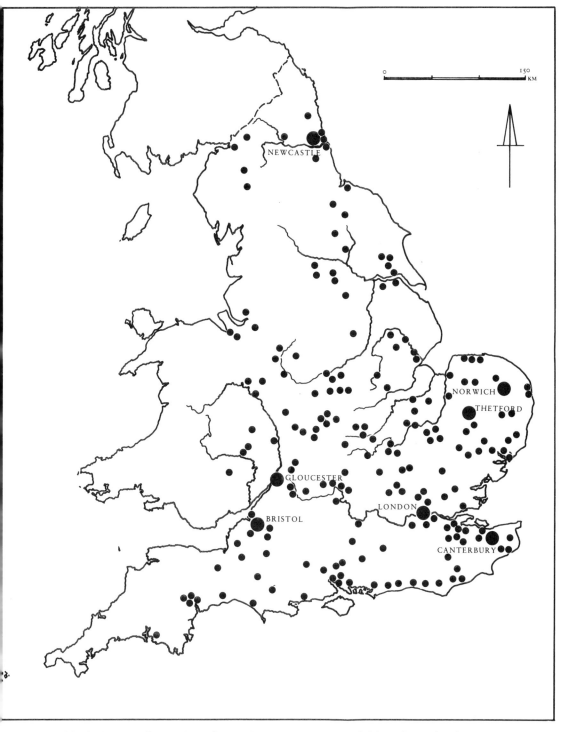

36. Distribution map of excavations of monastic sites 1956–80.   Compiled from the 'Medieval Britain' section of *Med. Archaeol.*

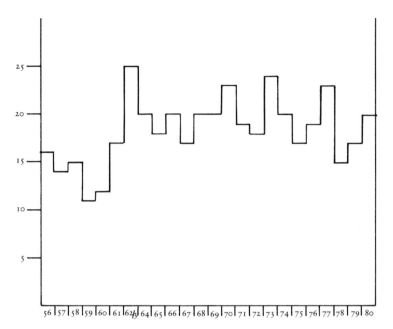

37. Chart showing the number of excavations per year on monastic sites 1956–80. Compiled from the 'Medieval Britain' section of *Med. Archaeol.*

of the archaeologist than they did fifty years ago.[3] It will be seen below, though, that even today only a handful of the post-Conquest monastic sites excavated between 1956 and 1980 have concentrated on features other than church and cloister.

Since 1956 more than 400 excavations have taken place on 171 monastic sites (including friaries) in England (fig. 36). As fig. 37 shows, excavations have remained fairly constant in numbers throughout, with very little fluctuation over the period and no dramatic decrease in recent years. This is in marked contrast to excavations on other types of site (see figs 10, 56, 70, 84) and may be the result of the changing emphasis from claustral to monastic industrial sites noted above. The distribution of excavations among the houses of the various religious orders (whose origins, development and differences in attitude are described below) is shown in fig. 38, where it can be seen that the most favoured sites have been those belonging to the Benedictine monks (40 sites), Augustinian canons (37), Cistercian monks (21) and Dominican friars (19). The professed aim of most of the excavations even during this period has been to recover the plan of church and claustral buildings as, for example, at Faversham, Kent, where the plan of the Cluniac priory was revealed, or at the Benedictine nunnery of Elstow, Bedfordshire, where the plans of church and cloister as well as buildings to the south of them were discovered.[4] Friaries (for the friars in England see p. 103) have also been excavated in search of plans. Their

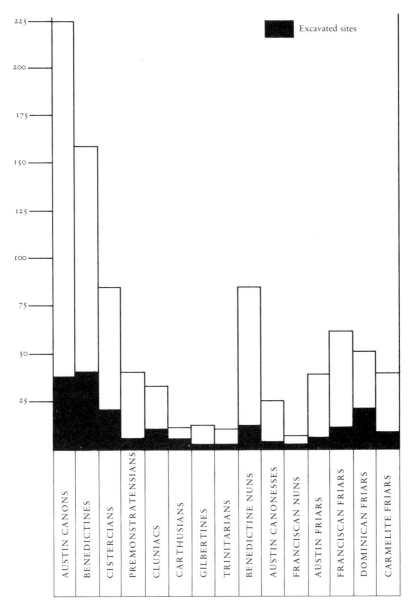

225 —
200 —
175 —
150 —
125 —
100 —
75 —
50 —
25 —

Excavated sites

AUSTIN CANONS
BENEDICTINES
CISTERCIANS
PREMONSTRATENSIANS
CLUNIACS
CARTHUSIANS
GILBERTINES
TRINITARIANS
BENEDICTINE NUNS
AUSTIN CANONESSES
FRANCISCAN NUNS
AUSTIN FRIARS
FRANCISCAN FRIARS
DOMINICAN FRIARS
CARMELITE FRIARS

38. Chart showing the number of excavations per year on religious houses of the different monastic orders 1956–80. Compiled from the 'Medieval Britain' section of *Med. Archaeol.*

positions in or on the fringes of medieval towns have meant that these houses suffered particularly badly during and after the Dissolution and their sites are now often known only from documentary sources. Some, such as the Dominican Friary in Newcastle-on-Tyne, have a few, much modified, standing buildings which have been converted to modern secular uses;[5] others such as the Augustinian Friary, Leicester,[6] were known only from place-name evidence before excavation began.

The comparatively large number of recent excavations on urban friaries can be associated with the threats posed by the redevelopment of medieval towns in England in the 1960s and 1970s and may reasonably be regarded as one aspect of the archaeology of the medieval town (Chapter 6). Other sites have also benefited from excavation because of urban development. The best recent examples of this are Norton Priory, Cheshire (Augustinian canons), which is in the process of total excavation in order to form the centre-piece of a park for Runcorn New Town, and Bordesley Abbey, Worcestershire (Cistercian monks), which will perform the same function for Redditch New Town.[7] These two sites are being excavated as part of a 'rescue' project, though the enlightened attitude of their respective town authorities have enabled them also to be approached with research in mind. As a result, they have given us far more information than forced and hurried 'rescue' excavations which would have, of necessity, been confined to the discovery of churches and claustral complexes. Norton and Bordesley tell us about these aspects, but their excavation has also concentrated on the ancillary buildings within the precinct, and the economic and industrial processes involved in the running of a medieval monastic house. We shall return to them below.

Although most of our knowledge of medieval monastic sites comes from the excavation of church and claustral buildings, it is limited even in this field. In the nineteenth and early twentieth centuries archaeologists were usually content to reveal the foundations of the buildings which lay closest to the ground surface, and these were of course from the later phases of the monasteries, often almost immediately pre-Dissolution; the buildings that were erected on the sites in the initial stages of foundation were either not sought or not recognised. A recent work on Augustinian canons has emphasised this deficiency[8] and archaeologists are becoming increasingly aware of what still remains to be learned about the history and development of the medieval monastery.

The physical remains which caught the attention of nineteenth-century anti-quarians, and still exert a fascination on modern scholars, are the manifestations of a religious ideal which originated in the eastern Mediterranean during the earliest Christian centuries, where hermits and anchorites lived in isolation far from the distractions of the world. This eventually developed into an organisation where groups of men or women lived together in communal simplicity, following a common disciplinary rule (*Regula*) and honouring an abbot or abbess as their head. Those who entered into the monastic state cut themselves off from the world so that they could devote their time to prayer and worship, to save their own souls and, less importantly, those of the secular population.

Although the monastic ideal had been current for several centuries, it was not until St Benedict founded his famous house at Monte Cassino near Naples at the beginning of the sixth century and formulated his code of conduct to which his monks had to conform (the *Rule of St Benedict*)[9] that monasteries began to proliferate in Western Europe. St Benedict's rule laid down that a monastery should be a totally self-sufficient unit, both economically and administratively, so that there should be minimal contact with the world beyond the enclosing walls around the monastic precinct. Within those walls there should be all that was necessary for sustenance, whether it be in the form of food production or the maintenance of footwear and clothing, and no work done within the precinct walls should be directed towards any end other than the immediate well-being of those within. It is difficult today to appreciate the single-mindedness of the men and women who entered monastic houses in the Middle Ages, but if we want to understand the heritage they left behind we must bear in mind their initial attempt at self-sufficiency and also their belief that monasteries served no other function than 'to provide an ordered way of life based on the teaching of the gospel'.[10]

The Rule of St Benedict laid down a strict timetable of religious observances, and of other activities, such as the number and quality of meals, when feet or hair should be washed and at what date a fire could be lit in the warming house (*calefactory*). Unfortunately the Rule is not specific about the rooms or buildings which were thought necessary to house a monastic community, but it is possible to conclude, both from the Rule itself and other rather later sources,[11] that from the beginning there must have been a church, refectory, dormitory, cloister, chapter-house, warming house, kitchen and other ancillary buildings. At the earliest period not all these structures need have been present together on any one site and their arrangement does not seem to have been standardised in England until at least the tenth century. From then onwards they formed the standard plan up to the Dissolution in England (and to the present day elsewhere) and can be illustrated by many of the building foundations exposed by modern excavation. A good idea of the profusion of buildings that might be found within a monastery is given by the plan preserved in the Abbey of St Gall, Switzerland,[12] an idealised lay-out of an early ninth-century abbey (fig. 39) in which the church is shown as the dominating feature, closely followed by its associated cloister garth and monks' quarters, but where there are also barns, stables, granaries, fowl-houses, buildings for coopers and turners, a mill, a kiln and even shops, all within an encircling precinct wall. It is unlikely that this plan was ever followed in its entirety at any monastery, and it was not fully carried out at St Gall itself, but it stands as a 'blue-print' for all later monastic houses which conformed to the Benedictine Rule and shows graphically what might be expected from the excavation of a monastic site.

Monasticism following the Benedictine Rule arrived in England in AD 597 with St Augustine, who founded the monastery of SS Peter and Paul at Canterbury almost immediately upon his arrival. Monasteries were already known in the Celtic west of Britain and Ireland, where Christianity was introduced almost two centuries

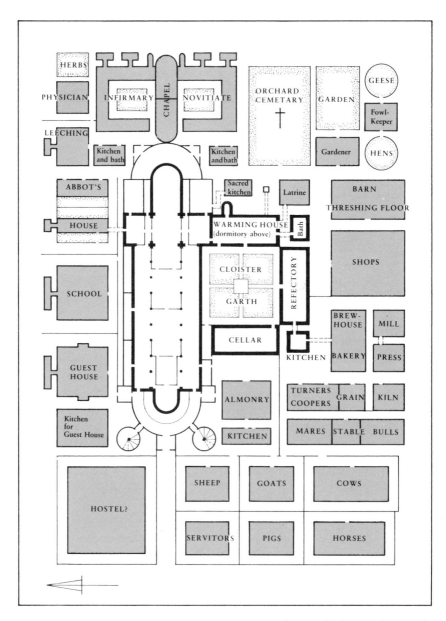

39. The idealised lay-out of a ninth-century monastery, St Gall, Switzerland. Many features of the plan can be seen in the monastic houses of the later Middle Ages.   After Horn and Born 1979

40. Monks' cells on the 'Celtic' monastery of Skellig Michael situated on an island off the west coast of Ireland.

earlier than in lowland England, which was under the dominance of the pagan Anglo-Saxons from early in the fifth century A D. The monastic houses of the Celtic west are known best from research and excavations in Ireland,[13] where they often consisted of little more than a huddle of dry-stone buildings surrounded by a precinct wall and were usually situated in an isolated and often desolate spot (fig. 40). They appear to have had little uniformity of plan, and bear very little comparison with the monastic houses built to conform to the Benedictine Rule. Several of these so-called 'Celtic' monasteries are known from lowland England and at least two have been excavated: Glastonbury, Somerset, and Burgh Castle, Norfolk.[14] There were many more, particularly in Northumbria, which were flourishing institutions when St Augustine arrived in Kent with his Benedictine ideas. Both types of monastic organisation coexisted uneasily until about the middle of the seventh century when the Benedictine form became paramount in England, and the number of new foundations rapidly increased to include such wealthy and famous sites as Monkwearmouth and Jarrow, Northumberland, which have recently been excavated.[15] The seventh- to ninth-century structures which were revealed through excavation at Monkwearmouth and Jarrow proved to have been elaborately constructed in stone and decorated in some cases with sculpture, painted wall-plaster and coloured window-glass. The domestic build- ings were aligned on the church but do not appear to have conformed to the lay-out which figures on the St Gall plan (fig. 39) and which was adopted in England in the tenth century.

Monastic life continued uninterrupted in England until the later ninth century, when Viking raids on the wealthy but undefended monasteries, mainly on the coast, seem to have been responsible for the practical cessation of monastic life by the time of King Alfred.[16] Monastic houses were abandoned and left to decay. Although the Viking raids are blamed for this, perhaps we should consider another factor – the gradual fading of religious fervour. We shall encounter this factor below when dealing with the reformed orders of the tenth century and later (pp. 98–9); new reforms, new orders are ushered in with enthusiasm, thousands flock to join their cause, but after a time that burning fervour wanes, laxity sets in and the beginning of the end is in sight. Perhaps such was the case with the Anglo-Saxon monasteries of the late ninth century, and the Viking raids just tipped the balance into total dissolution. It is possible that archaeology could help to solve this problem by finding, for example, evidence to show that monasteries were destroyed, rather than merely becoming decayed from lack of use. At Jarrow, a layer of burnt material was discovered overlying some of the seventh- and eighth-century buildings, but the excavator is unwilling to attribute this to the destruction brought about by Viking raiders.[17]

The subsequent revitalisation of English monasticism came in the late tenth century, inspired by similar but rather earlier developments on the Continent, and found expression in 970 in the *Regularis Concordia*, the outcome of a meeting at Winchester presided over by Archbishop Dunstan of Canterbury, who had already overseen the refounding and replanning of Glastonbury Abbey.[18] The *Regularis Concordia* gave the outlines of the plan to which newly founded, or refounded, monastic houses should conform, and mentioned the buildings which the monastery should include, mainly those listed above p. 81 and shown in the St Gall plan. The aim, to formalise adherence to the Benedictine Rule in England, succeeded to a great degree, with the establishment of thirty-five houses for men and nine houses for women by 1066.[19] A glimpse of the physical planning of the tenth-century houses can be gained from the excavations at the New Minster, Winchester, and St Augustine's Abbey, Canterbury, where parts of the claustral arrangement have been exposed.[20]

The next stage of monastic development in England came with the Norman Conquest, which resulted in both the foundation of many great Benedictine houses (such as Battle Abbey founded by William the Conqueror himself on the battlefield of Hastings, the high altar being positioned where Harold fell), and the introduction of reformed orders of monks from the Continent. Until about AD 1200 monastic religious fervour was at its height, with the foundation of more than a thousand houses in England. In the thirteenth century much of this enthusiasm was transferred to the friars (fig. 41), the first contingent of whom arrived in 1221.[21] These were Dominican or Preaching friars and, like the Franciscans who were shortly to follow them, they lived a life much more in contact with the general

41. Fifteenth-century representation
of a Franciscan friar (MS Douce
104, f. 46).

population than did the older-established orders, whose existence was confined within the monastic precinct walls and who are consequently known as enclosed orders. This was at least one of the reasons why the friars dominated the religious life of the second half of the Middle Ages; they brought religion to the people, particularly to the urban populations where poverty, misery and, of course, illiteracy were rife.

This is not the place to describe in detail the many different religious orders, enclosed and unenclosed, which proliferated in England in the post-Conquest period. This has been done with great scholarship and lucidity by many authorities, notably David Knowles, whose books are standard reference texts and essential reading for any student of either the history or the archaeology of monasticism.[22]

42. Watercolour by John Sell Cotman (1782–1842) of the Benedictine abbey of Croyland (or Crowland), Lincolnshire, from the south-west, showing the church before restoration.

Innumerable other works have dealt with monasticism in general[23] or with specific orders.[24] Here we will concentrate on the physical remains of monastic houses culled from excavation, but a few lines on each of the orders are necessary to put the excavated results into context.

The Order of Benedict has been mentioned frequently as that to which English monks and nuns belonged in the pre-Conquest period. The Norman Conquest saw a marked increase in the number of foundations, particularly in the first sixty years of Norman rule, and it is to this order that most of the wealthiest abbeys of the Middle Ages belonged, e.g. Tewkesbury, Gloucestershire; Evesham, Worcestershire; Malmesbury, Wiltshire. Most of them were situated in the rich countryside of southern and central England, well endowed with money and land by the Norman aristocracy and, generally, looked on with favour by the royal house (fig. 42). Many of them also served as parish churches for neighbouring centres of population and in this way became involved with the local laity. The monks, it is true, were not always popular with their parishioners, but they must have been sufficiently so for many towns and villages to fight for the preservation of all or part of the monastic church as their parish church at the Dissolution. As a result, the churches of Benedictine monasteries often remain totally or partially intact; for example, at Pershore, Worcestershire, the present parish church consists of the chancel, presbytery, crossing tower and south transept of the monastic church. At Shrewsbury, Shropshire, the nave of Holy Cross is all that remains, and at Rumburgh, Suffolk, the aisleless church is the only sign of the small Benedictine priory that once stood there. Examples such as these could be multiplied many times.

In contrast, the claustral and other buildings of Benedictine houses have frequently disappeared totally, usually through being treated as quarries after the Dissolution, when their stone was carted away for use in secular buildings elsewhere. The best-preserved Benedictine monastic buildings today are those of the greater houses whose churches served as cathedrals during the Middle Ages (so-called 'cathedral monasteries', a peculiarly English development whereby the bishop of the diocese was also the abbot of the monastery), for example Durham and Canterbury; or those whose churches were raised to the status of cathedrals by Henry VIII in 1541, for example Gloucester and Chester. The buildings preserved at these cathedrals conform to the classic Benedictine lay-out ultimately derived from St Gall and give us the best idea of the appearance of a large medieval monastery at the time of the Dissolution. The buildings on the outer fringes of the precinct are not usually preserved, although the gatehouse set in the original monastic precinct wall often still stands, as at Canterbury, leading into what is now the cathedral close. To discover what these peripheral buildings may have been like we must turn to the smaller Benedictine houses where they have not been preserved above ground but where they have been revealed through archaeological excavation. It is unfortunate that there has been so little recent excavation in the great Benedictine monasteries. Bury St Edmunds, Suffolk, is virtually the only house where extensive excavation has taken place in recent years,[25] and most of the excavated evidence quoted below is from the monastic foundations which were of lesser rank in the Middle Ages.

At Elstow, Bedfordshire, a Benedictine nunnery, extensive excavations have revealed the total plan of the church (the nave of which is still in use as a parish church, although the east end was demolished in the sixteenth century), the cloister and the buildings around it, the infirmary to the south-east of the cloister and a complex of outbuildings to the south. The outbuildings stood on marshy ground which was drained sometime after 1200 when the stream which skirted the site was canalised. They were built either of timber or of a construction which involved stone foundation walls with timber-framing above. A fourteenth-century stable block defined the area on the east. Information about this could only be revealed by excavation, as all the buildings have been destroyed to foundation level, probably at the Dissolution. The plans of peripheral building are only likely to be recovered where large areas of open land are preserved today. This is obviously not possible where monastic sites occupy land which is now heavily built on. Elstow is fortunate in that it lies on the fringes of the town of Bedford where intensive modern development has not taken place. Most urban monastic structures – and many Benedictine monasteries fall into this category – have been destroyed beyond recovery by post-sixteenth-century developments, so it is unlikely that many of the outer-precinct features will ever be revealed, even by the most thorough excavation.

Another valuable contribution made by excavation is the knowledge that it gives of the phases of construction of the buildings themselves. Where the buildings are still standing, as in the cathedral sites mentioned above, they fossilise the monasteries at a certain period, usually that of the immediately pre-Dissolution phase. Excavation can tell us how the sites developed through the centuries from their foundation. At Elstow, for example, it is possible to see how an originally fairly modest twelfth-century cloister was expanded during the fourteenth century, when the prosperity of the nunnery was at its height. The artifacts and pottery found within the excavated structures can tell us about the fluctuating wealth and external contacts of the house during its existence and, in some instances, about the industrial processes carried on within the precinct wall. We shall return to this aspect of the archaeology of monasteries later (p. 104).

The period which saw the greatest expansion of Benedictine houses in post-Conquest England also saw the growth of the Cluniac Order, which reached great heights on the Continent but never became overwhelmingly rich or influential in England, with only thirty-two houses being founded. The Cluniac order grew from the house founded in 910 at Cluny in Burgundy in an attempt at reorganisation after the decline in standards of the late ninth century which had been aggravated by the incursions of the Vikings. The primary ideal of the monks of Cluny was to revert to the original tenets of St Benedict which, in their opinion, had fallen into disuse during the turmoil of the previous century. The form which the Cluniac ideal took was to place increasing emphasis on the liturgical aspects of monastic life; progressively more and more time was spent in elaborate church services, and less on the manual labour which St Benedict had considered essential if monasteries were to remain self-sufficient. During the tenth century the abbey of Cluny became ever more influential in France, with its abbot being sent to revitalise those Benedictine houses which seemed to have grown lax and ineffectual. Although the aim was not to proselytise, Cluny naturally acquired adherents in this way and other monastic houses began to follow the so-called 'Customs of Cluny'. Cluny itself acquired wealth through bequests from royalty and aristocracy, enabling it to build its spectacular church and domestic quarters, which culminated in the middle of the twelfth century with a church said to be the largest in Christendom. Very little of this stands above ground today to give an idea of its immense size and beauty; but excavations have done much to supplement what is known from documentary sources and the few surviving architectural fragments.[26]

Early in the eleventh century the Customs of Cluny were codified and acknowledged by the Pope as a Rule, so that from 1049 onwards it is possible to speak of the Cluniac Order. For the next sixty years St Hugh, an Englishman, was the

Abbot, and under his leadership the order expanded rapidly in France and abroad, so that by the time of his death there were about fifteen hundred houses throughout Europe. The strength of the order lay in its ability to attract bequests from the pious laity and also novitiates of high social and intellectual standing. It remained an essentially aristocratic order with a strictly hierarchical and feudal organisation. The Abbot of Cluny was the head of the order; all the other houses were dependent upon the mother house and each had a prior, not an abbot, as its head. Hence, Cluniac houses were all, apart from Cluny itself, priories not abbeys. The tight control exercised by Cluny on its dependencies led to a cohesive organisation which was part of the order's success, but at the same time prejudiced its popularity in countries such as England, where close allegiance to a foreign head was regarded with suspicion and where such priories were known as 'alien'. In the fields of art, architecture and scholarship, however, the Cluniacs were pre-eminent, and even in England, one of their less successful provinces, their influence may be seen.

The first house of the Cluniac Order in England was founded in 1077 at Lewes, Sussex, by William de Warenne, one of the Conqueror's Norman supporters.[27] Of the other thirty-one houses founded in England that of Bermondsey was probably the most influential, and it was raised in status from a priory to an abbey in 1381 when it relinquished its association with Cluny to become a denizen (native) rather than an alien monastery.[28]

Cluniac houses conformed to the Benedictine plan. Their originality of approach lay in the splendour of their buildings, marvellous examples of which may still be seen today in the churches of Vézelay, La Charité-sur-Loire or Moissac in France. In England such exaggerated splendours were probably never achieved, but some of the ruined fragments which survived the almost total destruction of Cluniac houses at the Dissolution testify to the elaboration and magnificence with which they must have graced the English countryside. The west front of the priory church at Castle Acre, Norfolk, for example, or the *lavatorium* (washing place) at Much Wenlock, Shropshire (fig. 43), give some indication of what an English Cluniac house must have looked like.

Unfortunately, none of the Cluniac churches were preserved as parish churches at the Dissolution, and they and their claustral buildings suffered particularly badly thereafter. In general, only their plans remain, recovered by excavation in the early years of this century. Recent excavations (i.e. 1950–80) have been few, and have tended to concentrate on church and claustral buildings; excavations at Pontefract, Yorkshire, in the 1950s and Faversham, Kent have been the most extensive, the latter providing some evidence for economic buildings.[29] The lack of excavation of the non-claustral buildings is disappointing, particularly in view of the detailed knowledge of the running of a Cluniac monastery which has been culled from documentary sources.[30] Although excavation has produced the plans of those Cluniac priories which are in the guardianship of the Department of the Environment (e.g. Castle Acre and Thetford in Norfolk; Much Wenlock, Shropshire), regrettably little work has been done on the outer precincts of any Cluniac priory

43. Carved stone panel from the
lavatorium of Much Wenlock
Priory, Shropshire (Cluniac).

and much still remains to be learned. The site of the priory at Lewes, Sussex, for example, would prove a particularly interesting study. There has been some excavation here in recent years, but this has concentrated on the areas where fragmentary remains still stand above ground.[31] The southern area of the precinct remains free of modern buildings (although there are tennis courts and a children's playground) and would undoubtedly reveal remains of prime importance for an understanding of the total lay-out of a Cluniac priory in England, particularly significant perhaps because of Lewes's position as our first Cluniac foundation.

In 1128 the first house of the Cistercian Order in England was founded at Waverley in Surrey;[32] it was followed by the Yorkshire monasteries of Rievaulx (1132) and Fountains (1132), and thereafter foundations came thick and fast until there were seventy-six houses in England and Wales by the end of the century. The Cistercians take their name from their first monastery founded in 1098 at Cîteaux in Burgundy, where a small group of monks, originally from Molesme, attempted to live a life dedicated to what they believed to be the original, strict ideals of St Benedict. The Cistercians were the first truly 'reformed' order. They were rebelling against the declining standards which they perceived in the Benedictine and Cluniac houses of the time, and set out to live a life of asceticism and hardship, which, although initially viewed with suspicion, soon proved overwhelmingly popular, not only in France but elsewhere in Western Europe. Their great charismatic figure was St Bernard, Abbot of Clairvaux (d. 1153) whose puritanical zeal and fulminations against the decadence of the world attracted innumerable fervent adherents to the Cistercian cause.

One of the most important tenets of the Cistercian Rule, embodied in its charter, *Carta Caritatis*,[33] was that the houses should be founded in desolate places, far removed from the habitations of men, and that austerity and poverty should be followed both in the lives of the monks and in the buildings of the monasteries. A lack of adornment marks the earliest Cistercian buildings that are preserved (Bernay and Fontenay in Burgundy, for example); they are in marked contrast to the exuberant buildings of their Cluniac counterparts.

Despite the original intentions of the Cistercian founders, the order soon became both rich and powerful. Its appeal to the intelligentsia and aristocracy of the twelfth century meant that the numbers of monks and monasteries increased rapidly, so much so that in 1152, when there were 340 houses in Europe, the General Chapter (governing body) of the Cistercian Order called a halt to all new foundations lest the original ideals should be diluted. After that the rate of expansion slowed down, but new houses were still being founded until the end of the Middle Ages. The initial impetus and enthusiasm led to the acquisition of wealth by the monastic houses almost despite themselves. Most of the wealth was in the form of land, often superficially poor and unprofitable, which the Cistercians handled with consummate skill, draining bogs, clearing heaths and establishing sheep-runs. It has often been said that the Cistercians ushered in the first agricultural revolution. Most of the physical labour entailed was carried out not by the monks themselves but by lay brethren (*conversi*), who lived either within the monasteries or on outlying farms or granges (p. 103). They were not fully professed monks but, rather, illiterate labourers who were willing to exchange the freedom of the secular world, with all its discomforts, for an assured though circumscribed life within the precinct walls. It was thanks to the lay brethren that the lands of the Cistercian abbeys were changed from wildernesses to profitable fields and they outnumbered by many times the professed (or 'choir') monks in the heydey of Cistercian monasticism. For example, at Rievaulx in the mid-twelfth century there were 140 choir monks and between 500 and 600 *conversi*. Special quarters were set aside for them in the monasteries and this entailed a change of the formal Benedictine arrangement around the cloister (fig. 35). In Cistercian houses the monastic refectory is usually set at right angles to the south cloister walk, rather than alongside it, so that the west wing of the cloister could be used for housing the lay brethren (see the lay brothers' range at Fountains, fig. 44).

Although the first Cistercian house in England was founded in Surrey, the truly great and wealthy houses were those established in the remoter areas of the country where neither Benedictine nor Cluniac monasteries were common and where there was sufficient unpopulated and uncultivated land. The Yorkshire abbeys of Byland, Fountains, Kirkstall, Rievaulx (fig. 45) and Roche are examples of Cistercian abbeys that grew to financial power as a result of successful sheep-farming on hitherto unprofitable land; their ruins attest to the money lavished on church and domestic quarters during the height of their economic ascendancy.

At the Dissolution the Cistercian houses suffered, like others, from being sold

44. Reconstruction drawing by Alan Sorrell of the Cistercian abbey of Fountains, Yorkshire, in the fifteenth century. The lay-brethren's range runs southwards from the west front of the church.

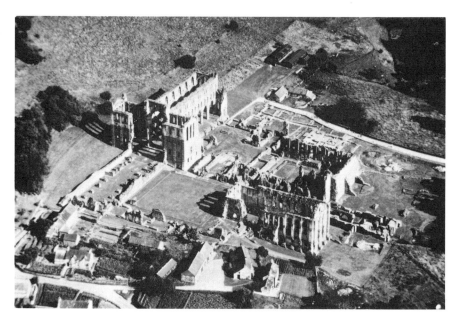

45. Aerial view of Rievaulx Abbey, Yorkshore. As usual in Cistercian houses, the refectory lies at right angles to the cloister.

off to speculators, but their usually isolated positions often saved them from being totally demolished for building-stone, and their claustral buildings are usually better preserved than those of other orders, although their churches, which were not usually converted to parochial use, mostly stand today as gaunt and roofless ruins. There are exceptions to this, however, as at Abbey Dore, Herefordshire, where the chancel, crossing and transepts still serve as the parish church, or, in contrast, Meaux, Yorkshire, where the entire monastery is totally destroyed.

The houses of the Cistercian order proved particularly attractive to those nineteenth-century English antiquarians who began the serious archaeological study of monasteries, and since about 1850 many plans, descriptions and excavation reports have been published.[34] The standard plan of the Cistercian abbey is known from these works, from ruined standing buildings and from those Cistercian abbeys which still exist today on the Continent (Bernay and Fontenay, for example). It is only from very recent excavations, however, that evidence has begun to emerge of the buildings of a Cistercian monastery in the so-called pre-masonry phase.

It has always been assumed that, following in the footsteps of their founders at Cîteaux, as soon as the Cistercians arrived at the site of a new monastic house their first activity was to put up timber buildings to serve as temporary church and living-quarters while labour and money were being collected for the permanent stone buildings. Traces of these temporary buildings have only recently been discovered for the first time at Bordesley Abbey, where timber slots and post-holes suggest the initial stage of construction of the church and some preserved timbers reused as grave covers are thought to have come from temporary domestic quarters around the claustral area.[35] With the refinement of archaeological technique we can hope for more such information and, already, similar timber structures have being found elsewhere (p. 102).

When a monastery was being converted from timber into masonry the building-stone must in most cases have been brought from some distance beyond its boundaries. Excavations at the Cistercian abbey of Kirkstall in Leeds have thrown light on the way the building-stone was transported by the discovery of a timber quay south of the refectory and some 60m north of the present course of the River Aire. It was probably used for unloading building-stone which is known to have come from Bramley Fall quarry, which lay some distance away upstream.[36] Subsequently, the quay went out of use and the area on the riverward side of it was reclaimed by dumping rubbish above and beyond it.[37] This aspect of land reclamation on a monastic site may be compared with the methods employed extensively in medieval ports (pp. 181–7) and illustrates the practical side of monastic organisation. It is paralleled by recent discoveries at Reading Abbey.

The Benedictines, Cluniacs and Cistercians all lived in houses whose architectural arrangement is anchored in the Benedictine Rule and the St Gall plan. There was one order of monks which diverged very radically from this arrangement: the Carthusians, whose extremely strict rule forced each monk to live in individual cells around a great cloister. The first house of the Carthusian Order was founded by St Bruno at La Grande Chartreuse near Grenoble in southern France in 1084. Although living in a community, strict isolation and silence were enjoined upon the monks who spent most of their time in their cells, meeting together only infrequently for communal worship or meals. The dominance of church, refectory, etc., so characteristic of the Benedictine arrangement is therefore missing from Carthusian houses, where the great cloister takes their place as the main architectural feature. The first house in England was founded at Witham, Somerset, in 1180[38] but the excessive austerity of the rule ensured that it never became widely popular, and only ten houses are known from England. Several have been excavated: Charterhouse, London, and Mount Grace, Yorkshire, being the best examples.[39] Investigation has been largely concentrated on the conventual buildings, although a certain amount of interest has been displayed in the monastic water systems, for which together with their gardening, the Carthusians were famed.

The final major order which influenced English religious life in the Middle Ages was that of the Augustinian or Austin canons, whose Rule was devised by St Augustine of Hippo in the early fifth century. It differed from the other orders in that the canons were not necessarily enclosed, there being *canons regular* who lived in monasteries, and *canons secular* who lived outside and acted as priests, mainly for some of the cathedral churches such as Lincoln, Sarum (Salisbury) and York. Both regular and secular canons differed from monks by taking holy orders; it was not until fairly late in the Middle Ages that it became customary for monks also to be priests.

The Augustinian canons first arrived in England at the end of the eleventh century and they spread rapidly, rivalling Benedictines in popularity and numbers. Their houses resembled the normal Benedictine plan but their churches were often simpler in design, often with only a single aisle, or even none. On the whole, the Augustinian houses did not approach those of the Benedictines for wealth and splendour, although some, such as St Bartholomew, Smithfield, London, now preserved in part, were as magnificent as any Benedictine house.

As fig. 38 shows, Augustinian houses have been the second most popular objective for excavation over the past twenty-five years, and since 1971 Norton Priory in Cheshire has eclipsed all others in the extent and detail of its investigation. The entire plan of the site has been revealed through excavation, and it has been possible to establish the different chronological phases from its origins in 1115[40] until the Dissolution and beyond. Many outstanding architectural features have been discovered by the excavation of this site, notably the fine mosaic-tile floor of fourteenth-century date in the crossing and transepts of the church.[41] The remains of temporary, pre-masonry accommodation have also been discovered at Norton. Two superimposed timber buildings were found beneath the later masonry cloister; the first, built shortly after the establishment of the priory, had wattle-and-daub walls supported by upright wall-posts, and was soon replaced by a longer aisled building with wattle-and-daub walls. The conversion to masonry can clearly be seen here, for at the end of the twelfth century stone foundations were inserted under the wooden posts.[42]

In addition to the four main orders described above a number of minor orders flourished to a greater or lesser degree in medieval England. They include such orders as Tironensians, Premonstratensians, Gilbertines and Trinitarians, to name but a few, but they all bear close affinities with either the Benedictines or Cistercians whose rules they either followed or approximated to. All the orders mentioned above, apart from the Carthusians, had houses of both monks and nuns, although the former were more common. The Gilbertines had double houses, that is, both monks and nuns lived in the same precinct, but were separated both in their domestic arrangements and in church.

The final groups of religious houses which must be mentioned here are those of the friars who arrived in England in the first half of the thirteenth century and rapidly overtook the enclosed orders in popularity. They established their houses in or on the edges of towns, with the result that very little remains in the way of standing buildings, and in many instances the site is known from documentary references alone. In recent years the investigations of friaries has gone hand in hand with the increase in urban excavations and knowledge of their claustral arrangements has consequently improved. In almost every instance recent excavations have concentrated on the church and buildings around the cloister; the outer precincts are usually inaccessible because of later urban development and there is little excavated evidence for economic or industrial buildings, although some have been discovered recently at Beverley, East Yorkshire[43]. The great strength of the friars in the later Middle Ages was their appeal to the mainly urban, labouring classes through their preaching; this led to the development of so-called 'preaching churches' with enormous naves which could hold the great congregations that the friars attracted. Such churches have been excavated, at Whitefriars, Coventry, for example,[44] and show how huge was their scale. In friaries, also, the masonry structures seem to have been preceded by timber ones and at the Dominican friary in Guildford, Surrey, a timber building beneath the later kitchen has been excavated and interpreted as temporary accommodation either for the friars themselves or for the masons who built the stone structures.[45]

Archaeology can also give us information on some of the methods employed in the construction and adornment of monastic buildings. Lime-kilns have been discovered at Tynemouth and Pontefract, a possible mortar mixer at Grove Priory, Leighton Buzzard, a mason's lodge at Bicester, Oxfordshire, and a building-workshop at Faversham.[46] A kiln for firing roof-tiles was excavated at Haverholme Priory, Lincolnshire[47] and kilns for floor-tiles are known at Meaux and Norton. The kiln at Meaux (near Beverley, Yorkshire)[48] was situated not in the abbey precinct but in the grounds of North Grange, about 1km away. Granges were a characteristic feature of the Cistercian economy,[49] organised mainly as independent farms to control the monastic lands and be responsible for their agriculture, but they must also have had an industrial function if the kiln at Meaux is anything like typical. When a monastic church was built it must have been floored with tiles produced nearby, in a grange as in the case of Meaux or, perhaps more often, within the precinct itself. At Norton Priory a kiln for mosaic tiles was discovered only about 50m north of the priory church;[50] this situation may well prove to be the more typical. At Norton, also, two bell-pits have been discovered within the precinct; these are but two of the increasing numbers of such features which have been discovered in recent years.

There remain two aspects of the archaeology of monasteries, both of which are treated more extensively elsewhere in this book: industry and agriculture. The former includes an excavated watermill at Bordesley, a forge at the grange at Waltham Abbey, Essex, and iron-smelting at Norton. The industrial methods used in monastic and secular sites do not appear to differ from each other and will therefore be discussed in Chapter 5. Agriculture, also, is more suitably discussed elsewhere as, although barns, granaries and stables have now been found on a number of sites (two timber-framed barns still stand at Faversham and other tithe-barns survive elsewhere), most large-scale agricultural activities must have been concentrated on the granges, many of which were similar to the moated farmsteads discussed in Chapter 1. Some, such as Badby, Northamptonshire,[51] consisted of elaborate masonry buildings on their moated islands, but many more, such as Stoke Goldington, Buckinghamshire[52] or Marton, Cheshire,[53] were simple buildings within small moated enclosures. The site of the preceptory (residence) of the Knights Templars at South Witham has many features in common with a grange or, as the excavator says 'the function of a preceptory such as that at South Witham was similar to that of a manor'. The site was totally excavated in 1965 and 1966[54] and consisted of a roughly rectangular embanked enclosure with fish-ponds and a mill on its periphery and large barns and workshops flanking an open courtyard.

The fact that such sites can be treated in a secular context shows how far the investigation of monastic sites has moved from the concentration on the essentially 'religious' buildings of church and cloister.

4. Castles

Perhaps the most evocative symbol of the Middle Ages today is the castle (fig. 46), usually, in popular imagination, a gaunt and ivy-covered ruin whose crumbling stone walls dominate the surrounding countryside. In fact, a castle today is more likely to be an unremarkable grass-covered mound in a field, with little on the surface to suggest that it was ever a fortress of any kind. The castle as a symbol of might and power is most suitably the subject of research based on historical documentation; the castle as a structure and a functional unit can most readily be seen from archaeological excavations and it is largely that aspect of castle-building and use that will be dealt with here.

Defensive strongholds have been built and used by virtually all societies throughout the ages, as the many impressive fortifications still remaining in Britain and on the Continent bear witness. Although Iron-Age hillforts, Roman legionary fortresses, Anglo-Saxon forts (*burhs*) and medieval castles all represent a particular population's need for defence against its enemies, the castle of the Middle Ages stands apart from earlier fortifications in both structure and purpose. The castle combined the functions of both dwelling and fortress; it defended an individual aristocratic family and its immediate retainers against attack and also provided a place of habitation and a focus for an administrative unit. It was 'the defended residence of a lord'. In this way it differed radically from its predecessors which were designed to provide places of safety for a large population, be it of peasants or soldiers, and could either shelter barracks or act as fortresses into which the surrounding population could flee in times of danger; they were essentially communal defences. The castles of the Middle Ages were not designed to meet such needs. They therefore occupied less space, and their protective walls encircled different types of buildings, usually with a great tower (known as a donjon or keep) as the focal point. The contrast in size between a Roman fort and a medieval castle is graphically illustrated by sites such as Pevensey, Sussex (fig. 47), where the Norman castle is tucked away in one corner of the vast area surrounded and

46. The motte of Arundel, Sussex, surmounted by a circular stone shell-keep and square wall tower.

47. Aerial view of the Saxon Shore fort of Pevensey, Sussex, with the Norman castle in the south-east corner. The small size of the medieval structure contrasts with the large area surrounded by the walls of the late Roman fort.

defended by the stone walls of the fourth-century Saxon Shore fort. Such a large area was necessary if the late Roman fortification were to function satisfactorily; the needs of the twelfth century were met, equally efficiently, by an area one tenth the size.

This changing form of fortification was not merely a reaction to the new methods of warfare and defensive needs introduced into Europe in the Middle Ages, but was rather a reflection of a new social organisation based on a system of vassalage and land-holding: feudalism. There has been, and still is, much controversy among historians about the origins of feudalism and the precise date when it crystallised as a system of government in medieval England.[1] Some see the seeds of feudalism in Anglo-Saxon England, others consider that it was transplanted in fully developed form from Normandy at the Conquest. Whatever the rights and wrongs of the argument, it is sufficient here to say that England had a feudal system during the High Middle Ages and that this manifested itself by the different strata of society being inextricably linked by bonds of loyalty. The great landowner and overlord in England was the king; he rewarded his followers by giving them lands, and in return they owed him loyalty and became his vassals. They in their turn secured the loyalty and vassalage of their followers by judicious gifts, and so on, until all the upper echelons of society were enmeshed within a web composed of mutual loyalty and responsibility. This system was one of delegation

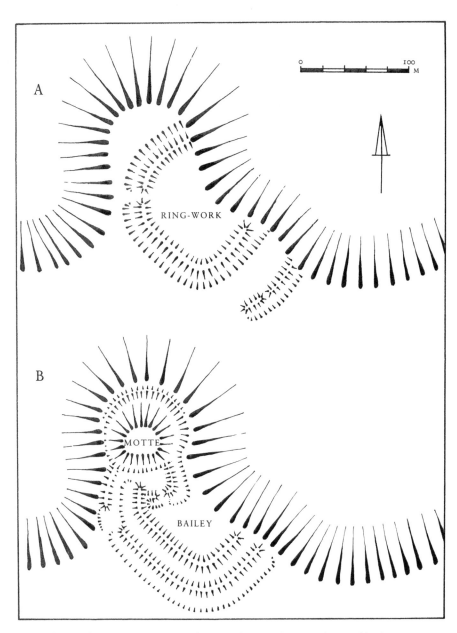

48. Castle Neroche, Somerset. The original ring-work (A) was later supplemented by the addition of a motte in the north (B).   After Davison 1972

from the central authority (the king) which ensured that armies could be raised and armed when called upon, and also ensured that the king had ultimate control over all his people; it 'institutionalised personal relations'.[2]

The castle was central to this system. It was not only the strong-point whereby the lord kept a grip on his lands, the mustering point where troops might gather in time of emergency, the centre where taxes might be paid, but it became the very symbol of lordship itself, whereby the delegated power of the king could be seen throughout the land. So the medieval castle became more than the sum of its parts. Its defensive capabilities, although important, represented but one aspect of the importance of the castle, which came to embody the power and might of the rulers of medieval England.

The earliest medieval castles that we know in England were mainly constructed of earth and timber, and are of either the ring-work (fig. 48a) or the motte-and-bailey type. Both these forms of earthwork castle were built during the eleventh and twelfth centuries, and more than seven hundred castles with mottes and two hundred ring-works are known from the period AD 1066 to 1215.[3] The ring-work is the simpler form, consisting as it does of a bank and external ditch with palisade and defended gatehouse and some form of accommodation within the embanked area.[4] The second, and better-known, type of earthwork castle is the motte-and-bailey (fig. 48b), which dominated castle-building in England during the late eleventh and first half of the twelfth century. These structures consisted of an earthen mound (the motte) which was surmounted by a tower. At its base the motte was surrounded by a wet or dry ditch which served both for defensive purposes and as a quarry from which the material used in building the motte was dug. Beyond the ditch was a lower courtyard on natural ground level. This was the bailey, a roughly oval or kidney-shaped enclosure housing the castle's domestic buildings and defended by a ditch and an internal bank supporting a timber palisade. Many motte-and-bailey castles are still clearly visible today, the mottes in particular being proof against any but the most determined modern attempts at levelling. Surviving mottes have been grouped into types according to their height and shape[5] and they fall into three categories: greater than 10m in height (Type I), between 5m and 10m (Type II), and less than 5m high (Type III). The arbitrary modern division of metres seems justifiable here, as the 5m module corresponds very closely to the perch, a unit of measurement commonly employed in the Middle Ages (1 perch = $16\frac{1}{2}$ft = 5.03m) and perhaps, therefore, used as a basic unit in motte construction.

Roughly 10% of the surviving mottes in England are more than 10m in height (fig. 49); these huge earthen mounds topped by timber towers and palisades must have had a stunning impact on a conquered Anglo-Saxon population unused to such overt displays of power, and must have emphasised the prestige and status of the new Norman overloads. Slighter and less impressive mottes were also thrown up throughout England, but even these must have made an effect on the newly subservient population. Some motte-and-bailey castles must have been built

49. The motte at Thetford, Norfolk (Type I, more than 10m high). The motte lies within an Iron Age fort, the ramparts of which were used as defences for the bailey.

to control centres of communication and suppress local populations, others were no more than links in a chain of signal stations, but whatever their individual purposes they together coalesced to form a defensive and offensive network throughout the whole country.

Whatever their height, mottes are usually preserved today as squat, flat-topped, grass-covered mounds with their basal diameter at least double their height. Many of the highest mottes (for example Oxford, Norwich, Arundel or Windsor) are crowned with masonry buildings, but these are secondary, usually twelfth-century, additions which replaced an original structure, usually of timber. No such timber structure survives, but an idea of their appearance may be gained from illustrations on the Bayeux Tapestry of the eleventh-century castles of Rennes, Dinan or Bayeux (fig. 50), where the top of the motte is in each case surmounted by a tower and the lip of the motte encircled by a palisade. The skilful embroidery of the tapestry indicates that towers, palisades and even bridges were built of wood, and the point is emphasised most forcefully in the case of Dinan, where the surrender of the castle is being brought about by the threat of fire. Each of the five castles portrayed in the Bayeux Tapestry (Dol, Dinan and Rennes in Brittany, Bayeux in Normandy and Hastings in England) displays variations on the basic theme of tower, palisade and bridge, and it seems clear from this, as from the results of excavations which will be discussed below, that differences in constructional details should be expected within a simple overall framework.

Contemporary written evidence fills out the picture even more. An early twelfth-century account of the castle of Merchem, Flanders, says:

> It is the custom of the nobles of that region ... in order to defend themselves from their enemies to make a hill of earth, as high as they can, and encircle it with a ditch as broad and deep as possible. They surround the upper edge of this hill with a very strong wall of hewn logs, placing towers on the circuit, according to their means. Inside this wall they plant their house (*domus*), or keep (*arcem*), which overlooks the whole thing. The entrance to this fortress is only by a bridge, which rises from the counterscarp of the ditch, supported on double or even triple columns, till it reaches the upper edge of the motte (*agger*).[6]

50. Bayeux Castle, Normandy, as shown on the eleventh-century Bayeux Tapestry.

The outlines and appearance of the eleventh- and twelfth-century castle, therefore, can be reconstructed from contemporary documentation; archaeology can fill in the details and has shown, perhaps not surprisingly on the basis of the Bayeux Tapestry illustrations, that each castle so far investigated differs subtly from its neighbour. This point will be returned to below when recent excavations of castles are discussed (pp. 123–7).

Although most of the castles which were built in the early years of Norman rule had earth and timber as their building materials and were of the motte-and-bailey type – masonry was not commonly used until the middle of the twelfth century – stone castles were put up in exceptional cases where either defence or status demanded it. The Tower of London, for example, was built of stone soon after the Conquest, probably in the 1070s, and, although much restored, it stands today as an example of the Normans' ability to build great stone towers, an ability which is also displayed in some of the castles in their homeland. The closest English parallel to the Tower of London is the castle at Colchester, Essex, a sturdy stone tower resting squarely on reused Roman foundations, which was built at the same time as the Tower of London, presumably to guard the eastern approaches to the City from possible attack by enemies from across the North Sea. A few other castles were built in stone during the eleventh century: Ludlow, Shropshire, with its great stone gatehouse, looking westwards to Wales; the magnificent hall-keep of Chepstow, Gwent, dominating the southern crossing of the Wye; the gatehouses of Richmond (Yorkshire) and Exeter castles; the stone walls of Rochester, Kent, and perhaps the stone keep at Canterbury.[7] But these stand as exceptions, for there is no doubt that by far the greatest number of castles erected in the years after the Norman Conquest were composed predominantly of earth and timber.

The stone castles of the late eleventh century were forerunners of the next stage of castle development in England, whereby the early timber structures surmounting and encircling motte-and-bailey castles were replaced by stone. The motte with its timber tower provided defence through height and a vantage point from which to dominate the surrounding countryside. Both these purposes could equally well be served by a stone tower, which had the added advantage of being less likely to be destroyed by fire. Throughout the first half of the twelfth century we see the earthwork castle being replaced by the stone keep, a rectangular stone tower with immensely thick walls supplemented by buttresses along its faces and at the corners, a sloping plinth at the base, virtually no windows and an entrance at first-floor level (fig. 51). Many such towers survive today as symbols of Norman power, and range in size from the magnificent structures of Rochester, Kent, or Castle Rising, Norfolk, to the slighter but still impressive examples such as Goodrich, Herefordshire. They were founded four-square on the ground, not on mottes whose unconsolidated earth would form an unstable foundation for the solid masses of masonry, and they stood within baileys which for the most part were still surrounded by timber palisades and ditches.

Norman keeps were totally defensive structures, built to withstand siege. A

51. The mid-twelfth-century stone keep of Kenilworth Castle, Warwickshire. The large windows are later insertions.

water supply was essential and usually provided by a well opening into the ground floor of the keep. The ground floor had no external access and usually served as storage basement and kitchen. Dwelling-quarters lay on the floors above, and were reached either by ladders, which could be moved from floor to floor, or by staircases contrived in the thickness of the walls. In some of the larger keeps, such as Rochester, each floor was divided by a spine wall, with the minimum of openings, so that specific areas of the keep could be isolated and defended in times of emergency. The whole design of the keep was aimed at strength, and to this end the features which might diminish the solidity of the building (windows, fire-places and so on) were kept to a minimum. They were virtually impenetrable buildings, but hardly designed for permanent occupation.

Paradoxically, the building of strong stone keeps in the twelfth century must have resulted not only from military needs but from the fact that by that time Norman England was sufficiently peaceful and well-organised for stone-quarries to have been exploited and a building industry to have grown up. The earthwork castles of the immediate post-Conquest period were built rapidly, from materials most available to hand, in response to a very positive threat from the native population. By the twelfth century the Normans had imposed their rule on the land sufficiently to allow a little more leisure in the construction of their symbols of

52. Reconstruction drawing by Alan Sorrell of the late thirteenth-century castle of Beaumaris, Anglesey, built by Edward I. The plan of the castle is symmetrical and defence in depth is provided by the curtain wall a few metres outside the central, defended, courtyard.

power, and some of the great stone towers of this period must have taken many years and much expertise to complete.[8] Some of them, indeed, can hardly have been completed before new advances in castle-building overtook them and made them redundant.

From the second half of the twelfth century onwards the centralised defensive keep lost its predominance, and a more offensive attitude was taken by castle-builders. The timber palisades of the eleventh and early twelfth centuries were replaced by stone walls (curtain walls). Stone towers were added to these, at first square as at Dover in 1180 – 90, so that arrow fire could be directed more effectively against attackers. Square or rectangular mural towers were soon replaced by ones circular in plan in an attempt to counteract the weak points presented by right-angle corners, and the stone castle finally achieved its culmination by the late thirteenth and early fourteenth centuries in the castles of Edward I (Harlech, for example, or Beaumaris, fig. 52) built to quell the Welsh. These so-called concentric castles consisted of several lines of defence formed by curtain walls only a few yards apart. The idea of the central defensive point, such as the keep, had by then long been abandoned, and an attack on a castle was met by a counter-attack from a garrison ranged around a fairly long perimeter wall.

The two centuries following the reign of Edward 1 and the building of his Welsh castles saw a steady decline both in the construction of castles and their use. This is not to say that great and defensible fortifications were not built at the end of the Middle Ages, for there are a number of magnificent examples, such as Bodiam in Sussex (fig. 1), Raglan in Gwent and Herstmonceux in Sussex, where power and might are displayed in splendid architectural style. But it is increasingly evident that castles were being regarded more as dwellings than as military structures; walls are thinner, windows are larger, more decoration is employed. Castles were becoming more comfortable places to live in. Kenilworth castle, Warwickshire, presents a splendid example of this changing attitude. Its twelfth-century keep still stands as one of our finest exemplars of the might and solidity of a heavily-defended Norman tower, yet across the courtyard lies John of Gaunt's hall, built at the end of the fourteenth century with huge, traceried windows with no possible defensive function (fig. 53).

Building materials were also changing. By the fifteenth century brick was replac-

53. Large traceried windows in the late fourteenth-century Gaunt's Hall at Kenilworth Castle.

54. South front of Herstmonceux Castle, Sussex (fifteenth century); the structure is of brick with stone facings. Gun-loops are visible in the gatehouse towers.

ing stone as the favoured material in parts of England. Herstmonceux shows this to perfection (fig. 54), as do the great tower of Tattersall, Lincolnshire, and the gatehouse of Oxburgh, Norfolk. Military features such as battlements, draw-bridges and gun-loops (the equivalent of the earlier arrow-slits) are still incorporated into the design of these buildings, but it is difficult to imagine their being of more than decorative use. What we are witnessing here is the transformation of the medieval castle into the Tudor mansion and, finally, the aristocratic country house.

The development of the castle and its strategic importance in medieval warfare have been studied in depth by many scholars, and the subject can be pursued by consulting the works and bibliographies listed at the end of this book.[9] There have also been many studies of individual castles based on documentary and architectural evidence, and some masonry castles have been investigated archaeologically (particularly those in the guardianship of the Department of the Environment). Much of this work belongs to the realm of historical and architectural rather than of archaeological research, so the remaining pages of this section will be devoted to some of the new information which has emerged from the archaeological excavation of early, particularly earthwork, castles and to the problems which many of these excavations were designed to solve (fig. 55). Much modern archaeological work has concentrated on questions concerning the origin and development of castles in England in the years immediately after the Norman Conquest. Views held by scholars since the start of the study of earthwork castles in England at the beginning of this century have recently been called into question, and new models have been propounded and tested. This interest culminated in the project on the early medieval castle sponsored by the Royal Archaeological Institute,[10] which encouraged, and partly financed, research into five castles: Baile Hill, York; Bramber, Sussex; Hastings, Sussex; Hen Domen, Montgomery; and Sulgrave, Northamptonshire. These sites were chosen either because they had well-documented foundation dates or possible pre-Conquest, Anglo-Saxon origins. Interim reports of the excavations appeared in *The Archaeological Journal* in 1977, and volume I of the definitive report on Hen Domen has recently been published,[11] but unfortunately financial constraints prevented the project from realising its full potential and the motte-and-bailey castle of Hen Domen is the only one of the five where excavation continues. The project raised more problems that it solved, but it had the virtue of crystallising interest in the early castle in England and providing a focus for archaeological research. It is interesting to note that the time when the Royal Archaeological Institute's project was under way coincided with a peak in earthwork castle excavation in general (fig. 56) and the two cannot be unconnected.

Until the 1960s the theories about the origins and development of earthwork castles had gone unchallenged since they were first put forward by Mrs Armitage in her book *Early Norman Castles of the British Isles*, published in 1912. The received opinion, based largely on her fundamental work, was that the motte-and-bailey castle was introduced into England in 1066 by William the Conqueror, and that this form of castle was well known and fully developed in Normandy for half a century or so before that date. The castle was considered a post-Conquest, Norman and feudal institution, even though a handful of castles do appear to have been built in England during the reign of Edward the Confessor (r. 1042 – 65). Edward was brought up in the Norman court while the Danish kings were occupying the throne of England and his sympathies were biased towards Normandy even after his accession on the death of Harthacnut. Those Norman courtiers who accompanied him to England in 1042 were rewarded with wealth and land, much of it along the borders of Wales, and it is there that we first hear of *aene castel* being built by 'foreigners' in 1051.[12] This was probably in Hereford, and was followed by apparently similar structures elsewhere in that county: Ewyas Harold and Richard's Castle. The castle of Hereford was destroyed in the nineteenth

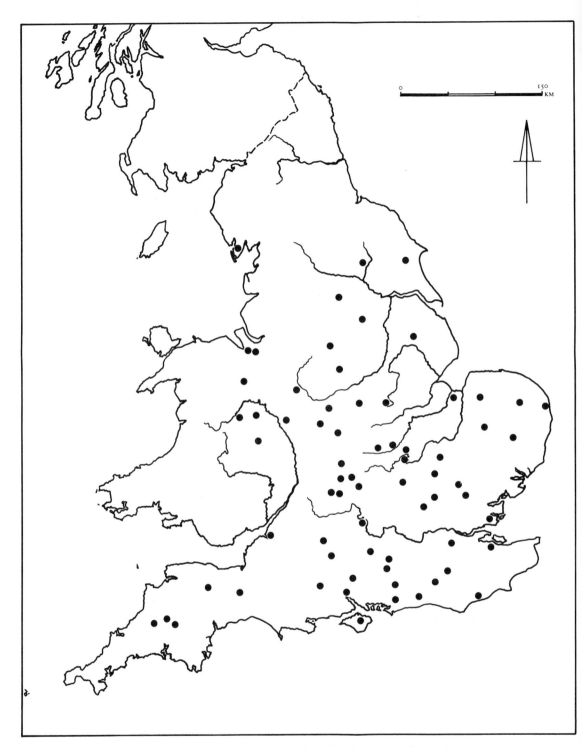

55. Distribution map of excavations of earthwork castles (ring-works and mottes) 1956–80.
Compiled from the 'Medieval Britain' section of *Med. Archaeol.*

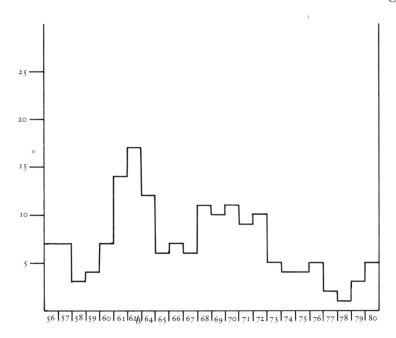

56. Chart showing the number of excavations per year on earthwork castles 1956–80.   Compiled from the 'Medieval Britain' section of *Med. Archaeol.*

century, but the other two sites remain today as mottes. Ewyas Harold has not been investigated, but Richard's Castle was excavated in the 1960s in the hope of discovering the lay-out of this probable pre-Conquest castle. Unfortunately, the huge motte there proved to have been greatly modified after its initial construction (fig. 57) and, although other extremely interesting information came to light, the castle of the 1050s remained undiscovered.[13]

Although these castles are mentioned in the *Anglo-Saxon Chronicle,* they are not described in detail, and it is far from clear what the Old English word *castel* really meant. Should we be looking for a motte-and-bailey or a ring-work? Presumably some form of earth and timber construction is implied by the word as masonry buildings were rare in Anglo-Saxon England, other than in ecclesiastical contexts, and a stone *castel* would surely have been specified by the compilers of the Chronicle. There are several other enigmatic references (Clavering, Essex, and Dover, Kent) which point to possible castles of pre-Norman date, but there is insufficient evidence on the ground to be confident of either, and there are not enough hard facts to support the existence of castles in England in any number before the Norman Conquest.

This view fits in well with the opinion that feudalism and castles go hand in hand (pp. 107–9), but recent research has led to the suggestion that as the seeds of feudalism may have been present in Anglo-Saxon England, so also may have been

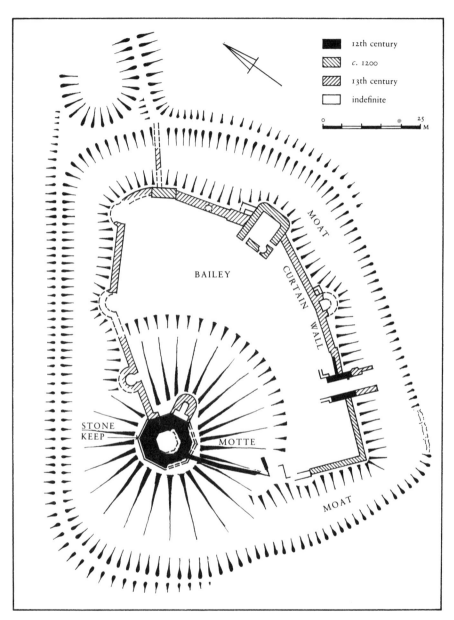

57. Plan of Richard's Castle, Herefordshire, showing twelfth-century masonry within the motte and around the perimeter of the bailey. No evidence for a possible pre-Conquest castle was found by the excavations.   After Curnow and Thompson 1969

the roots of the castle; that, in fact, there may have been castles in England before the arrival of Edward the Confessor and his Norman favourites. Much of the reasoning in the controversy about the origin of the castle in England comes dangerously close to circular argument (castles are intrinsic to feudalism; feudalism was introduced by the Normans; castles are therefore Norman in origin) or to a pure matter of semantics (castles are defended residences of the lord; Anglo-Saxon lords, *thegns*, had defended residences; therefore there were castles in Anglo-Saxon England) and those not personally involved in the controversy might wonder why such strong feelings have been aroused. Nevertheless, much print has been expended on questions such as whether the Anglo-Saxons had castles, whether the motte-and-bailey was a Norman innovation, or whether it developed in England after the Conquest through the addition of a mound (motte) to a ring-work (which might already have been known to and built by the Anglo-Saxons in the pre-Conquest period). Such stuff is the very life-blood of scholarship and enlivens many an otherwise dry technical description. In this case it has fuelled not a few articles, acted as the spur to a number of excavations, and led to the selection of Sulgrave, Northamptonshire, as one of the subjects of the castles project mentioned above (p. 117).

Excavations at Sulgrave and also at Goltho, Lincolnshire, have produced evidence indicating that Anglo-Saxon residences may have been defended in some manner.[14] Both these sites were occupied during the tenth and eleventh centuries (and Goltho also a good deal earlier), when they each consisted of at least one large hall with ancillary buildings lying within an area defined by a timber palisade (Goltho, ninth and tenth centuries) or an earthen rampart (Goltho, later tenth century; Sulgrave, mid-eleventh century). Neither site has documentary evidence which could tell us of its status in the Anglo-Saxon period, but each may have been the dwelling of an aristocrat (or *thegn*). The well-known and often-quoted early eleventh-century reference to the qualifications for thegnly status ('If a ceorl prospered so that he possessed fully five hides of land of his own, church and kitchen, bell and *burhgeat*, a seat and special office in the king's hall, then was he thenceforth of thegn-right worthy')[15] has been assumed to mean that the dwellings of Anglo-Saxons with wealth and power must have been encircled by a defence, the *burhgeat* being the gatehouse marking the entrance through palisade or rampart. Hence, sites such as Goltho and Sulgrave, with their defences, would qualify as 'thegnly' residences or 'private *burhs*' and may be the Anglo-Saxon equivalent of the castle – presumably of ring-work type. It was on this basis that Sulgrave was selected for the Royal Archaeological Institute's castle project. Partial excavation of the site has confirmed that the hall at Sulgrave was defended in some measure in the pre-Conquest period, and that the hall itself was somewhat unusual in an Anglo-Saxon context by being partly built in stone; but is it justifiable on these grounds to claim Sulgrave as a pre-Conquest castle? Goltho displays equally unusual, but different, features. After the Conquest the site became first a manor house and, subsequently, in the early twelfth century, a motte-and-bailey castle.

There is continuity here between the pre- and post-Conquest periods, but does this mean continuity of status? It is obviously impossible to hypothesise too confidently on the basis of two excavations, and although other sites of possibly similar type have been excavated more recently (for example Faccombe, Hampshire; Raunds, Northamptonshire),[16] the question of Anglo-Saxon 'castles' must remain unanswered. It is becoming increasingly obvious, though, that the Anglo-Saxons did not concentrate exclusively on communal defences, and that the chain of large forts established through Wessex and Mercia in the late ninth and tenth centuries (the burghal fortresses or *burhs*) mainly in response to potential attack from the Danes did not stand in isolation, but were supplemented by 'private *burhs*' where the *thegn* and his family might be safe from their enemies, without having to flee to the nearest defended fortress.

The likelihood of there being defences of ring-work type in Anglo-Saxon England lends weight to Davison's suggestion that the motte-and-bailey castle may have developed in England at or shortly after the time of the Conquest.[17] In conjunction with this, Davison investigated some early earthwork castles in Normandy which were reputed to have been in existence long before 1066 and to have been models for the motte-and-bailey type of castle known in England after the Conquest.[18] Although this research has not yet been fully published, it seems clear (pers. comm. B.K.Davison) that the evidence for both the dating and the actual types of castles in Normandy in the early eleventh century is far from secure, and that there is little concrete proof that they were the prototypes of the motte-and-bailey castle in England. It is certain, however, that both masonry and earthwork castles were being built in parts of western France during the early eleventh century[19] and that at least some aspects of them must have influenced castle construction in England from the Norman Conquest onwards. It is Davison's contention that the modern scholar has too readily assumed that the eleventh-century castle in England was of the motte-and-bailey type, which was a direct copy of the originals in Normandy (and portrayed, for example, on the Bayeux Tapestry).

Several of Davison's excavations in England have also been designed to test the hypothesis of mound added to ring-work to form a motte-and-bailey, and in two cases he has shown conclusively that the motte was a secondary addition to an original fortification. At Castle Neroche, Somerset (fig. 48), the excavated structure consisted of three phases: the first, an Iron-Age (or perhaps Anglo-Saxon) earthwork, whose ramparts and ditches were subsequently used as the basis of a ring-work; this was finally supplemented by a motte, which had been abandoned by the twelfth century.[20] A section cut through the motte at Aldingham, Cumbria (fig. 58), showed that an early twelfth-century ring-work enclosing timber buildings was filled in to form a flat-topped mound in the mid-twelfth century. The mound was raised a further 2m in height during the early thirteenth century, when it was also revetted with timber, although abandoned unfinished.[21] Other evidence is gradually coming forward to show that the motte of a motte-and-bailey castle was

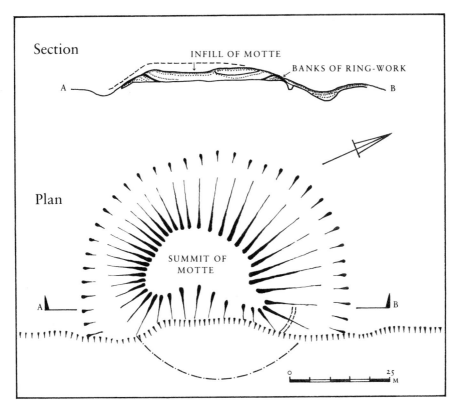

58. Section and plan of Moat Hill, Aldingham, Cumbria. The original ring-work (ramparts shown in section by heavy line) was converted into a motte in the mid-twelfth century. After *Med. Archaeol.* 1969

not necessarily always built as part of the castle's first phase, but it is not possible yet to come to any positive decision about Davison's ring-work theory.

As we shall see below, archaeological excavation of earthwork castles over the past three decades has added complexity to a subject which, before excavation, seemed to be simple in the extreme. In 1912 Mrs Armitage said that too little was known about earthwork castles for generalisations to be made. The same is even more true today. The archaeological study of early castles has been invaluable in amassing new and fascinating data, and we know much more about mottes, baileys and ring-works and their construction than was dreamed of in 1912, but it is still impossible to generalise, and virtually every site which has been excavated has produced different information. The potential of this study remains enormous, even after so many years of scholarly research.

Despite the long-standing interest in early earthwork castles, the first scientific excavation of a motte did not take place until the late 1940s, when Brian Hope-Taylor excavated the castle mound at Abinger, Surrey.[22] Until then our knowledge of the structures which originally surmounted the tops of earthen mottes was confined to early written references, and the illustrations of castles depicted in the Bayeux Tapestry. Both sources indicate that castles of the eleventh and twelfth centuries consisted of a high earth mound surrounded at its base by a moat and at its summit by a palisade encircling a wooden tower. Archaeologists and historians alike assumed that the mound of earth was thrown up first and the tower then planted on its top; excavation has shown that that method of construction was but one of a multiplicity of different forms employed in the construction of motte-and-bailey castles. Some of these will be described in the remaining pages of this chapter.

The excavation at Abinger, Surrey, revealed a pattern of post-holes on the top of the motte which indicated that a timber tower with an open ground floor had been erected on the summit once the mound had been built, and that the top of the motte had been encircled by a wooden palisade and wall-walk, with a simple gateway and access from the base of the motte by some form of ladder. Although two phases of construction could be discerned (early and middle twelfth century), the basic pattern remained the same throughout, and when occupied Abinger Castle must have looked very similar to the castle of Dol as depicted on the Bayeux Tapestry.

Abinger, then, showed that the motte was built first and the foundations of tower and palisade dug down into it, but other excavations have indicated that this was by no means the only method used when constructing a motte. The Bayeux Tapestry itself suggests that a different method might have been employed at Hastings, where the castle is shown under construction, with the tower already in position and the motte being thrown up around it (fig. 59). This could, of course, be a form of that artistic licence known in the Middle Ages where a number of consecutive actions are shown taking place simultaneously, but it could equally mean that the tower was indeed erected first, with its foundations reaching into the firm natural ground surface, and that a mound of earth was subsequently piled around its base.

A number of excavations have shown that this method of construction was not unknown to the Normans in England, and that there were an infinite number of variations on the theme. Towers built on the old ground surface and subsequently surrounded by an earth mound could also be built of masonry, as is shown by those excavated at Ascot Doilly, Oxfordshire, Aldingbourne, Sussex, Farnham, Surrey, or Castle Acre, Norfolk,[23] and some were designed in such a way that they could hardly have looked like mottes at all. The most spectacular example of all is the castle at South Mimms, Middlesex, excavated in the 1960s, where a timber tower was erected on a stone footing and surrounded up to first floor level by an earth mound which was itself encased in wooden shuttering. Access to the castle was by means of a timber-lined tunnel, about 8m long, which penetrated the basement

59. The building of the motte of Hastings Castle as depicted on the Bayeux Tapestry. The workmen appear to be piling a mound around an already-existing timber tower. The motte is shown with horizontal strata and apparently covered by a layer of some different substance.

of the tower. When it was complete the castle of South Mimms must have looked like a great timber tower surrounded by a timber ground-floor plinth (fig. 60), not in the least like the earth mound surmounted by a tower as we would think today. Although no other excavated motte has produced such a distinctive style of construction, it is worth bearing in mind that many of the seven hundred or so mottes which we know today as gently sloping grass-covered mounds may in fact have displayed quite a different profile in their lifetimes.

The castle at South Mimms is but an extreme example of the elaborate mottes which were being put up all over the country in the eleventh and twelfth centuries and whose construction we know in detail from a very small excavated sample. Once again, the depiction of Hastings motte on the Bayeux Tapestry can give us a clue to ways in which mottes were built. The embroidery there shows a mound evidently constructed in a number of horizontal strata, each separated by a well-defined but narrow layer of a different colour; overlying the whole there is yet

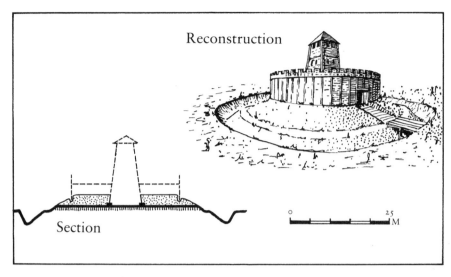

60. Section and reconstruction of the twelfth-century motte at South Mimms, Middlesex. After Davison 1979

another layer which appears to be encasing the total mound. Recent archaeological work has shown that the tower at Hastings could be a factual representation; is it possible, then, that the method of motte construction as shown by the tapestry could be equally well substantiated by archaeological excavation?

The motte at Hastings itself was excavated as part of the Royal Archaeological Institute's project at the end of the 1960s in the hope that this first documented motte in England after the Norman Conquest might reveal some evidence of the methods used in its construction which could be equated with the tapestry illustration. Unfortunately, as so often, the excavated evidence failed to tally with that from other sources, and an unconsolidated sand core was all that was revealed,[24] but excavations elsewhere have proved more productive. Some mottes were constructed of horizontal layers of earth or turf separated by brushwood (Baile Hill, York),[25] some of alternating layers of gravel and clay (Southampton) or clay and shale (Launceston, Cornwall). Some had their surfaces covered with clay (Northampton, Oxford and Winchester) or surrounded by wooden shuttering (Goltho, Lincolnshire, and Huntingdon). Some castle mounds were of unconsolidated and ungraded earth as the result of heaping up the spoil from their moats; some were of selected blocks of stone. The variations are innumerable and can only be traced through working through the 'Medieval Britain' section of *Medieval Archaeology*. There is as yet no synthesis of the archaeological evidence for early castle-building in this country. The excavations carried out so far suggest that it is still impossible to generalise about motte-construction in England and that although we have more detailed evidence than Mrs Armitage had in 1912 we are still no closer to making a comprehensible picture of it. In the years after the Conquest castles had to be built speedily with the materials most readily to hand; archaeological excavation has shown that virtually every castle-builder's response was different, conditioned by the circumstances of time and place.

The motte-and-bailey castle was one response to the need for castle building in the immediate post-Conquest generation. Most archaeological work in recent years has been concentrated on the motte, which appears to have been the focal point of most defensive works, but the long and painstaking excavation of the bailey at Hen Domen, Montgomery,[26] for the past two decades has shown that equally detailed information can be obtained from these so-called outer defences. The work at Hen Domen has shown that the baileys of motte-and-bailey castles must have been filled with buildings, ranging from chapel to kitchen to stable. This was the area where the life of the castle went on, while the motte, with its tower and palisade, remained undisturbed except for times of emergency. The motte remains today as a much more spectacular monument to the past, but the bailey must always have seen most life. As in many things, the modern scholar often pays more attention to the incidentals than the essentials of medieval life, and the motte has received a disproportionate amount of attention from recent archaeological work.

The excavation of earthwork castles continues, but at a much diminished rate. The same is true of masonry castles, where work is mainly confined to excavation in advance of consolidation by the Department of the Environment. The work done on these later medieval fortifications has hardly been mentioned here; many of them have a well-documented history (particularly when they were royal castles), and in other instances there are sufficient surviving ruins to allow interpretation of their function and use. The same cannot be said of the earthwork castles of the eleventh and twelfth centuries. Excavation is the only way of discovering what these castles looked like when they were in use. It should be clear from the brief summary given here that their present appearance bears little relation to their original form. Archaeology has a great deal to offer in filling out the picture of medieval England, not least through the contribution it has already made to our knowledge of an aspect of medieval life which must have affected every member of the population in the generations immediately after the Norman Conquest.

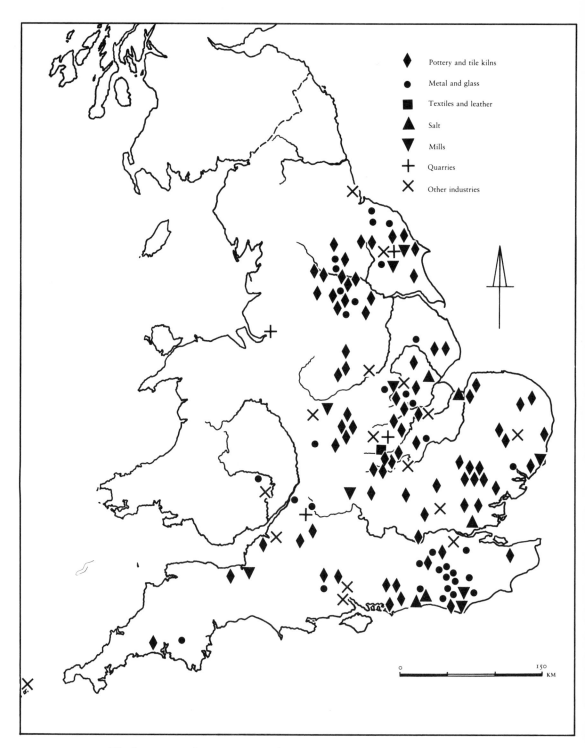

61. Distribution map of excavations on industrial sites 1956–80. Compiled from the 'Medieval Britain' section of *Med. Archaeol.*

5. Craft and Industry

The crafts and industries which were the life-blood of medieval England have generally been poorly served by the archaeologist, who has until recently shown a peculiar lack of interest in this most important aspect of medieval life. Reports in the 'Medieval Britain' section of *Medieval Archaeology* show how unimportant 'Industry' has been compared with most other aspects of excavation (fig. 61) and this is particularly unfortunate as this is a subject which could contribute greatly to our knowledge of the medieval economy. In the words of the historian P. D. A. Harvey the archaeological investigation of industry and industrial sites would result in 'greater returns than any other work on the period's archaeology, simply because it fills such a gap in the written records'.[1] Some of the archaeological evidence for crafts and industries known at present is summarised below; it is patently an incomplete summary, for some activities, such as that of the armourer, the jeweller, the coiner, the worker in precious metals, are omitted altogether, and other trades, such as that in bone and horn, are given but a brief mention. For these the archaeological evidence remains slight and most space has been devoted to those industrial processes where archaeology has contributed new information.

Much more remains to be done on this subject, and the gaps in our knowledge can only be accentuated by a survey of this type. It is encouraging, though, that the Council for British Archaeology has recently published a research report entitled *Medieval Industry*[2] and is now running a series of seminars on industrial subjects. This aspect of medieval archaeology is at last beginning to be given the treatment it deserves.

TEXTILES

Although during the Middle Ages woollen cloth-making was 'probably the most important of all manufacturing enterprises, as an employer of labour, of capital, of technical expertise, and of business skill',[3] medieval cloth-making has been almost totally neglected by archaeologists. Not only are the textiles themselves likely to be preserved only in anaerobic conditions where bacterial activity has not destroyed them, but the equipment of textile production was also usually made of organic materials, notably wood, which similarly demand special conditions for preservation. Little then remains of the medieval cloth-making industry, its tools and its products. The ever-increasing excavation of waterlogged sites in the past decade or so has, however, produced more evidence and the archaeologist is consequently more capable of supplementing the historian's study of the medieval cloth-making industry.

Trade in cloth, which is so well documented, has, on the other hand, been a popular study for historians,[4] who have, with few exceptions, tended to deal more with the administration and organisation of the industry than with the methods employed in textile manufacture. Nevertheless, it was L. F. Salzman,[5] working from written records, who first summarised the manufacturing process. E. Carus-Wilson continued his work[6] and first dealt with some of its physical aspects, using as her evidence sculptures from the Lane Chapel, Cullompton, Devon, which depict aspects of cloth-finishing.[7] Carus-Wilson also pointed out the importance of the development of the fulling-mill in the English textile industry, suggesting that once cloth could be fulled in an industrialised manner rather than being trampled in fulling-pits (p. 134) commercial cloth-making became centred in the countryside, where streams suitable as a driving-force for the fulling-mills could be found, and that the previous historically attested ascendancy of urban cloth-making declined.[8] This view has since been disputed,[9] but the medieval archaeologist might be able to resolve the controversy. Is it possible to discover fulling-mills (which are mentioned in documents from the twelfth century) and, once discovered, is it possible to distinguish fulling from any other milling practice? It is shown elsewhere (p. 162) that the mill at Bordesley Abbey was used for providing power for industrialised processes; could fulling have been one of these? And is there any archaeological evidence to suggest that cloth-making became more common in rural sites after the thirteenth century? Archaeology could here make a positive contribution to a historian's dispute.

The processes involved in making woollen cloth (the most commonly produced and used textile in the Middle Ages) began with the shearing and selection of woolfells (sheepskins), the quality of which would be reflected in the quality of the finished product. Different parts of England were noted for their different qualities of wool, but no true selective breeding policy seems to have been carried out, although large-scale stock movements (between, for example, monasteries of the same order) suggest that some form of breeding was being practised in order to produce finer wool.[10] Iron sheep-shears of types very similar in shape to those in use up to mechanisation this century were used. Some shears have been discovered through excavation,[11] but they are best known from illuminated manuscripts such as the twelfth-century Canterbury Psalter.[12]

After shearing, the wool had to be cleaned by beating and washing, and then prepared for spinning into yarn by carding or combing. Carding of wool with short fibres (or staples) was done with a wooden implement set with short metal hooks, or perhaps with teasels; larger iron teeth in a wooden frame were used for combing longer staples. Archaeological traces of carding and combing are few, as the metal teeth which are likely to be the only preserved parts of the implements used could easily be mistaken for nails or other unidentifiable iron objects, although teeth from carding combs have been found in some urban sites. In certain circumstances, also, the remains of teasels should be recognisable.

Spinning the carded or combed wool into yarn was the next task, one which seems normally to have been undertaken at home by both women and men using distaff and spindle. The spinning-wheel, for which we have no archaeological evidence, is depicted in manuscripts from the fourteenth century (for example, the Luttrell Psalter).[13] It was probably introduced into England earlier,[14] but may not have come into common use in households until after the close of the Middle Ages, for there is a great deal of evidence that spindles were used for spinning throughout the medieval period. The equipment needed for spinning by hand was simple: a wooden rod (distaff) on which to carry the raw wool, another wooden rod often slightly thicker in the middle and hooked at one end (spindle), and a weight (spindle-whorl) which was slipped over the spindle to act as a 'fly-wheel' to keep the spindle rotating while the raw wool was being drawn out into yarn. Spindle-whorls were commonly made of stone, baked clay, bone or lead and are therefore more frequently preserved in the ground than the wooden distaffs and spindles which are their essential counterparts. Whorls have been found at every period and in every region where cloth was made by non-industrialised means, and the medieval period in England is no exception. Distaffs and spindles may be preserved in favourable circumstances and in King's Lynn, Norfolk, a complete spindle with its hooked end, stone whorl and spool of thread was discovered.[15]

The virtual ubiquity of spindle-whorls in domestic contexts throughout the entire medieval period suggests that spinning was a cottage industry which continued even after the introduction of the spinning-wheel. It may have been producing the yarn for weaving into cloth to meet the immediate needs of the family, though, as we shall see, there is very little evidence for domestic weaving in England in the High Middle Ages.

Until the High Middle Ages weaving on an upright loom, which could stand either in the dwelling-house or a subsidiary outbuilding,[16] was the usual method of producing textiles, presumably purely to satisfy the needs of the household. The main archaeological evidence for upright looms consists of loom-weights. These are perforated stones or pieces of baked clay used to keep the warp (vertical) threads taut so that the weft (horizontal) threads could be woven through them. Such looms (warp-weighted looms) were in common use throughout the prehistoric and early medieval periods[17] and even up to the twentieth century in some parts of Scandinavia,[18] but in most parts of Europe they were superseded in the

Middle Ages by the horizontal or treadle loom, which needed no loom-weights to keep its warp taut.

It is common to find loom-weights in habitation sites up to the end of the Saxon period, although by the eleventh century there are indications that the upright, warp-weighted loom was either beginning to go out of use or that its warp was being tensioned by a wooden bar rather than a collection of weights.[19] Loom-weights are rarely found on domestic sites of the post-Conquest period but two twelfth-century kilns for their production were found at Rochester, Kent.[20] It is assumed that the upright loom with its warp threads held taut by heavy loom-weights was either no longer an everyday piece of furniture in the medieval English household, or that looms of this type had been replaced by the horizontal loom where weights were no longer necessary. A horizontal loom takes up much more space than an upright one and is therefore less likely to be used in normal domestic conditions.

The horizontal loom was introduced into Europe some time during the early Middle Ages, although the precise date is disputed. There are manuscript illustrations of treadle looms from the thirteenth century and later, but there is no archaeological evidence from English medieval sites to substantiate this dating. The best archaeological evidence for the horizontal loom comes from excavations in the USSR and Poland. In Novgorod, USSR, the waterlogged conditions preserved medieval timber structures and a multitude of wooden artifacts,[21] including the remains of horizontal looms such as treadles, oval shuttles and heddle rods attributed to the thirteenth century. Remains of a treadle loom have also been discovered in medieval Gdańsk, Poland,[22] where fragments of woollen textile which could only have been woven on a treadle loom have also been found.[23] East European discoveries such as these seem to date from the thirteenth century, but it has been argued that an innovation such as the change from upright to horizontal loom must have occurred earlier in Western Europe (introduced there from the Near East via Italy). A twelfth-century date for the adoption of the horizontal loom in Western Europe has, therefore, been suggested by some authorities,[24] but an even earlier date is postulated by others.[25] Although there is virtually no archaeological evidence in England for the horizontal loom, pieces have been recovered from excavations in Sigtuna and Lund, Sweden, from the twelfth and thirteenth centuries respectively[26] and there seem to be good grounds for believing that the horizontal loom was being introduced into Western Europe by the eleventh century at the latest.

The replacement of the upright by the horizontal loom was probably a protracted process, for it has been argued that a certain type of cloth known as 'haberget' was being produced in England on an upright loom until the thirteenth century.[27] The word 'haberget' does not occur in documents after the end of the thirteenth century, and Carus-Wilson suggests that the term went out of use when the practice of weaving this particular type of cloth on an upright loom stopped. The absence of loom-weights from thirteenth-century and earlier contexts suggests that the upright loom may have gone out of use much earlier than this, and that if a cloth such as 'haberget' was woven on such a loom it could not have been on a warp-weighted loom housed in a domestic environment (for which there is no archaeological evidence) but rather in a specific production centre which concentrated on the production of this type of cloth. It would be unrealistic to expect excavations to reveal such a specific site; what can be said from the excavated evidence is that loom-weights are generally absent from excavated domestic sites from the eleventh century onwards and there is therefore no archaeological evidence for the use of the warp-weighted loom after that date.

The adoption of the horizontal loom in preference to the upright type was an important step in the development of the medieval cloth industry. It enabled cloth-making to move away from its essentially domestic base, where the weaving of woollen textiles aimed to produce sufficient cloth to clothe the immediate family, to an industrial organisation where cloth of unlimited length could be produced for a commercial market. Weaving therefore moved out of the home to a commercial centre and it could be that at the same time spinning became commercialised. But it is interesting to see from excavated evidence that although there is a total absence of loom-weights in the excavated material, spindle-whorls continue to be found until the end of the Middle Ages. This must suggest that for some reason spinning remained a domestic industry while weaving became centralised and commercialised.

The only other pieces of equipment from archaeological contexts which can certainly be associated with weaving are the perforated bone needles which occur on almost all excavated urban sites and which are generally called 'pin-beaters'. They have been compared with the double-ended polished, but not perforated, bone objects from Anglo-Saxon sites[28] which seem to have been used for adjusting individual threads in the weft of the cloth. The shape of the medieval examples is not strictly comparable with those from the Anglo-Saxon period (fig. 62) but can be equated with recent ethnographic examples,[29] where a perforated bone needle is used to adjust the weft. Even if the medieval bone needles were not used

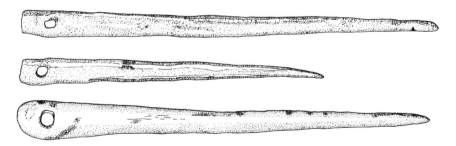

62. Perforated bone needles or 'pin-beaters' used in weaving.

specifically as pin-beaters they 'are most likely to be weaving tools, to whichever use they were put'[30] and their frequent occurrence on medieval sites suggests that, despite the lack of loom-weights, weaving was not completely unknown to the medieval household.

After weaving, the cloth needed to be thickened, or fulled, either with the mechanised help of a mill, of which we have little archaeological evidence, other than the fulling-mill at Fountains Abbey[31] or by the more ancient and traditional method of trampling the cloth in vats filled with water and fuller's earth, a clay-like substance still used today as an absorbent of the grease and oil of cloth. It is unfortunate that Professor Carus-Wilson's exciting theory about fulling-mills (p. 130) has not so far been substantiated by archaeological investigations, but it is certainly an idea which could be followed through by archaeological fieldwork. It is thirty years since the theory was put forward; surely it is high time that an archaeologist attempted to give some physical credence to it. Evidence for fulling has, however, been produced by excavations at Winchester,[32] where there is also documentary evidence for fullers,[33] and in the City of London, where excavations at Swan Lane produced hearths surrounded by fuller's earth, probably from the pits still in operation at Nutfield near Redhill, Surrey (pers. comm. G. Egan).

By fulling, the woven cloth was shrunk so that its density and strength were increased and the cloth 'felted', often to such an extent that the original pattern of weave was obliterated. Once fulled, the cloth was hung out to dry on tenter frames where it was stretched taut to achieve the correct dimensions, a most necessary measure as the sizes of cloth were laid down by law (first recorded in 1196, Assize of Measures) and checked during the final process of *aulnaging*, whereby governmental officials, aulnagers, could pass or condemn the quality and size of the cloths. Tentering took up a great deal of space and specific areas of towns were set aside as tenter grounds.[34] Several such grounds have been discovered in Bristol[35] and Winchester,[36] where post-holes in rows up to 16m long indicated the drying-racks and where the characteristic implements, the tenterhooks, used for attaching the cloth to the wooden frames were also found.[37]

After stretching and drying, the cloth was finished by being teased and sheared. The surface of the cloth was raised with the spiky heads of teasels mounted in a wooden frame[38] and finally sheared off by very large-bladed nap shears to make a smooth, in some cases almost velvety, surface. The finer the cloth, the more care had to be taken in the final shearing, which was done while the cloth was still slightly damp. The cloth was then sent to the aulnager who would seal the cloth with a leaden seal if it were up to standard for sale on the open market. Some medieval leaden seals have been discovered in excavations in Bristol[39] and on the Continent, for example in Amsterdam,[40] but many more have been discovered as casual finds, particularly on the Thames foreshore. Medieval leaden seals for cloth consisted of two discs which were clipped around the edge of each piece of cloth and attached by a split rivet. The discs carried motifs which included the initials of the aulnager and the town in which he worked, and, as the dies from which they were produced seem to have been engraved by craftsmen who also worked at the Exchequer engraving coin dies, there is a distinct similarity between the designs on seals and those of contemporary coinage. This helps to date the leaden cloth seals, the earliest of which that have been preserved belong to the second half of the fifteenth century. Cloth was certainly sealed at an earlier date than this, but the seals have not yet been recognised. This may be because wax rather than lead was used in the early years of the practice.[41]

Wool could be dyed at virtually any stage of its manufacture into cloth – as raw wool, after spinning or after weaving. Many of the leaden cloth seals found on the Thames foreshore seem to cluster around the known sites of medieval and later dyers' workshops, and suggest that cloth was being dyed there in the piece after aulnaging. Other excavated evidence also supports this. Dyers' workshops have been found in Bristol, Winchester and Fountains Abbey,[42] for example, where the requisite equipment of a supply of fresh water and hearths for heating the dyeing vats (usually of lead) has been found. At Winchester, also, there is evidence at the Lower Brook Street site of the relationship between the thirteenth-century dyeing workshop and the dyer's house in an area of the town where the somewhat noisesome residues of dyeing did not too much disturb the other inhabitants. According to documentary sources the dyes in most frequent use were woad, madder and grain, all of which were imported from the Continent in large quantities, although woad and madder were also cultivated in England. The discovery at Baker Lane, King's Lynn,[43] of a concentration of seeds of dyers' greenweed (*Genista tinctoria*), used extensively in the Middle Ages as a dye which produced a yellow colour when used alone or green when combined with woad, is one of the few examples of the archaeological recovery of such evidence for vegetable dyes. It should be possible to extract similar information from the soil samples taken by environmental scientists at urban excavations about other plants used in this manner, and analysis of textiles themselves may produce similar information.[44]

Although the archaeological evidence for cloth production in England in the Middle Ages is not extensive, enough information is now available for us to attempt to reconstruct the processes involved in changing wool from its raw state to finished product. Future excavations, particularly in towns, where most of the processes seem to have taken place, should increase our knowledge greatly over the next few years and supplement what can also be culled from documentary sources and illuminated manuscripts. Archaeologist and historian could here work hand in hand to produce a detailed picture of the methods involved in the most important industry of medieval England.

Textiles other than woollen cloth are not well represented in the archaeological record although we should expect to find the remains of linen, either in the form of fragments of finished cloth or the equipment used, as have been discovered for an earlier period.[45] Excavations at Novgorod, USSR, showed that only 10 of the 484 textile fragments which were selected as the basis for research were linen.[46]

This suggests that the quantity of linen worn in medieval Novgorod was small in proportion to the amount of woollen cloth and may therefore be difficult to discover. Linen also seems to be particularly prone to decay under archaeological conditions. In the Netherlands, for example, linen was particularly badly preserved even where woollen textiles were found in relatively good condition, and the same may be true on English sites.[47] This is probably also the case with silk fabrics (only 4 of the 484 investigated samples at Novgorod were silk), but excavations have produced evidence for the use of silk in medieval England, for example at Southampton and Northampton, where fragments from clothing and narrow silk braids used perhaps as shoe-laces have been found.[48] All these pieces are thought to have been imported already woven into cloth, presumably from the Near East. There is so far no evidence for silk-weaving in this country until the post-medieval period,[49] and there is similar uncertainty about medieval silk-weaving elsewhere in north-west Europe.[50]

The study of preserved fragments of cloth, as distinct from the study of the manufacturing processes themselves, has increased considerably in recent years as a result of the emphasis on excavations in waterlogged sites in medieval towns. On the Continent much work has already been done in this field, for example, in Sweden,[51] in Poland[52] and the USSR.[53] From these studies it is possible to establish whether a textile has been woven on a horizontal rather than a vertical loom, and whether it is of native manufacture. Fewer studies have been made on textiles found in England, but there have been some interesting discoveries; for example, a piece of cloth found in front of the thirteenth-century wharf at Thoresby College, King's Lynn, is thought to have been woven in Iceland, to have been, in fact, the *wadmal* which is frequently mentioned in documentary sources of the fourteenth century and earlier[54] as coarse cloth used as packing material around other, more fragile, goods.[55] At Novgorod it was possible to establish that the woollen cloth discovered in the earlier levels was made from imported English wool and that from later contexts from Spanish wool. Excavations on waterlogged sites, particularly those along the Thames waterfront in the City of London (p. 186), are producing increasing amounts of preserved textile fragments which will greatly add to our knowledge of English textiles in the Middle Ages.

The fragmentary remains of textiles which have so far been discovered on medieval sites in England can give us some idea of the way in which the cloth was made up into clothing, but little information has yet been found concerning styles of dress in different periods of the Middle Ages. For this we must turn to pictorial material (fig.63), either from illustrated manuscripts[56] or from sepulchral monuments and brasses which show the dress worn among the upper strata of society.[57] Combining this form of evidence with the physical remains from excavation is the ideal method of producing a picture of the finished products of the medieval textile industry. Other non-archaeological evidence can also be used in this way. For example, the eleventh-century manuscript, the *Gerefa*, lists the equipment needed for cloth-making on an aristocratic rural estate of that date.[58] The equipment noted

63. Scene from the Luttrell Psalter, showing rustic fashion in dress (Add. MS 42130, f. 171).

there should also be relevant to that textile production in the post-Conquest period which was carried on as a cottage industry before the introduction of the truly industrialised production of the thirteenth century and later.

LEATHER

The provision of leather, particularly for footwear but also for other items of clothing such as belts, purses, etc., was an important service industry of the towns in the Middle Ages and one for which there is a good deal of archaeological evidence.

Leather was made mainly from the hides of cattle, although goats' and pigs' skin was also used. The process of leatherworking began with the selection of the hides, which was presumably done in the countryside, rather than from live animals which had been conveyed to the towns 'on the hoof'. After de-hairing and tanning, the hides were used by shoemakers (cordwainers), cobblers and others for their finished products. De-hairing and tanning were unpleasant and foul-smelling processes which were carried on at the extremities of towns where there was an adequate water supply and where the effluents would disturb the smallest number of people. In Winchester, for example, in the early twelfth century tanners and parchment-makers mainly occupied the two streets in the city with the best water supply and which lay down-wind of most of the inhabited area.[59] Excavations in Lower Brook Street, Winchester (*Tannerstret* in the twelfth-century Winton Domesday) produced substantial timber-lined pits of eleventh-century date, which were probably used as tanning pits at that time, but by the end of the thirteenth century the properties previously occupied by tanners were used by cloth-makers and dyers (p. 135), suggesting a migration of the more unpopular industry away from a site which by that time was well within the built-up area.

Pits for the preparation of hides before tanning have been found by excavations in Kingston-upon-Thames[60] and Winchester; here a pit which contained hairs from sheep, goat and cattle may not have been a de-hairing pit itself but one which received the refuse from such activities. Close to this pit in Winchester were others which had originally held liquid, including one which had a type of platform above it from which may have hung hides during the course of tanning.[61] Tanning pits have been found elsewhere (London, Chester and Nottingham, for example) and some brick-built tanning vats are still preserved in the Cistercian monastery of Rievaulx, Yorkshire (fig. 64).

Not only high-quality hides were selected for tanning, although these must obviously have produced leather and finished products of a better standard. The leather discovered at the Augustinian Friary, Leicester, for example, showed that many shoe soles were made of cow-hide perforated with holes from warble flies, which must have infested the animals when alive; this may indicate that the leather discovered in this site was of poor quality, produced for and used by the poorer members of society amongst whom the friars may have numbered.

The tools used in tanning are not often found from excavations.[62] At King's Lynn, for instance, even though there is considerable evidence that hides were tanned in the town, the only implement found which might have been used in

64. Brick-built tanning pits at Rievaulx Abbey, Yorkshire.

leather preparation was an iron sleaker used to force dirt out of hides. There is, on the other hand, much more excavated evidence for the end-products of the leatherworkers' trade. The current emphasis on the excavation of sites where organic material is preserved has resulted in the discovery of large quantities of medieval leather footwear, mainly in the form of boots and shoes. Many complete boots and shoes have been discovered and it is now possible to see how they were made, what leather was used and how styles changed from one century to another. As is the case with textiles, the study of leather has been much more advanced on the Continent over the past few decades and in some places (e.g. Gdańsk, Poland)[63] the discovery not only of the leather shoes but also of the wooden lasts on which the shoes were made has enormously advanced our knowledge of medieval footwear. A tenth-century wooden last is known from York,[64] but later examples are so far unknown in England.

Work in the Netherlands has also helped to elucidate the medieval shoemakers' craft,[65] as have comprehensive analyses of finds from Swedish sites[66] which have aimed to distinguish regional variants in boot and shoe production. In England excavations such as those in King's Lynn, London and many other places over the past couple of decades have illuminated this aspect of medieval life. Many sites have produced so-called cobblers' waste in sufficient quantities to suggest that the mending of shoes was an everyday domestic chore carried out in most urban, and many rural, households. The making of the shoes themselves, however, was a much more specialised craft which must have been a centralised and commercial process carried on in workshops in specific areas of a town. Signs of such workshops have been discovered in twelfth- and thirteenth-century Dublin[67] and excavations in Skien, Norway, uncovered a thirteenth-century building fitted out as a shoemaker's workshop, complete with wooden lasts of several sizes, leatherworking tools and leather offcuts.[68]

The type of shoe made throughout medieval Europe was that known as the 'turn-shoe' in which the upper, often of supple goatskin, was sewn onto the sole, normally of cow-hide, and then the whole turned inside out so that the sewn seam was concealed. Many different types of shoe and boot are known (fig. 65) but they conform to similar basic patterns both in this country and abroad. Some are very elaborate, with cut-out or stamped patterns decorating the uppers and with a multitude of different methods of fastening (lacings at the front or side, straps, buckles and so on). Some excavated examples also show the exaggerated pointed toes so often depicted in late medieval manuscripts or effigies. The pictorial evidence has led historians of fashion to believe that pointed shoes were a purely late medieval phenomenon, but recent excavations have shown that such shoes were worn throughout virtually the whole of the Middle Ages and were not confined to any one specific period.[69]

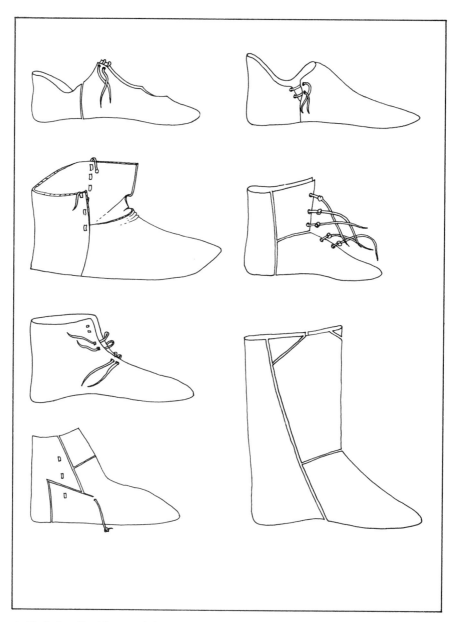

65. Typical medieval boots and shoes.

BONE AND HORN

The manufacture of objects from bone and horn is well attested by excavations in medieval towns in England and abroad. Numerous horn-cores of sheep and goats found in places such as King's Lynn and Stamford[70] suggest that the outer sheath was considered of value to the medieval craftsman, who removed it from the core by boiling and then used it to make various commodities, such as buttons or knife-handles. This must have been a modest and perhaps part-time activity which is seldom noted in contemporary documents.

Bones were also used to make a multiplicity of small objects ranging from spindle-whorls to dice, from combs (fig.66) to buttons. Offcuts and prepared blanks for many such objects are frequently discovered on excavation sites; their ubiquity in urban surroundings suggests that bone-working was, like horn-working or cobbling, an activity indulged in by many households.

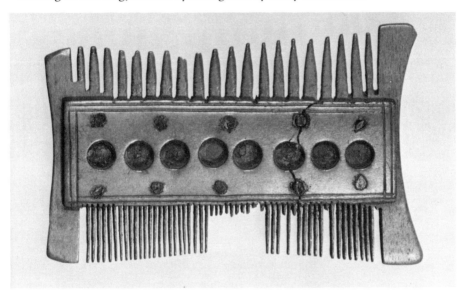

66. Double-sided bone comb from London.

WOODWORKING AND CARPENTRY

England is fortunate in the number of buildings which have survived, albeit often in modified form, from the medieval period (fig. 67). The framework of the walls of many secular domestic structures was made of timber, largely oak, and that of their roofs entirely so. Surviving ecclesiastical buildings also employ timber

67. Timber-framed buildings in Lavenham, Suffolk.

extensively in their construction, in this case mainly in roofs and towers as the walls of most surviving medieval churches and cathedrals are usually, though not always, of masonry. Medieval carpentry, therefore, is a subject which can be studied from standing buildings and which has been worked on extensively in recent years. There have been attempts to date buildings by the methods of construction used, notably typologies of joints have been proposed[71] and methods of roofing analysed as chronological indicators, but there is as yet no agreement among the protagonists of the various methods of dating. This study belongs to the realm of vernacular architecture rather than archaeology, and will not be pursued further here, but it is interesting to note that the science of dendrochronology has also been employed in these architectural studies and has produced tables of dates of the felling of timbers for particular buildings. Archaeology has also provided excavated examples of carpentry which can be dated both by conventional archaeological means and by extensive use of dendrochronology on preserved medieval timbers. The preservation of the evidence is of course dependent on anaerobic conditions in the ground and most examples come from excavations in waterlogged sites,[72] notably those along the Thames waterfront in the City of London[73] or from moats of castles or manors.[74]

Most interest has been concentrated on the types of joints used in the timber frameworks of buildings but careful scrutiny of the surfaces of the timbers from both standing structures and archaeological sites can also give invaluable information about the tools and methods of medieval structural carpentry. Unseasoned tree trunks were normally split with iron wedges to form planks which were then adzed into shape. Saws seem to have been only rarely used on large timbers, but at Black-friars Priory, Gloucester, saw-marks and adze-marks visible on the roof timbers suggest that the trees were sawn into planks soon after felling, and then shaped with an adze or perhaps a broad-axe once the sawn timbers had seasoned sufficiently to prevent further distortion.[75] This method of preparing structural timbers seems to have been an uncommon one in the Middle Ages, when the smallest possible trees for a given purpose seem to have been selected and used without seasoning.

Further evidence for the types of tools used in medieval carpentry has been adduced from the methods of construction used for church doors and standing structures[76] and from tools in use by carpenters up to the present day.[77] A great deal of information can also be obtained from medieval illustrations, such as the late eleventh-century Bayeux Tapestry, where the ship-building scene shows the use of broad-axe, adze and breast-auger[78] and an illustration from the 'Bedford Hours' showing the construction of a timber-framed house where saws, planes, hammers, mallets, chisels and augers can be seen.[79] There are innumerable illustrations of this type in both English and Continental medieval manuscripts; the collation of such information is badly needed for it would throw a light on a topic which has so far been poorly served by archaeological remains.

Carpenters' tools from excavations in England are regrettably few, either because they have not so far been recognised, or, more probably, because they were not thrown away after their useful life expired but were reworked into other implements. This must have been the fate of many iron tools in the Middle Ages and the most likely reason for the dearth of such finds in medieval excavated sites. Some such tools are known, though, and axes, adzes, augers etc. have been found.[80] Saws are less common, but a thirteenth-century example has been found on the Isle of Wight[81] and a fifteenth-century saw-pit discovered at Barton Blount, Derbyshire.[82]

Excavations have, however, produced evidence for woodworking on a smaller scale for the manufacture of domestic equipment, particularly that which supplemented pottery for household use (known as treen). Once again, the wooden objects themselves are likely to survive only in waterlogged conditions, and the number of sites on which they have been found is small. Wooden objects were probably also used as firewood once they had outlived their original usefulness, and so we should not necessarily expect to recover them in large quantities from archaeological sites, whatever the conditions of preservation. In Trondheim, Norway, for example, sites which have preserved the remains of timber-laid streets and wooden buildings in excellent condition[83] have produced remarkably few small wooden artifacts. The excavator thinks that this results from their being used as fuel at a time when wood was becoming scarce (pers. comm. C. Long), even though there was still sufficient timber in the neighbourhood to build large structures.

Wooden bowls have been recovered from many excavated sites in England such as Southampton, King's Lynn, Gloucester and Durham.[84] They seem mainly to have been turned on a lathe, probably the reciprocating pole-lathe which was already in use during the pre-Conquest period[85] and which has left traces in the form of tenth-century lathe-turned cores in places such as Coppergate, York.[86] No similar finds have so far been published from medieval sites of the eleventh century of later and, similarly, tools used in lathe-turning have not yet been recognised, but it seems reasonable to assume that lathe-turned objects of the Middle Ages were produced in this way.

Coopering must also have been a common activity (fig. 68) for barrels were used as containers for many commodities, the most important perhaps being wine. This was shipped to England in large barrels[87] and then sold or distributed inland in containers of varying sizes. Remains of barrels in the form of staves or tops have been found on many sites, such as Southampton, where late thirteenth-century examples have been discovered and virtually complete barrels are fairly often found as linings to wells.[88]

68. Manuscript illustration of a cooper at work (Harleian 1892, f. 29c)

GLASS

The archaeological evidence for medieval glass-making in England is slight and unsatisfactory. In the pre-Conquest period glass vessels are a relatively common find in the richer pagan Anglo-Saxon graves[89] and coloured window-glass has been discovered on monastic sites from the seventh-century onwards[90] and on the secular, but royal, site of Old Windsor,[91] but the vessels mostly seem to have been imported into England from the Continent[92] and the production methods of window-glass remain obscure. There is sufficient evidence from the Anglo-Saxon monasteries of Monkwearmouth and Jarrow to show that window-glass was made within the monastic precincts,[93] but no glass-making furnaces have been found there. The only examples of such structures from an Anglo-Saxon context are those excavated in the ninth- or tenth-century levels at Glastonbury Abbey, Somerset. Recent excavations in tenth-century York and Lincoln[94] have found crucibles with deposits of glass on their interiors, probably the remains from bead-making, and similar finds from Saxon Southampton[95] suggest that glass beads were also made there in the ninth century. It seems unlikely, though, that the cullet (raw glass) itself was made in these places, but rather that the beads were made by remelting old glass, perhaps sherds from old and broken vessels. This practice is known from elsewhere in Europe, notably Scandinavia,[96] where glass beads were undoubtedly made in large quantities, and at many other places in the early Middle Ages where beads were manufactured but where no glass-making furnaces are known. A find of cullet from tenth-century Gloucester, though, indicates that glass was being made from raw materials at least in one place in Anglo-Saxon England (pers. comm. J. Bailey).

Our knowledge of glass-making in England in the post-Conquest period is little better, even though the use of glass, particularly for glazing, increased considerably from the twelfth century, when the newly constructed cathedrals and greater churches were embellished with coloured window-glass,[97] and by the end of the Middle Ages glass was also being used for windows in secular buildings. The use of glass vessels as table-ware was also on the increase throughout the Middle Ages. Most of our evidence for this comes from illuminated manuscripts (for example, the dining scene in the Luttrell Psalter),[98] as the glass of the High Middle Ages is less durable than that of earlier periods (being made from silica and woodland ash rather than marine ash) and decays rapidly in archaeological conditions. However, glass vessels have been discovered on some excavated sites of the eleventh to fifteenth centuries.[99] Many of these vessels are of foreign origin (particularly at Southampton);[100] window-glass, particularly the coloured type, was also imported from abroad and the general impression is that, although some glass must have been produced in England during the Middle Ages, it was of a poor standard, and higher-quality products were obtained from the Continent (fig. 69).

There is some positive evidence, however, of glass production in England in the Middle Ages, mainly from the Surrey and Sussex Weald.[101] Much of the evidence

69. Glass-making in fifteenth-century Bohemia (Additional MS 24189, f. 16).

comes from documentary sources, such as the grant of land *c.* 1226 to Laurence the Glass-maker at Chiddingfold, Surrey, where an archaeological site with fragments of glass and crucibles has also been discovered.[102] Chiddingfold seems to have been the centre of glass production in the medieval Weald and residues from manufacture have been discovered in the surrounding area. One of the difficulties in pinpointing this activity from physical remains, however, is that the glass-makers seem to have been 'semi-nomadic',[103] and so few permanent structures are likely to have survived. A medieval glass-house has been excavated at Blunden's Wood, Surrey, where three glass-furnaces, an associated working surface and fragments of pale green window- and vessel-glass were discovered.[104] This site was dated to about 1330 by the scientific method of remanent magnetism and to the first half of the fourteenth century by pottery types; it seems to be representative of the types of glass-house current in England until the end of the sixteenth century. Several sixteenth-century glass-works of a similar sort have been excavated (Bagot's Park, Staffordshire for example; Alfold, Surrey)[105] but they fall outside our period. The site at Blunden's Wood with its furnaces for fritting, melting and annealing glass 'is really the only survivor from before 1500 of an enigmatic and somewhat intangible activity'.[106]

CERAMICS

The two industries about which we know most from archaeological sources are those of pottery-making and tile-making. The reports of excavated industrial sites published in the 'Medieval Britain' section of *Medieval Archaeology* show clearly that the investigations of these types of site far outweigh the combined numbers of all other excavated industrial features (fig. 70) and it is only recently that interest in other forms of medieval industrial activity has begun to assert itself. There are many publications which deal specifically with the medieval ceramic industry, and even general works on archaeological aspects of medieval England concentrate on the production of pottery and tiles to the virtual exclusion of other industrial activities;[107] the subject will, therefore, be dealt with here only in its broader outlines. Detailed discussions of pot and tile types and their manufacture can be pursued through the references cited in this section and through publications such as *Medieval Ceramics*, the organ of the Medieval Pottery Research Group.[108]

Our evidence for the ceramic industry in the Middle Ages comes largely from

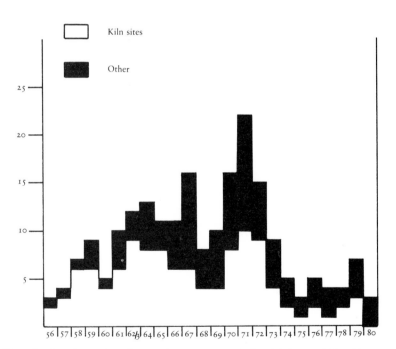

70. Chart showing the number of excavations per year on industrial sites 1956–80 with excavations on pottery and tile kiln sites shaded. Compiled from 'Medieval Britain' section of *Med. Archaeol.*

excavation, although relevant material can also be culled from documentary sources.[109] These indicate, however, that neither the potter nor the tiler was of high social standing in the Middle Ages, and written references to them and their trades are few. Although it is becoming increasingly obvious that written sources can reveal more than previously realised about the mechanics of pottery and tile distribution archaeology is still the main source of information. This comes mainly from the excavation of individual kilns or, more rarely, groups of kilns with associated buildings which may have been workshops or factories. For example, the kilns and buildings at Laverstock near Salisbury are thought to have made up a pottery-producing centre which supplied the neighbouring Clarendon Palace.[110] The kilns at Lyveden which lay within the confines of a peasant croft probably represent peasant craft production with a relatively limited marketing area, mainly confined to the East Midlands,[111] and at Danbury, Essex, there was a tile-making 'factory' which produced floor- and roof-tiles for commercial distribution through-out Essex.[112] Sites such as these, where both kilns and ancillary buildings have been excavated, tell us most about the medieval ceramic industry, but until recently archaeologists have tended to concentrate on the excavation of individual kilns, disregarding the essential working areas which surrounded them. The excavation

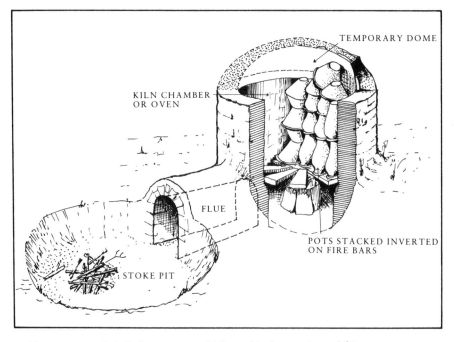

71. The reconstructed single-flue open-topped kiln used in the experimental firings at Barton-on-Humber. The pots are stacked inverted on a raised floor. The tunnel-shaped flue runs from stoke pit to kiln.   After Bryant 1977

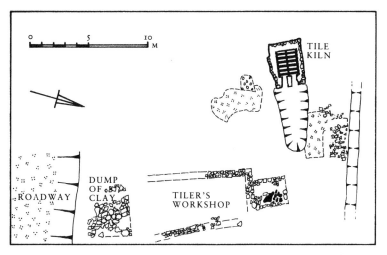

72. Peasant toft at the deserted medieval village of Lyveden with tiler's workshop
and tile kiln; evidence for tile-making as a peasant craft.   After Steane and
Bryant 1975

of isolated kilns has made it possible to build up a typology[113] and to establish the
methods used in their construction and firing, and experimental firings of reconstructed kilns (fig. 71) have also been used for the same ends.[114] More recently it
has been acknowledged that a reasonable idea of the entire process of pottery or
tile manufacture, the distribution of the finished product and the social and
economic organisation of the industry can only be obtained by the investigation
of total ceramic-manufacturing complexes and their hinterlands. Only a few of
these complexes have so far been investigated,[115] but their archaeological
importance is now acknowledged and it is unlikely that the excavation of individual kilns isolated from their industrial environs will be encouraged in the future.

Archaeological evidence shows that almost without exception the manufacture
of pottery and tiles in the Middle Ages was carried on in the countryside and was
probably a seasonal activity practised by craftsmen who supplemented their livelihood by agriculture, who were, in fact, essentially peasants with an additional skill
(as at Lyveden, for example; fig. 72). There are, however, some few examples of
pottery being made in towns in the Middle Ages and one might in those instances
think of the potters as being of an urban artisan class who presumably, similar to
their rural counterparts, supplemented their living in other ways. The production
of floor-tiles fell into a somewhat different category (pp. 157–8), as their manufacture for a specific contract (the flooring of a secular palace or a monastic
church, for example) seems to have been the rule at least in the early years (i.e.
the thirteenth century) of the floor-tile industry.

Until roughly A D 1100 it was customary for pottery-making centres to be situated

149

in towns, with particularly good evidence for this in the towns of midland and eastern England, where thriving pottery industries developed in the tenth and early eleventh centuries. Towns such as Thetford, Norfolk, Torksey, Lincolnshire, and Northampton[116] bear witness to this urban concentration which, for reasons perhaps associated with the availability of raw materials, particularly fuel, and the fire risk, was changed some time in the eleventh or twelfth century into a more dispersed rural distribution. The rural emphasis continued throughout the Middle Ages, and most excavated pottery kilns (for example, fifty-four out of the sixty-two sites reported in the 'medieval Britain' section of *Medieval Archaeology* 1956–80) are situated in the countryside. The most notable exception to this is Stamford, Lincolnshire, whose pottery industry was probably the most flourishing of all in the pre-Conquest period and where pottery continued to be made in an urban context until the end of the thirteenth century. Reasons for the decline of the industry in Stamford have been suggested (competition from outside markets, availability and cost of raw materials and labour, the degree of innovation in technology and style),[117] but what is more interesting is why the industry survived as long as it did in its urban environment. It will be seen elsewhere in this chapter that Stamford supported other industries (iron working, for example) in the Middle Ages, and it is salutory to remember that, although of paramount importance to the archaeologist today, the potters of Stamford were probably relatively unimportant in the overall economy of the town.

The production of roof- and floor-tiles was also an essentially rural craft, with kilns, particularly for floor-tiles, either being built and used at sites where the floors were to be laid (for example, Clarendon Palace, Norton Priory and Meaux Abbey),[118] or constructed as part of a commercial enterprise as at Danbury or Penn.[119] Although some glazed ceramic floor-tiles are known from a few ecclesiastical sites in England before the Conquest (e.g. St Albans, Bury St Edmunds, Winchester, All Saints, Pavement, York),[120] they did not come into frequent use until the thirteenth century and even then were confined to ecclesiastical or royal buildings.[121] It was not until the fourteenth century that floor-tiles became common in secular buildings, and then only in the richer merchants' houses.[122] That date saw the establishment of tile 'factories', specialising in the mass-production of floor-tiles which were distributed over a wide area from a commercially organised centre; these centres, however, remained based in the countryside.

The manufacture of pottery in the Middle Ages was essentially regional in character. The basic raw materials, clay for the pots and fuel for firing the kilns, were obtainable in virtually all parts of the country and the less essential materials, such as lead and copper for use in glazes, were probably equally easily obtainable in the form of scrap metal. Pottery was, therefore, made in most areas of England throughout the Middle Ages and, although regional differences can be discerned either by eye or through scientific analysis, basically the same methods seem to have been used throughout. The shapes of the pots produced were also virtually

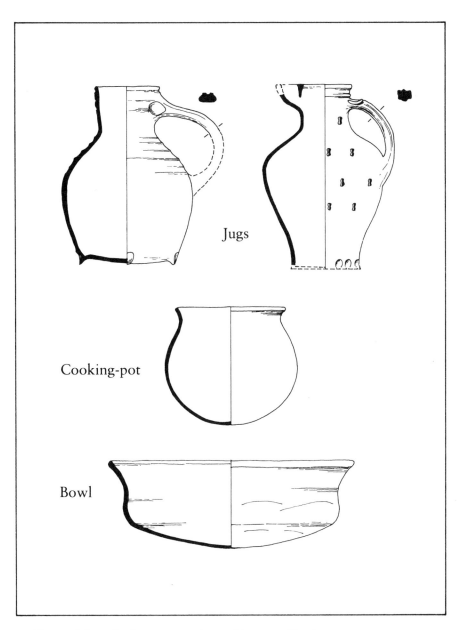

Jugs

Cooking-pot

Bowl

73. Characteristic medieval pottery types: jug, cooking pot and bowl.

74. Aquamanile in the shape of a mounted horse from Ditchingham, Norfolk. Aquamaniles were used as water-containers for washing hands at table.

identical, and few in number. Until the later part of the Middle Ages the jug, the 'cooking pot' and the bowl were the usual forms (fig. 73), with more elaborate hollow-wares, such as the aquamanile (fig. 74), or domestic equipment, such as lamps and candle-sticks, occurring only rarely. Cups and plates were unknown, their function presumably being fulfilled by wooden vessels (treen), but some small jugs may have served as drinking pots.[123]

Distribution maps of known pottery kilns[124] and kiln sites inferred from documentary or other non-archaeological sources[125] indicate that pottery-making was widespread throughout medieval England. Clay suitable for pottery-making occurs in most parts of the country, but usually needs to have another substance added to it to make it of the right texture for holding shape when formed into a pot. This additive is known as 'temper' or grog' and may be sand, grit, pounded shell, chopped straw and so on. It can often be distinctive to one kiln site and therefore diagnostic in establishing the place of origin of a pot. The clay had also to be weathered before use. This could be done either by leaving the clay in heaps over winter, or by steeping it in water in a pit, such as those discovered at Lyveden, Northamptonshire, and Olney Hyde, Buckinghamshire,[126] where areas for storing and settling clay were also found. The clay would then finally be prepared by wedging (forcing as much air as possible out of it) until it was in a fit state for throwing into the required shape. Virtually all medieval pottery was thrown on a wheel, although some, such as that made in the early thirteenth century at Lyveden, was hand-made and only trued up on a turntable[127] or, as at Chilvers Coton, Nuneaton, Warwickshire,[128] thrown bodies could be finished by the addition of necks made in the 'coil' technique. Moulds were never used, and therefore each pot is a unique product which may display slight differences from its fellows even though it is basically of the same design.

The common culinary wares of the Middle Ages (called by archaeologists bowl and cooking pot, but see Moorhouse 1978 for the multifarious uses of these types) were frequently unglazed, but the jugs, which must often have been designed to grace the table, were very often highly decorated (fig. 75) with lead glaze, coloured slips or even three-dimensional figures.[129] All these forms of decoration were added to the pots before firing, at the 'leather-hard' or 'green' stage; they were then fired in an updraught kiln. There are no examples of biscuit firing from medieval England although this method of firing a pot before the application of glaze (which necessitated a second firing once the glaze was applied) is known from medieval pottery kiln sites in Denmark (pers. comm. N.K. Liebgott).

The types of kilns in which medieval pottery was fired are well known from

75. 'Face-jug' of Scarborough ware found in King's Lynn, Norfolk.

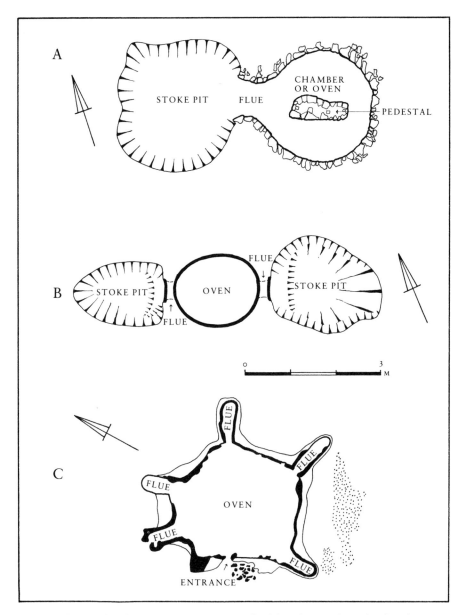

76. Ground plans of medieval pottery kilns: A) single-flue kiln (Olney Hyde, Buckinghamshire);
B) double-flue kiln (Laverstock, Wiltshire); C) multi-flue kiln (Potterton, Yorkshire).   After (A)
Med. Archaeol. 1968; (B) Musty *et al.* 1969; (C) *Med. Archaeol.* 1964

excavations, which have revealed the plans, but less often the superstructures, of many hundreds of kilns. They have been divided into types on the basis of their ground-plans and the numbers of flues and stoke pits,[130] but are all basically of the updraught type already known in the Roman period.[131] The single-flue kiln (fig. 76a) was well known in the pre-Conquest period in those areas of England where wheel-thrown and kiln-fired pottery was made[132] and seems to have continued in use throughout England until some time in the thirteenth century, when it was superseded in places by the double-flue type (fig. 76b), whose advantage probably lay in the more even distribution of heat from two sources (fires in the flues). The multi-flue kiln (fig. 76c) appears to be confined to Midland and northern England and to occur from the thirteenth century onwards, but there is not a simple chronological progression from one type to the next, as single-flue kilns continue after the introduction of the double-flue type (e.g. Olney Hyde and Lyveden) and all three types are present simultaneously at the great pottery-making complex of Chilvers Coton, near Nuneaton, Warwickshire.[133] The multi-flue types are generally greater in capacity than either of the other forms and more suited to the use of peat or occasionally coal as a fuel, the single- and double-flue kilns generally being fired with brushwood.

Those parts of a kiln most commonly revealed by excavation are the stoke pits, flues and firing chambers (or ovens) all of which were dug down into the ground. The oven was surrounded by a wall of clay or stone lined with clay, which defined a generally circular or oval area. The wall was pierced by the requisite number of openings forming the flues, which joined the interior of the ovens to the stoke pits. During firing, fires were lit in the flues. The stoke pits were used for storing fresh fuel and for holding the ashes which were periodically scraped out of the flues. The ovens may either have a 'raised' and pierced floor supported by some form of pedestal (as in the Type 1b single-flue kilns and Type 2c double-flue kilns of Musty's (1974) typology) or, as in other double-flue types and multi-flue kilns, have no internal structure. In the latter cases pots for firing were stacked, inverted, directly on the ground-level floor; in kilns with raised floors the pots would be stacked, also inverted, on the fire-bars of the raised floors and the fires, first lit in the flues, probably pushed into the oven itself (fig. 71). Methods of stacking the pots can be inferred from the few examples of kilns which still contained part of their last firing load when excavated (e.g. Laverstock kiln 6),[134] from patches and scars on floors and fire-bars and from the direction which glaze has 'crawled' on some decorated vessels. Modern experimental firings of kilns have all used this method of stacking.

The firing of a kiln was a long process which demanded knowledge and skill. The temperature in the oven had to be raised gradually, first to drive out residual moisture in the bodies of the pots and then to achieve maturing point of the clay (*c.* 1000°C). This seems to have taken about twelve hours; an equivalent length of time was then needed for the kiln to cool down. Great care needed to be taken in all these operations, and the comparatively large numbers of spoilt pots (wasters) found on kiln sites suggest that the difficulties were by no means always overcome. The pots might be overfired or underfired, often as a result of their positions in the kiln, they may explode through an excess of moisture or too great a proportion of temper in their clay, glaze may not adhere properly to the body of the pots, and so on. Modern experimental firings of reconstructed kilns have produced such wasters in abundance and testify to the difficulties inherent in the process. Experimental firings have also tried to solve the problem of the superstructure of medieval kilns, remains of which are far less common from excavation than are their foundations. Recent work by G. F. Bryant[135] at Barton-on-Humber has suggested that the kilns may have been open-topped, that is, with permanent vertical walls of some height which, after stacking were capped with a temporary covering of tiles, broken potsherds or turf. According to Bryant this method of construction enables a kiln to be stacked with pottery more easily than in a kiln with a solidly built dome and is therefore preferable, but this point is difficult to prove archaeologically.

Although pottery and tiles seem occasionally to have been fired together, tile-making was usually a specialised industry with its own techniques and types of kilns. The methods employed in their manufacture have been studied by a number of scholars, notably E. S. Eames;[136] a number of kiln sites have been excavated and there have also been experimental firings of reconstructed kilns. Research into the subject is well advanced, thanks largely to the pioneering work of Mrs Eames over the past three decades, and the publication of a corpus of all known medieval floor-tiles in England (fig. 77) is well advanced.[137] New information is still coming forward, but the emphasis is beginning to fall more on social and economic aspects of tiles and tilers than on the pure assembly of data.

Apart from the few pre-Conquest examples mentioned above (p. 150), glazed floor-tiles are not found in England until the end of the twelfth century or the early thirteenth, when they seem to have been introduced into royal and monastic circles from France. Many newly founded Cistercian abbeys in England had their churches paved with mosaic tiles which formed highly decorative floors in a variety of colours, mainly yellow, brown and green[138] and it is from monasteries such as Byland and Fountains, Yorkshire, that much of our surviving evidence comes (fig. 78). Other religious orders, however, also used mosaic tiles for their churches and an 80m² area of tiles *in situ* has been discovered in recent excavations at Norton Priory, Cheshire, and attributed on coin evidence to the beginning of the fourteenth century.[139] These mosaics were made up of a variety of simple geometric shapes; a more elaborate type of mosaic known as *opus sectile* composed of often naturalistic designs of men and animals was also made, an excellent example being that still in position in Prior Crauden's chapel in Ely Cathedral.[140] Remains of *opus sectile* floors have also been excavated at Norton Priory and Old Warden Abbey, Bedfordshire.[141]

The production of mosaic and *opus sectile* tiles with their many different shapes and sizes must have been difficult and time-consuming (for example, the 40,000

77. Medieval floor-tiles with heraldic designs.   After E. Eames 1980.

separate tiles needed to pave the choir, chancel, transepts, the east chapel, the first
bay of the nave and the chapter house at Norton Priory must have necessitated
54 firings of the kiln and taken perhaps two summers to complete). The floors
themselves were also complicated to lay. This must be one of the reasons why
mosaic tiles were never adopted for production on a large scale, the simple square
form being used for later mass-production. Mosaic tiles were therefore made in
response to 'special orders' and must have been manufactured as close as possible
to the site where the floor was to be laid. In 1972 a kiln for the production of the
mosaic tiles used at Norton Priory was discovered no more than 50m from the
north wall of the church. It was a rectangular structure with clay walls, which also
incorporated wasters and pebbles, and two parallel arched flues. The superstructure had been damaged by ploughing but the reconstructed kiln used for
experimental firings in 1977 and 1978 was given slightly sloping sides and left with
an open top.

   The experimental firings of the kiln suggested that its capacity was about 750
tiles and that the amount of brushwood needed for fuel amounted to about 600kg
for a complete firing of twelve hours' duration. A less well-preserved kiln for firing
mosaic tiles is known from North Grange near Beverley, Yorkshire. Although lying
about 1km from the Cistercian Meaux Abbey, the kiln must have produced the tiles
for the abbey church, founded in the mid-twelfth century but rebuilt and repaved
between 1249 and 1269. The capacity of this kiln may have been slightly greater
than that at Norton and there may also have been other kilns within the precinct
itself, so the number of firings and length of time involved in the paving of Meaux
Abbey may not have been as great as that suggested for Norton. Unfortunately,
evidence from the North Grange kiln was insufficient to carry out an assessment

78. Designs made up of mosaic floor-tiles.

on the lines of that at Norton, but somewhat similar and detailed work has been done on the so-called tile 'factory' at Danbury, Essex, which was the centre of a commercially-organised tile industry in the late thirteenth and early fourteenth centuries.

Pottery and tiles are used by the archaeologist both as important sources of evidence for dating and as indication of trading connections. Certain tiles can be very precisely dated by the designs that they carry (often heraldic and therefore attributable to a specific family at a certain time) and by documentary references to their being made for flooring a specific building (Clarendon Palace, Westminster Abbey or the Cistercian monasteries, for instance). They can, therefore, be used as chronological indicators with a reasonable degree of confidence. Pottery, on the other hand, must be used for dating only with very great caution. As early as 1963 John Hurst published a warning to this effect when writing about the pottery from the extremely fully documented White Castle, Gwent,[142] but archaeologists have continued to use pottery as the main dating evidence for their sites. Only recently has it been fully recognised that the extreme conservatism of potters and the pronounced regionalism of their production makes dating based on pottery extremely dubious. Methods such as those now being used in London, where the pottery associated with waterfront structures suitable for dendrochronological analysis can be given reasonably precise dates, the increased use of thermoluminescence and the intensification of studies of regional types should help to refine the dating capabilities of the pottery which is found in such abundance on virtually every medieval site. Unfortunately this refinement still lies in the future and at present pottery as a chronological indicator is an extremely blunt instrument.

The validity of pottery and tiles as indicators of trade is perhaps not so much in question, although recent work on documentary sources has shown there to be a close association between the siting of kilns, the distribution of kiln products and the owners of the land on which both kilns and products are found[143] which gives an added dimension to the simple interpretation of distribution maps. The distribution of pottery from one area to another is usually attributed to trade both within England and beyond. Amplification of this may be found in Chapter 6.

IRONWORKING

Ironworking is one of the few industrial processes of medieval England which have been investigated in depth, but even so much work still remains to be done. The survival of the residues of iron smelting and smithing is comparatively good in archaeological conditions and the importance of iron-production to the English economy of the Middle Ages and earlier has long been recognised by archaeologist and historian alike.[144] Evidence for smelting and smithing in the Anglo-Saxon period has been summarised elsewhere[145] and that in Roman Britain also studied.[146] The High Middle Ages have recently been similarly served by Crossley[147] and

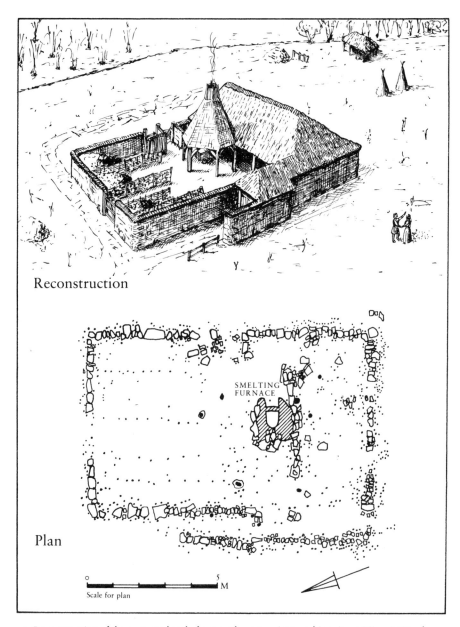

Reconstruction

Plan

SMELTING
FURNACE

0   5
                M
Scale for plan

79. Reconstruction of the excavated early fourteenth-century ironworking site at Minepit Wood, Rotherfield, Sussex.   After Money 1971

Tylecote.[148] Interest in this subject has been even more pronounced on the Continent, particularly in Scandinavia[149] and in Eastern Europe,[150] where metallographic analysis of iron objects is very far advanced.

The two basic raw materials necessary for iron-production are iron ore and coal or charcoal, which was used both as fuel and reducing medium. Iron ore occurs in many areas of England either in the form of bog or lake ore or as deposits of carbonate, hematite or limonite ores.[151] Bog ore can be obtained in the form of nodules from wet areas, but the other types of ore demand mining of some type; in Anglo-Saxon and medieval England this mining usually took the form of surface working in bell-pits, the remains of some of which can still be seen.[152] Smelting generally took place in rural areas where both iron ore and fuel were easily available (for example in the Weald of Surrey, Sussex and Kent),[153] and where the fire risk was less than in heavily populated settlements (fig. 79). But that this was not always the case is shown by excavations in Stamford, Lincolnshire, where an eleventh-century iron-smelting site was discovered in the High Street.[154] In this case, however, the requisite ore occurs close to the site and charcoal (also used for firing the pottery kilns present in the town; p. 150) must have been easily available; as with Stamford's urban pottery kilns, the danger of fire must have been disregarded. The iron-smelting site at Stamford produced evidence of many of the activities involved in iron-production which have also been noted on other excavated sites, notably the early fourteenth-century site at Minepit Wood, Rotherfield, Sussex.[155]

Before smelting, iron ore was roasted in a furnace and then crushed into pieces of suitable size. Roasting furnaces have been discovered at a number of sites including Stamford, Lincolnshire, Minepit Wood, Sussex, Beeston Regis, Norfolk,[156] and Lyveden, Northamptonshire. Ore-roasting furnaces vary in type from simple depressions in the ground with heat-hardened surfaces, as at Stamford, to more elaborate three-sided stone structures surrounding low clay platforms, such as roasting furnace II at Minepit Wood, which has been likened to the late medieval ore-roasting furnaces depicted by Agricola in *De Re Metallica* of 1556,[157] or circular patches of stones as at Lyveden.

Smelting took place in bowl furnaces or small shaft furnaces which sometimes had a channel for tapping off the slag. Excavated remains are generally insufficient for reconstruction of the furnace superstructure, but furnaces may have been of the low-shaft type (Stamford), the domed type (High Bishopley, Co. Durham)[158] or high-shaft type,[159] all of them developments from the primitive bowl furnace.

Ore and charcoal (sometimes coal in the later medieval period) were placed in the furnace and heated up to between 1100°C and 1300°C with the aid of bellows. The nozzles of the bellows were protected from the heat by clay sheaths (tuyeres), which are frequently found on iron-smelting sites, occasionally still in position at the base of the furnace. Tuyeres are, characteristically, perforated lumps of clay with a highly baked or vitrified surface on the side exposed to greatest heat, but occasionally they are of stone or even reused pieces of slag. When a sufficient temperature was reached in the furnace the impurities in the ore liquified and separated from the iron to form slag and a porous lump of iron (the bloom). In furnaces with slag-tapping channels the slag could be run off as liquid, leaving the iron bloom at the bottom of the furnace. This method did not produce iron of any great purity and it is noticeable that smelting slag found on medieval sites contains a high proportion of iron and that the iron blooms often contain a great deal of slag.

The next stage in the process was to heat up the bloom in a bloomery hearth and to hammer out as much as possible of the residual slag so that the iron was as pure as possible. Bloomery hearths have been discovered on a number of medieval sites in England even where there is no evidence for smelting, and it is likely that in many cases the two processes were physically separated. By the fourteenth century there is evidence for water power being harnessed to drive the hammers used to force out the slag (the earliest example so far known is the fourteenth-century watermill at Chingley, Kent,[160] but that at Bordesley Abbey may be even earlier). This naturally increased efficiency and more examples of water-driven bloomery hammers are known from the fifteenth century, by which time iron-production was being practised on a larger scale than previously. The introduction of the water-powered bloomery was a late phenomenon in England in comparison with the Continent, where water-powered hammers are documented as early as the early twelfth century, and until its appearance ironworking in England had remained essentially the same for many centuries, even though the demand for iron for tools and weapons must have increased enormously. This demand must have been met by an increasing number of small smelting sites, even though our knowledge of them from archaeological sources is still slight. Many of the sites must have been in the countryside away from habitation but some were situated in villages (Lyveden, Northamptonshire), individual manors (Alsted, Surrey)[161] or towns (Stamford). These are rare exceptions, however, to what must have been an essentially isolated rural craft.

In some cases iron smelting must have been carried on as a commercial enterprise, but in others, particularly in a monastic or manorial setting, it was probably intended to supply immediate domestic needs. Both the village smelting site of Lyveden, and the urban one of Stamford could have been manufacturing raw iron for a commercial market; at Alsted, however, the smelting furnaces were associated with a small manorial complex which was probably the only customer for the smelted iron, and at Bordesley the abbey and its granges must have been the consumers.

Evidence for the smithing or forging of iron is much more widespread in both urban and rural situations. The raw material used by the smith was usually in the form of rods or bars of a size appropriate to the tool or implement to be made. Such raw material has been discovered at Waltham Abbey, Essex, where a monastic forge was excavated.[162] Evidence of forging, in the shape of rough blanks for tools such as chisels and a sledge hammer, was also found there, but on the whole such discoveries seem fairly rare on medieval excavations in England and most of our information comes from forging hearths, hammer scale (or slag) and finished products.

The slag which is found on many sites may be either smelting slag or smithing slag (hammer scale). It is difficult to distinguish between the two by eye, but scientific analysis of the slag's structure shows it to be more often the residue from smithing or forging.[163] Few sites have produced slag from both activities (that at Godmanchester, Huntingdonshire, is one of the few exceptions)[164] and the archaeological evidence suggests that smelting and smithing were generally carried out in different places. Smithing was common on many types of site; the hammer scale can be either from working iron rods or bars into implements or from the re-working of worn-out implements into new ones. The former is more likely to be part of a commercial enterprise; the latter a domestic activity for the refurbishing of objects for household use. As the two activities are difficult to distinguish from archaeological evidence alone it is seldom possible to establish which was being practised at a particular site unless the remains of the forge itself is found.

The forging of iron bars into implements demands a number of structures, the remains of which can be discovered by means of archaeological excavation. The most important of these are the forging hearths, which could be at either ground or waist-high level,[165] the water tank or 'water-bosh' for dousing and cooling tools, and the anvil. These features are seldom all found together on excavated sites, but at Goltho, Lincolnshire, a small timber building of late fourteenth- to early fifteenth-century date enclosed a forging hearth with a hood or chimney, a clay-lined water-bosh and another hearth. At Alsted, Surrey, a forge with smith's dwelling produced an elaborate ground-level forging hearth and the stone base for an anvil. At Waltham Abbey[166] post-holes representing the remains of a tool rail and a support for bellows were discovered, along with a tapering tube which probably came from the bellows themselves. Such fragmentary information can be combined to produce a rounded picture of medieval iron forging which can be supplemented by illustrations in contemporary manuscript of English and Continental origin[167] which show the methods used in making knives, tools, nails, wire and so on (fig. 80). Few of the specialised tools illustrated in the manuscripts have been discovered in post-Conquest sites in England, although they are well known from Viking-Age discoveries in Scandinavia (the Mästermyr hoard from Gotland, for example)[168] and surely remain to be discovered on English medieval sites.

Metallographic analysis of iron objects can add considerably to our knowledge of medieval iron smithing. As so often, England has lagged behind Scandinavia and Eastern Europe in this aspect of study, although for the past twenty years Professor Tylecote[169] has been trying to make British archaeologists appreciate the importance of the metallographic analysis of iron objects. This has long been understood elsewhere; at Novgorod, for example, the methods used in making knives from the tenth to the fifteenth centuries were worked out by metallurgists[170] and their findings have considerable importance for the rest of Europe.[171]

Some of the few published examples of iron objects which have been analysed metallographically are the knives from Goltho, Lincolnshire,[172] where four different methods of constructing an iron knife blade can be distinguished. The knives at Goltho were made by combining iron and steel (iron which, through carburisation and heat treatment, has absorbed more carbon and which is therefore tougher and can be sharpened to a cutting edge). Steel was more difficult to produce than iron and used sparingly whenever possible. The methods used for the Goltho knives were either to sandwich a plate of steel between outer plates of iron so that the steel could protrude and be sharpened into a cutting edge, to tip the iron with steel, to envelope the entire iron core with steel or to amalgamate iron and steel (by piling) to make a homogeneous blade. All four methods are known from the Roman period and later and are therefore not a medieval invention. They must have been used throughout Europe and can be seen wherever knives have been analysed by scientific means (for example at Novgorod).

In England much still remains to be done on the investigation of medieval ironworking. The pioneering work of Professor Tylecote in the metallurgical field is only gradually being built on, and fieldwork in search of iron mining, smelting and bloomery sites such as that carried out in South-East England by the Wealden Iron Research Group could be extended to other parts of the country with profitable results.

80. (Opposite) Illustration from *Das Hausbuch der Mendelschen Zwölfbruderstiftung zu Nürnberg*, c. 1500. The cutler, Ulrich Promauer, is shown finishing knives and small weapons by filing, hardening, polishing and hilting them. He is working at an iron anvil set in a wooden block and behind him is a bellows-driven waist-level forging hearth.

6. Towns and Trade

Although only a small proportion of the population of medieval England lived in towns, urban centres exerted a disproportionate influence on the social and economic life of the country throughout the Middle Ages. They were centres of government, of industry and commerce; they acted as market centres for the surrounding rural areas, and their demand for agricultural products acted as a stimulus to the production potential of their hinterlands. In this way, town and countryside in the Middle Ages were inextricably bound together, and strictly speaking the two should not be separated in any discussion. Towns do, however, display characteristics which set them apart from their rural contexts and there is some justification in treating them as subjects in their own right. The history of the medieval town has fascinated historians since Maitland's *Township and Borough* of 1898, and archaeologists have become more and more bound up with the subject since the Second World War. The amount of information that has been amassed by both historian and archaeologist is enormous, and synthesis within the short space of a chapter in a book of this type is quite impossible. All that I can hope to do in the following pages is to summarise some of the more important aspects of recent archaeological work on medieval towns, and indicate lines which the interested reader might pursue through further reading and research.

In recent years medieval towns have been the subject of cross-disciplinary studies, with historians, archaeologists, architects, environmental scientists and a host of other specialists combining their individual skills in an attempt to work out the history of specific towns or to generalise about the origin and development of the urban settlements of the Middle Ages. The quest into urban origins has led to discussions about the definition of a town and increasing emphasis on the contacts between a town and its hinterland. The origin of towns in Anglo-Saxon England has been studied in depth over the past decade and urban development in the post-Conquest period has occupied medieval archaeologists for even longer. To a great extent the history of medieval archaeology since the Second World War is the

81. Excavations in The Lanes, Carlisle.

history of archaeology of the medieval town. More energy, and certainly more money, has been expended on urban excavation than on the excavation of any other type of site. This has largely been the result of archaeologists taking advantage of modern urban redevelopment which has provided an opportunity for excavation on an unprecedented scale (fig. 81). As the rate of urban renewal slows down and the number of potential archaeological sites in towns diminishes, it is now time to attempt to evaluate what we have learned from excavations in medieval towns and to look to the future.

Archaeological excavation is but one means of investigating the history of medieval towns in England, for we are fortunate in possessing an almost unparalleled collection of documentary sources relating either to individual towns or to towns within a national context. Most of the preserved written records, though, date from no earlier than the fourteenth century and archaeology is the prime source for many towns before that date. For this reason much archaeological work has been devoted to investigating the origins of towns and their early development.

The historical sources for medieval towns are far too extensive for more than a very sketchy outline to be presented here. Lists of sources for urban history useful to the archaeologist have been published elsewhere and this is not the place to go into a detailed discussion of their significance.[1] Any archaeological investigation of a medieval town needs to begin with research into the historical sources, beginning with Domesday Book for the eleventh century, and governmental records such as Pipe Rolls, Patent Rolls, Close Rolls, Fine Rolls and so on for the twelfth and thirteenth centuries. Some ecclesiastical documents also survive from this early date and provide information on the origins and topography of some individual towns. By the fourteenth century records kept by the towns themselves begin to be preserved in greater numbers. They are often of private property transactions (the selling, exchanging or bequeathing of land) from which much information can be extracted about the lay-out of the town, the street names, the occupations and social status of the inhabitants. There are also documents relating to the land owned by the town corporation itself which may detail the general day-to-day upkeep of an urban community or specify such things as the provision and maintenance of defences. The survival of documents varies greatly from town to town. Some of the best-preserved records are from medieval ports such as King's Lynn, Hull and Southampton,[2] where documentary evidence has recently been used to supplement that from archaeological investigations, and from Oxford where a detailed map of the medieval town has been compiled from documentary sources.[3]

From the seventeenth century onwards there is cartographic evidence such as John Speed's *Theatre of the Empire of Great Britain* (1676) which consists of county maps, each with an enlarged plan of one or more towns (fig. 82). The standard of early English cartography is not high compared with European examples and it is not until about two hundred years later that maps become really useful. In the early decades of the nineteenth century many new maps were drawn up in connection with the payment of tithes, new regulations concerning health, sanitation and so on, and they cover many of the larger towns of the time. Fortunately many of these maps record towns before the great nineteenth-century urban expansion resulting from the Industrial Revolution, and probably fossilise medieval urban topography, which remained virtually unchanged until later that century. By 1890 the Ordnance Survey had completed its first edition of 25-inch-to-the-mile (1:2500) maps of British towns which now form the basis of much modern topographical work, such as the series of maps and plans of historic towns in the British Isles.[4]

Archaeology was not used as a source for urban history in England until after the Second World War when derelict sites in cities such as London and Canterbury[5] were excavated on a modest scale. Even then, Roman rather than medieval features were the preferred objectives and it was not until the late 1950s and early 1960s that excavations of medieval urban sites became common. Before that time there had been some excavation in Oxford, Southampton, York, and a handful of

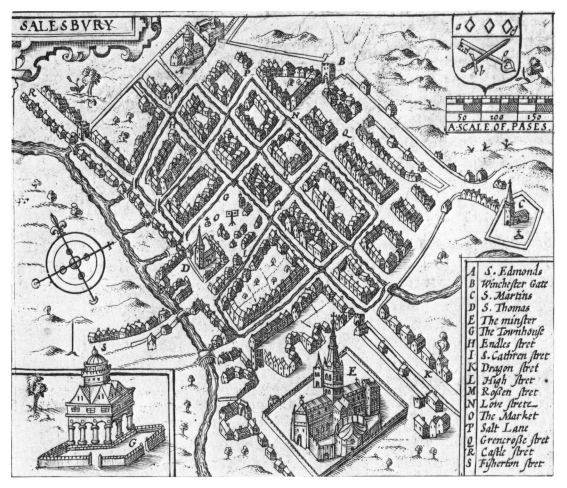

82. Map of Salisbury from John Speed's *Theatre of the Empire of Great Britain* (1676).

other towns,[6] but the first deliberate attempts at large-scale and co-ordinated urban archaeological programmes only came to fruition in the first half of the 1960s with Martin Biddle's long-running excavations in Winchester[7] and the less spectacular but no less important excavations in Stamford, Lincolnshire,[8] and King's Lynn, Norfolk.[9]

These pioneering efforts were the forerunners of the urban excavations of the 1970s when both the number of excavations carried out (fig. 84) and their scale increased enormously.[10] Much of this increased activity stems from two very significant publications of the early 1970s, *The Erosion of History: Archaeology and Planning in Towns*[11] and *The Future of London's Past*[12], which together influenced the outlook of archaeologists and urban planners not only in Britain but over large parts of continental Europe. In Scandinavia, in particular, the two works have been very influential and have led to the initiation of co-ordinated projects on medieval towns in Sweden, Finland and Denmark,[13] and large-scale work in Norwegian towns such as Oslo, Tønsberg and Trondheim.[14] Before then the importance of excavating medieval towns had long been appreciated by individual archaeologists in many countries; for example, in Norway Asbjørn Herteig had been digging in Bergen since the early 1950s;[15] Novgorod, USSR, had been the scene of very extensive excavations;[16] and the port of Gdańsk, Poland, was thoroughly researched in the early 1960s[17]. However, it was not until the 1970s that overall research policies were formulated in response to the increasing threat to historic towns from modern town-centre development.

The type and scale of response has varied from country to country. In Sweden a project sponsored and financed by both private and public funds is studying all the medieval towns in the country and publishing works which summarise the present state of knowledge and the potential for future research in each town. These publications, under the general project title of *Medeltidsstaden*, are designed as working documents which show the archaeological potential of individual towns and which must be taken into account by commercial interests who intend to redevelop existing town centres. They describe the archaeological work that has already taken place in the town and attempt to reconstruct the medieval topography on the basis of both archaeological evidence and information culled from other sources, such as bore-holes, drain-digging, pipe-laying and so on. By combining all these forms of information it has been possible to reconstruct part of the history of the towns over the past thousand years and also to point to areas where the strata containing potentially significant archaeological information lie undisturbed and where archaeological excavation may therefore be most productive. The newly initiated project on medieval towns in Finland is modelled precisely on the Swedish format, but in Denmark a more selective approach has been favoured. There ten towns have been chosen as pilot projects; each represents a particular type of medieval town development and their history is being traced through surviving written evidence as well as from archaeological information. Small excavations have been carried out on a research basis to answer specific problems which have arisen from studies of the towns and the aim of the project is to produce definitive summaries of Danish urban development in the Middle Ages.

Although two English publications acted as stimuli for the national projects in Scandinavia they have not resulted in similar nationwide projects at home. The Council for British Archaeology set up its Urban Research Committee in 1970 to act as a focus for research into towns,[18] but no overall plan directing the aims of urban research has so far emerged. A large number of surveys of the medieval towns

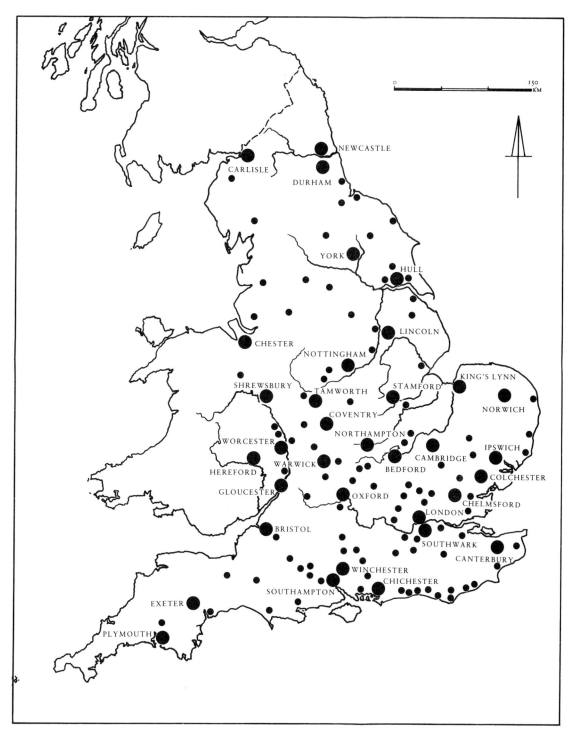

83. Distribution of excavations in towns 1956–80.   Compiled from the 'Medieval Britain' section of *Med. Archaeol.*

of specific counties have been published, mainly by the archaeological units for the counties in question (for example Wiltshire, Avon, Oxfordshire and Cornwall),[19] but by no means the whole country has been covered and many of our medieval towns remain as uninvestigated now as they were when *The Erosion of History* was published in 1972. Even though the threats to English medieval towns from commercial redevelopment are diminishing, because of both the economic recession of recent years and the increasing activity of the conservation lobby which have succeeded in slowing down the destruction of our historic town centres, the urban heritage of medieval England remains in jeopardy.

This is in part the outcome of the only general 'policy' on towns that has ever been implemented and the direct result of our current economic conditions. Virtually all excavations in medieval towns in England have been, and still are, 'rescue' excavations financed largely by central government through the Department of the Environment. Although some few towns have had large-scale and extensive excavation programmes (fig. 83) and many towns have seen the excavation of a single site, the vast majority of towns with medieval origins have had no excavation at all. Most of those excavations which have taken place have been in response to threatened redevelopment of sites, and were often undertaken with inadequate time and financial backing. This has meant that it has seldom been possible to select

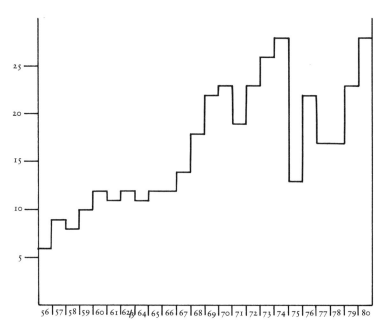

84. Chart showing the number of excavations per year in towns 1956–80. Compiled from the 'Medieval Britain' section of *Med. Archaeol.*

sites in towns on a problem-solving basis and that many questions about medieval towns remain unanswered. Since 1956 there have been excavations in more than a hundred medieval towns, most of these since 1970 (fig. 84), but in only about thirty towns have the excavations been of such a scale that an element of research or problem-orientation has been possible.

Furthermore, in recent years it has become the policy to concentrate finances from the central purse on a small number of towns which are considered to have been of 'international' importance in the Middle Ages. Places such as Canterbury, Lincoln, London, Norwich, Oxford, Southampton, Winchester and York immediately spring to mind, although some others have also been the scene of fairly extensive investigation, and places such as Bedford,[20] Bristol, Carlisle, King's Lynn, Stamford and Worcester[21] must also be considered significant from an archaeological point of view. The argument leading to the adoption of this policy of concentration is essentially one of cost-effectiveness, based on the wealth of archaeological deposits in these large urban settlements and therefore the amount of information and number of finds retrieved from each cubic metre of earth excavated. This attitude is suspiciously close to treasure-hunting and many archaeologists would argue that the validity of excavated information cannot be estimated on the 'number of finds per pound spent' scale. By pouring money into large and spectacular excavations the grant-giving authorities have concentrated on a few sites to the detriment of hundreds of others in smaller provincial towns which may never have achieved 'international' importance but which are of intrinsic significance for our knowledge of life over most of medieval England. There can be no doubt that a national policy for the investigation of medieval English towns is needed, but this policy should be formulated on the basis of other criteria than pure cost-effectiveness. There are some seven hundred towns in England with medieval foundations; a few were undoubtedly of international significance in the Middle Ages, but by far the greater number were of importance only for their immediate hinterland, for which they acted as centres of communications, market places and so on. From the viewpoint of most of the population of medieval England all towns were equally important, and it is therefore essential that the archaeologist today should look with an unbiased view into all types of medieval town and not concentrate on one to the detriment of another. The *Medeltidsstaden* project in Sweden shows that this is possible; each town is being treated on its merits and no one town is being given overweighted importance.

As there has never been any national policy for the excavation of medieval towns in England the archaeological coverage is naturally patchy, and the highly diversified nature of the evidence obtained by urban excavation makes synthesis difficult. This is further compounded by the comparative lack of publication of the sites dug over the past twenty years. Urban excavation is time-consuming and expensive, and the publication of the usually very complex sites is equally so. Therefore, in many cases, publication is inevitably slower than one could wish and although interim reports appear fairly regularly in the 'Medieval Britain' section of *Medieval*

Archaeology and in local journals, definitive reports appear much less frequently.

These factors combine to make it essential for research priorities for urban archaeology to be formulated and adhered to. As methods of excavation become more sophisticated, so excavations become ever more expensive to stage and the choice of sites therefore more crucial. The Urban Research Committee of the Council for British Archaeology has published several papers on research priorities which refine the method of selection of sites mentioned above and suggest a problem-orientated approach to urban excavations. If these suggestions were adopted nationwide there would be a much better chance of a cohesive picture of the origins and development of the medieval town emerging from the multifarious excavations which have been undertaken so far.

Despite its shortcomings, the archaeology of the medieval town in England has contributed enormously to our knowledge of life in England in the Middle Ages. We know much more now than we did thirty years ago about the topography of medieval towns, their industrial potential and the standard of living of their inhabitants. We also have a much better idea of their Anglo-Saxon antecedents and of the continuity from the pre-Conquest to the post-Conquest town. Many towns of the High Middle Ages were new foundations on virgin sites, deliberately sited to act as centres of population or markets or for strategic or economic reasons,[22] but a large number of them originated in the pre-Conquest period, particularly in the tenth and eleventh centuries, when towns were being founded or were developing for both military and economic reasons.

Before we pursue farther the archaeological evidence for towns it is necessary to establish precisely what is meant by 'town' in generally accepted terms so that pre-Conquest and post-Conquest towns may be equated. Until fairly recently the English historians' view has been that when a borough charter confirming rights and privileges (of land tenure, taxation, markets, etc.) was granted to a settlement by the king then that settlement was elevated to the status of a town.[23] The term 'town', therefore was almost purely legal and administrative in definition. A wider interpretation has been adopted lately, however, and the most recent historical synthesis of English medieval towns states:

> A town is a permanent human settlement with two chief and essential attributes. The first is that a significant proportion (but not necessarily a majority) of its population lives off trade, industry, administration, and other non-agricultural occupations. Because of the occupations practised within it the town is likely to serve as some kind of centre for the surrounding area – generally in marketing, possibly in administration. The second essential attribute of the town is that it forms a social unit more or less distinct from the surrounding countryside.[24]

This definition of a town by an historian closely corresponds to the criteria suggested in *The Erosion of History* (p. 9) as archaeologically acceptable indicators of urban status:

1. Defences
2. Internal street plan
3. Market
4. Mint
5. Legal existence, as indicated by borough charter
6. Situation: the settlement may have a central position in a network of communications
7. Population: a town often has a high density and size of population compared with its surroundings
8. Diversified economic base with concentration of crafts and long-distance trade
9. House plot and type: a town may be divided into long, narrow plots of land ('burgage plots') on which 'urban' buildings are constructed
10. Social differentiation: a wide range of social classes, particularly a 'middle class'
11. Complex religious organisation: there may be more than one parish church or other institution, particularly monastic
12. Judicial centre for courts of national or local status

Not all these criteria can satisfy an archaeological definition, which must rely on material evidence alone, but many of the features suggested here could be discovered by archaeological investigation and it has been suggested that if a settlement fulfils three or four of these criteria it may then be assumed to be a town.[25]

This definition of terms is particularly significant in the investigation of pre-Conquest towns and the tracing of urban development in England during the post-Roman period. Occupation in towns appears to have ceased with the abandonment of Britain by the Romans some time in the early fifth century, and there is little to suggest either the reoccupation of Roman towns or the foundation of new urban centres until the seventh century, when ports such as Ipswich and Saxon Southampton[26] began to flourish on sites not previously occupied. At much the same time some form of urban life began to re-emerge in old Roman towns, particularly in those which became the centres of dioceses in the newly Christianised country. It is argued that these latter fulfilled primarily administrative and ecclesiastical functions until the end of the ninth century and that it was only then that they acquired a sufficient density of population and the associated economic functions for them to be described as true towns.[27] It is here that the question of definitions and criteria becomes important, for if we accept that a town must have a permanent and relatively dense population and a diversified economic and social base, then there were very few towns in Anglo-Saxon England until the late ninth or early tenth centuries when settlements combining economic, administrative and even defensive functions began to multiply.[28]

By the time of the Norman Conquest England was fairly well provided with urban centres[29] and the arrival of the Normans does not appear to have made any

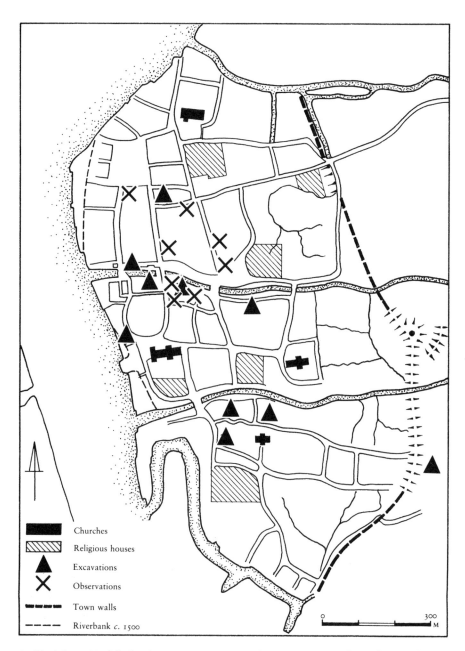

Churches

Religious houses

Excavations

Observations

Town walls

Riverbank *c.* 1500

0   300
                 M

85. King's Lynn, Norfolk showing excavations 1963–70. St Margaret's Priory lies in the central area of the town.

appreciable difference to the extent of urbanisation of the country.[30] Indeed, much of their activity was inimical to urban life, for Domesday Book records many instances of tenements within towns being destroyed for the foundation of castles, and the building of churches also led to some destruction.[31] The twelfth and thirteenth centuries, though, ushered in another period of urban expansion, not only in England but throughout Europe as a whole, resulting from a growth of population and increasing trade. Trade and towns go hand in hand and as both long-distance and local trade continued to expand so new towns continued to grow up, either as a result of deliberate plantation[32] or natural growth.[33] In particular, many English ports which grew to eminence in the Middle Ages were founded at this time and benefited from long-distance sea-borne trade with the Continent, Scandinavia and the Mediterranean lands.

Much archaeological work has recently been devoted to investigating the origins of medieval towns. Emphasis has been laid on those towns which were founded during the Anglo-Saxon period and where documentary evidence for their early years is scanty. A number of these have been mentioned in the previous pages, but some towns which originated in the eleventh century or later have also been investigated recently, although generally not on such a large scale.

The dominant interest is pre-Conquest urban settlements is partly the result of the lack of written evidence for that period in comparison with the increasing wealth of documentation relating to towns in the later medieval centuries. This documentation has formed the basis for historical works on post-Conquest towns in general[34] and histories of individual boroughs (for example, King's Lynn, Norfolk, and Canterbury),[35] it is so prolific that it is often thought that there is little to add to it by archaeological investigation. This belief has been held of all aspects of the medieval town, not merely the question of their origins, but I hope that the following pages will show that it is an erroneous opinion.

The east coast port of King's Lynn, Norfolk, for example, has excellently preserved documentary sources from its foundation in the eleventh century which have served as the basis for accounts of the town written by historians from the eighteenth century[36] to the present day.[37] The historical information was taken as the starting point for a campaign of excavations carried out from 1963 to 1970[38] which set out to investigate various aspects of the medieval town, including that of its origins. When excavations began little was known of its earliest history beyond a brief reference to *Lun* and *Lena* in Domesday Book,[39] and the first bishop's register of Norwich.[40] These implied a late eleventh century foundation by Bishop Herbert of Norwich of a priory and market place between the Purfleet and the Millfleet (fig. 85), possibly associated with an existing small settlement (*Lena*). To the south of the Millfleet the settlement of South Lynn (which remained an independent borough until 1546, when it was merged with its northern neighbour) had a church founded before 1100, but no evidence to suggest a population of any size before the establishment of St Margaret's Priory further north. The assumption was that the earliest evidence for the town should be sought in the area immediately around the Priory, and the programme of excavations was organised on this assumption.

Excavations in selected areas of the town, however, showed that the earliest settlement did not lie around the late eleventh-century priory, as documents suggested, but further south in South Lynn, where a site near the church of All Saints produced evidence of occupation from earlier in the eleventh century.[41] This is one instance of archaeological evidence both supplementing and amending knowledge from historical sources for a town that is exceptionally well documented, and gives the lie to the assertion that the excavation of medieval towns well known from historical documentation is merely providing information which confirms what we know already.

The question of the continuity of the post-Conquest town from its Anglo-Saxon, or even Roman, predecessors falls outside the scope of the present work, for it is largely concerned with the continuation of urban life from the Roman period into that of Anglo-Saxon domination. The development of the town in the Middle Ages is more relevant to our theme and is also a question to which archaeological investigation has provided answers. Urban development can be divided broadly into two aspects: topographical and economic, both of which can be expanded by excavated evidence. Urban topography has been particularly favoured by an archaeological approach and much of the rest of this chapter will be devoted to various aspects of it.

Excavation has shown that it was not unusual for towns to be founded on sites which were not immediately suitable for occupation. Very often drainage and land-reclamation schemes had to be put into effect before urban development could take place and these can be seen in the form of ditches dug to drain low-lying land between natural drier ridges, as at King's Lynn,[42] or to dry out waterlogged deposits as at Kingston, Surrey.[43] Marshland was also reclaimed by raising the ground level by deliberate deposition of clay or gravel (Waltham Abbey, Essex, Lincoln and Stafford),[44] and sites beside the sea or rivers were often protected by artificially constructed banks (Bedford, Durham, and Shrewsbury).[45]

After reclamation the ground would be laid out with a system of streets and associated plots of land surrounded by boundary fences (tenement plots), in which domestic buildings could be erected. Some streets were metalled with gravel or cobbles, and many were resurfaced a number of times within their medieval lifetimes. Tower Lane, Bristol, for example was remetalled five times from the twelfth to the fourteenth centuries[46] and this is by no means unusual. Some towns with Anglo-Saxon origins may have had their street plans laid out when the towns were first founded in the ninth or tenth centuries[47] and perpetuated throughout the Middle Ages, even up to the present day in some instances. In other cases the streets appear to have been laid out piecemeal, although their arrangement often seems to conform to a standard arrangement using the perch ($16\frac{1}{2}$ feet) as the basic unit of measurement (for example Colchester).[48]

The tenement plots which bounded the streets were usually rectangular in shape,

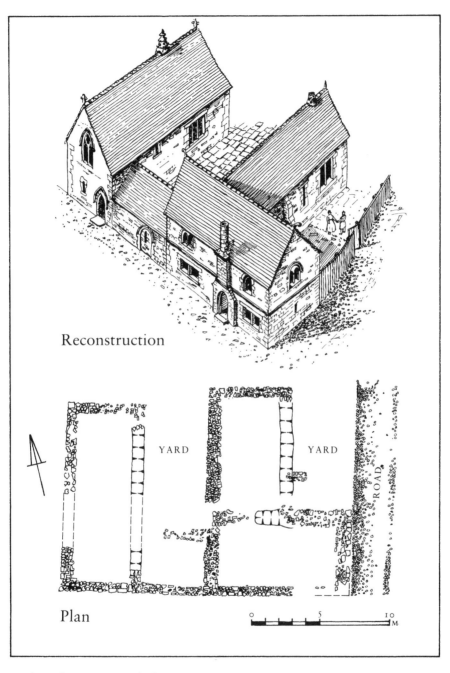

Reconstruction

Plan

0   5   10
M·

86. Plan and reconstruction of a fourteenth-century house at Flaxengate, Lincoln. After
R. H. Jones 1980

with their narrow ends flanking the street. They varied in width from one part of a town to another, with the narrowest situated in areas of greatest economic importance. Many excavations have established the dimensions of entire tenements, or groups of tenements, and show that almost without exception the boundaries remained unchanged from their initial establishment until recent times. In York this is even true of properties first laid out in the tenth century[49] and it is only in rare instances, as in Winchester, that property boundaries can be seen to change radically. In Tanner Street, Winchester, there is evidence for considerable fluctuation in the size and shape of properties during the course of the Middle Ages but this appears to be an unusual occurrence.[50]

The buildings which stood in these properties normally lay beside the street frontage, with open yards to the rear. Excavation has revealed entire or partial ground-plans of innumerable domestic buildings, some so detailed that hypothetical reconstructions can be made (fig. 86), and in some towns a few medieval buildings remain sufficiently intact for them to supplement the excavated information. As with rural domestic buildings, however, those which have survived in towns (Exeter, King's Lynn, Lincoln, Southampton or York, for example) tend to be buildings of the wealthy and our knowledge of the buildings of the urban poor must come largely from excavation. A terrace of tiny, one-roomed artisans' cottages near St Mary's Church, Tanner Street, in Winchester[51] is probably a better illustration of the standard of housing enjoyed by most of the population of a medieval town than any extant medieval domestic building anywhere.

It is impossible to generalise about the types of domestic buildings known from the excavation of medieval towns. It is commonly said that, as in villages, timber buildings were replaced by ones incorporating masonry in the thirteenth century, but there are examples of stone buildings in towns before that date, and timber-framed buildings were still being put up at the end of the Middle Ages. Stone certainly did become more common towards the end of our period, but it never succeeded in replacing timber as a primary building material over much of the country. Brick began to be used to supplement timber in the eastern counties during the fifteenth century but was used exclusively in very few buildings at that time (fig. 87). The building materials used throughout the Middle Ages were those most ready to hand and masonry consequently only became common in those parts of the country where building-stone was most easily accessible.

A glance at the 'Medieval Britain' section of *Medieval Archaeology* and the monographs on Flaxengate, Lincoln, or Shrewsbury[52] will show the wealth of information on medieval urban domestic buildings which has emerged over the past twenty years. This is yet another subject which is crying out for a broadly-based approach and one which would amply repay the attentions of a research student. There are many aspects of the archaeology of the medieval town to which the same comment might apply; in the field of urban topography only one topic has been subjected to generalised evaluation and scrutiny over the past few years – the development of waterfront and harbour areas in medieval ports (fig. 88).

87. The late fifteenth-century Hanseatic Warehouse at King's Lynn, built of brick and timber.

Excavations in medieval ports in north-west Europe have become increasingly common since the 1950s when Asbjørn Herteig began the investigation of Bryggen (the old Hanseatic wharf area) in Bergen, Norway. His excavations showed the great wealth of information that could be extracted from the waterlogged deposits lying along medieval waterfronts and, in particular, illustrated how the topography of ports had been influenced by the presence of waterways.[53] When Bergen was founded by the Norwegian King Olav Kyrre in AD 1070 the only land available for occupation was a very narrow coastal strip between the mountains and the sea, and over the centuries this was gradually increased by deliberate land reclamation until almost 100m of new land had been formed. Dwellings and warehouses were built on the newly formed land and wharves constructed against the seaward side.

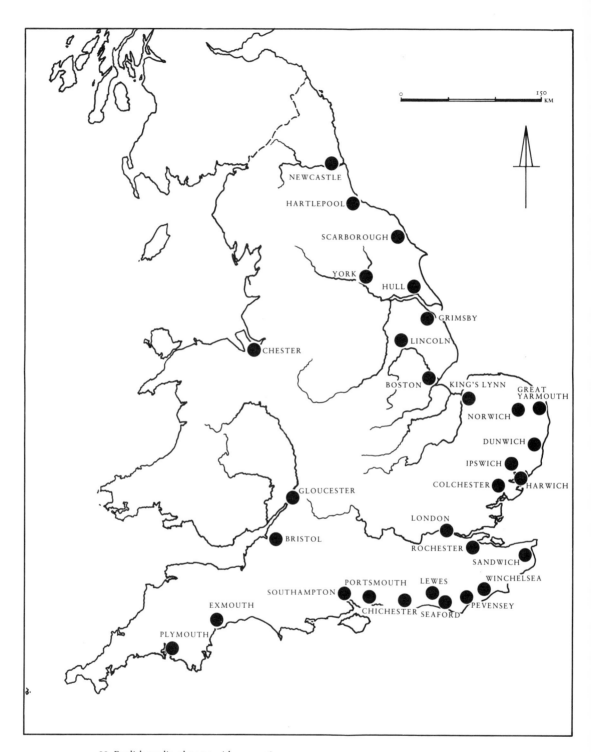

NEWCASTLE

HARTLEPOOL

SCARBOROUGH

YORK

HULL

GRIMSBY

LINCOLN

CHESTER

BOSTON

KING'S LYNN

GREAT YARMOUTH

NORWICH

DUNWICH

IPSWICH

COLCHESTER

HARWICH

GLOUCESTER

LONDON

BRISTOL

ROCHESTER

SANDWICH

WINCHELSEA

PORTSMOUTH

LEWES

SOUTHAMPTON

EXMOUTH

CHICHESTER

SEAFORD

PEVENSEY

PLYMOUTH

150
KM

88. English medieval ports with excavations.

89. Timber structures used in medieval land reclamation at Dordrecht, Netherlands.

After the discovery of this method of land reclamation in medieval Bergen similar discoveries were made by archaeological excavation in other medieval ports in north-west Europe, for example, Amsterdam, Dordrecht (fig. 89) and Staveren in the Netherlands, and Schleswig in Germany,[54] and it is now accepted as a phenomenon common to most medieval ports.

In England the feature was first noted at King's Lynn, Norfolk, where excavations revealed a short stretch of timber riverside wall of thirteenth-century date lying some 50m inland of the present bank of the River Great Ouse[55] and indicating considerable build-up of land from that date to the present day. More recent and much more extensive excavations in both coastal and inland ports in England have shown that land reclamation beside waterfronts was as common there as on the Continent in the Middle Ages, and much work has been done on the archaeological deposits in waterfront sites and, particularly, on the timber structures which they

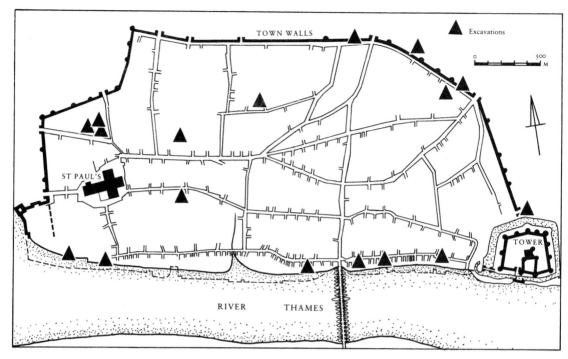

90. The City of London with sites excavated since 1974.

conceal. Brief reports on a number of English sites have been published in the proceedings of a conference on waterfront archaeology held in London in 1979[56] and more lengthy reports on specific ports also appear elsewhere (for example, Hull and Norwich)[57] but by far the most work has been carried out, and appeared in print, on large-scale excavations in the City of London.[58]

When *The Future of London's Past*[59] was published the archaeological potential of the banks of the River Thames was particularly emphasised, and excavation there became a major objective once the Department of Urban Archaeology was set up for the City of London in 1974 (fig. 90). Even before that date there had been excavations on the Old Custom House site near the Tower of London which had shown the wealth of timber structures and waterlogged deposits lying beside the Thames,[60] and a fifteenth-century stone-built dock had been discovered at Baynard's Castle near Blackfriar's Bridge.[61] Since 1974 ever-increasing effort has been concentrated on excavation of Thameside sites, culminating in 1982–3 with work at Billingsgate.[62]

The work in the City of London has shown that the north bank of the River

Thames has been pushed southwards some 100m since Roman times through a combination of deliberate reclamation and natural silting. The waterlogged condition of the archaeological deposits so formed are ideal for the preservation of organic materials such as leather, textiles and wood, and our knowledge of artifacts made from these substances has increased enormously since excavation began. The methods of construction used in the timber revetments which succeeded each other over the centuries (fig. 91) have been studied in depth and much new light shed on the skill of medieval carpenters. Tree-ring analysis of the often excellently preserved timbers has led to great precision in dating the various building techniques used[63] and, as many of these techniques were also employed in house-building, has led to better dating of some of the extant medieval buildings throughout the country.

The method of land reclamation most commonly used in the Middle Ages, not only in England but also in the Low Countries and Germany, was to build a wooden revetment on the foreshore some little distance in front of the existing river bank (fig. 92) and then to fill in the intervening gap with dumps of debris, very often domestic refuse presumably obtained from elsewhere in the town. By the end of

91. Medieval waterside revetments discovered at Trig Lane, City of London.

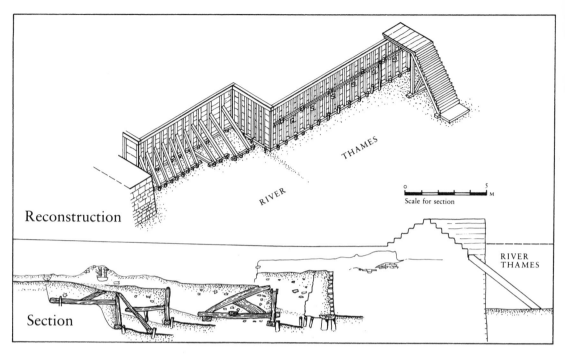

Reconstruction

Section

92. Reconstruction of the waterside structures at Trig Lane, City of London, showing the southward movement of the north bank of the River Thames through the repeated construction of revetments.   After Schofield and Dyson 1980

the fifteenth century stone was being used in London for revetments[64] but before that time timber was virtually the only building material employed. The precise dates for the timber revetments obtained by dendrochronology can be used to date the dumps of rubbish behind them and the artifacts that they contain. The investigation of waterfront sites in London and elsewhere is, therefore, not only producing information on methods of reclamation, building techniques and objects made of organic materials, but it is also turning up evidence for the dating of those objects and, above all, of pottery, which is found in great quantities in the refuse deposits. This is, of course, of great importance, as the archaeologist places enormous reliance on pottery for dating evidence and it is difficult to date pottery to within precise limits. Research into the potsherds found in the London waterfront excavations will help to resolve this difficulty, and should eventually enable a chronological sequence to be built up which will be of help to archaeologists not only in London but further afield.

Although it is now clear that the reclamation of land along waterfronts was common in all medieval ports throughout Europe in the Middle Ages, it is still far from clear why this activity was so common and so apparently important. There seem to be at least four reasons why so much effort was expended: to acquire more land on which to build, to obtain a greater depth of water beside quays, to counteract the threat to ports through silting and to prevent erosion of land and property by water. These reasons are probably to some extent interrelated. In Bergen, Norway, for example, land reclamation for building purposes was probably paramount, as it was at Amsterdam and Dordrecht, Netherlands,[65] but the desire to provide better facilities for shipping was probably also of importance. In King's Lynn all four factors probably played a part, and there the illegal disposal of rubbish in the river added to the difficulties presented by silting.[66] In London the need to maintain a sound river frontage is seen as the main motivation.[67]

The topographical importance of waterfront studies has been emphasised by more than one writer, and archaeological evidence has been combined with that from documents and extant waterside buildings to work out the types of riverside development in the Middle Ages (for example in London)[68] and the stages whereby a port reached its final form.[69] King's Lynn, Norfolk, is particularly fortunate in its quantity of medieval documentation and the number of medieval (mainly fourteenth- and fifteenth-century) waterside buildings which have been preserved, and it has proved possible to combine information from these with that from archaeological excavations in the town to produce a picture of waterfront development from the foundation of the town in the eleventh century to the end of the Middle Ages (figs 93, 94). This work shows that medieval King's Lynn was a dynamic settlement whose topography varied and whose area expanded from century to century. Changes such as this remind us that the medieval town was in a constant state of flux and, like the medieval village, can only be understood if all its fluctuating fortunes over a long span of time are studied.

Several other aspects of urban topography have been the subject of recent archaeological research, but not given the prominence accorded to waterfront studies. The construction of town walls from the thirteenth century onwards has been given some overall attention[70] and some excavations published in full (for example, Canterbury and Shrewsbury).[71] The walls of a few individual towns have also been studied in depth (King's Lynn for instance)[72] but the subject has on the whole excited comparatively little archaeological attention over the past thirty years. The same may be said of the medieval suburbs which grew up outside these walls or along the routes which radiated from towns. Their significance as indicators of a town's importance has been acknowledged[73] and some excavations have taken place in recent years (particularly in Winchester, pers. comm. M. Biddle) but they have so far failed to become the subject of intensive archaeological investigation. This is probably the result of 'rescue' demands, whereby sites in town centres are more likely to be excavated than those on the fringes of modern (and medieval) towns, and a further reason why a national policy of archaeological research priorities (pp. 172–9) should be encouraged.

One of the definitions of a town quoted earlier (p. 175) is that it is a settlement

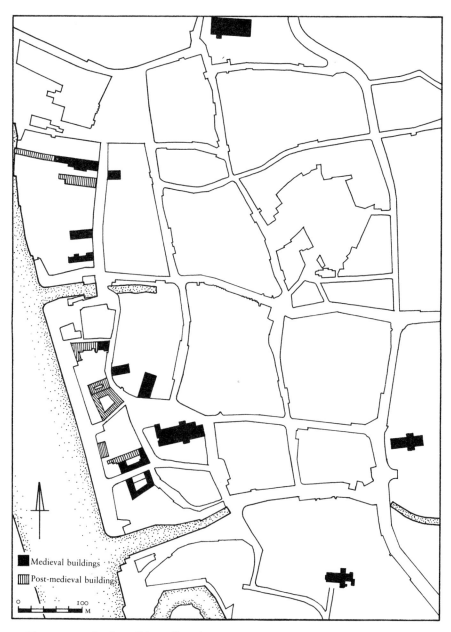

93. The extant medieval (twelfth- to fifteenth-century) and post-medieval (sixteenth- and seventeenth-century) riverside buildings in King's Lynn, Norfolk.

Medieval buildings
Post-medieval buildings
0   100
M

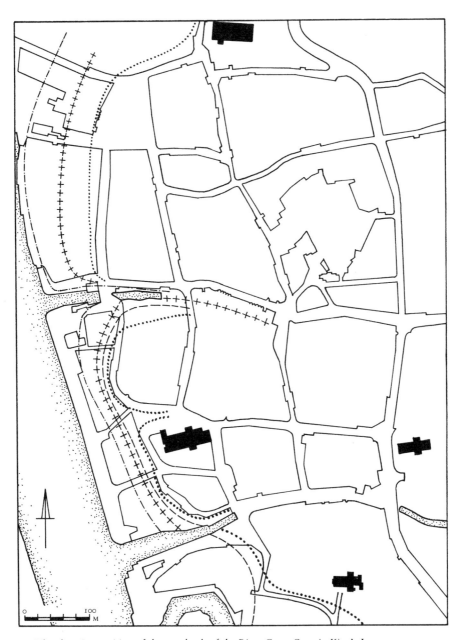

94. The changing position of the east bank of the River Great Ouse in King's Lynn
throughout the Middle Ages. The earliest, probably eleventh-century, bank lies furthest to the east.

with a diversified economy based on industry and trade rather than agriculture. Some of the industrial aspects of medieval towns have been discussed in Chapter 5, but the subject of medieval trade has only been touched on briefly.

Trade was the life-blood of towns, which either grew up spontaneously at natural centres of communications or were deliberately founded by a lord or landowner to take advantage of the commercial possibilities of an area. Once a settlement was granted a charter it could act as a market centre for its hinterland; the dramatic increase in the number of such market charters in the twelfth and thirteenth centuries is graphically illustrated by Platt (1976, fig. 4) where the county of Suffolk is shown to have had a dozen markets before 1100 but well over 60 by 1350. The growth in both trade and population which this presupposes was a phenomenon common to the whole of north-west Europe at the time and was succeeded by a period of contraction in the late fourteenth century, when the population declined drastically and the volume of trade diminished. Towns, both old and new foundations, played a vital part in fostering both local trade (the exchange of agricultural products for manufactured goods at local markets, for example) and long-distance trade, particularly in heavy and bulky commodities which were shipped around Europe as raw materials for a steadily increasing manufacturing industry. Great international fairs were held at places such as St Ives, Huntingdonshire, or Oxford and each town of any size held its annual fair, where merchants and goods from many nations could be found. International trade has long been studied by economic historians from the particularly well-preserved documentary sources which England is fortunate in possessing; local trade within England itself is less well documented and therefore less well known historically. Archaeology can add significantly to our knowledge of both types of trading activity, but makes the greater contribution where written evidence is either sparse or totally lacking. Hence, international trade before *c*. AD 1200 (when written evidence becomes common) or local trade throughout the entire Middle Ages (where written evidence, although it exists, is never common) should be given priority in archaeological research into medieval trade.

Although we know from historical documentation that the commodities traded both within England and beyond were extremely varied in type and source, the goods that we know from archaeological sources alone are limited to those which have survived in the ground for the past five hundred years or more. Objects made of organic materials (leather, wood, textiles, agricultural produce and so on) are only preserved in exceptional circumstances and pottery remains the most commonly discovered artifact on medieval archaeological sites. Pottery, therefore, has to be used as the archaeological indicator of trade but, although undoubtedly useful for this, we must always bear in mind that for the medieval merchant pottery must have represented only a tiny proportion of his trade.[74] We have little hope of discovering any of the wainscots, deal boards, bowstaves, slabs, spars, planks, pitch, tar, wax, ashes, beer, skins, linen cloth, yarn, thread, fish, cork, garlic, onions, beaver hats, hair and haberdashery which were imported into King's Lynn during the twelve months from 12 February 1396,[75] nor the costly cloths, spices, drugs, sugar, dyes, carpets, popinjays, wormseeds, salt, woad, fur, fish, haber-dashery, cabbages, oranges, apples, raw silk, compasses, antimony, soap and onion seed brought into London in 1420–1[76] although the metal goods, glass and gold which are also mentioned in the Customs Accounts might have a better chance of surviving. There is a much better chance of finding and also recognising some of the 'clay pots' brought into Hull from the Low Countries in the fifteenth century[77] and it is largely on finds such as these that the medieval archaeologist must base his assessment of trade.

Since Gerald Dunning's seminal paper on the trade in pottery around the North Sea was published in 1968 a great deal of work has been done on tracing long-distance trade routes through the finds of imported pottery on archaeological sites. This work has largely been concentrated on the discoveries made in coastal and riverine ports in England and abroad, and as excavation has continued so the information has increased and Dunning's postulated trade routes have been refined and modified.[78] The use of pottery as an indicator of trade must, however, remain only marginally important for the period after AD 1200, when we know so much more about international trade from historical documentation than we can hope to learn from archaeological sources.[79] Nevertheless, much can be learned from detailed study of pottery discovered in well-stratified and well-dated deposits such as those at Bergen, Norway, or in the City of London, for documentary evidence, although prolific, is by no means complete even for the later medieval centuries and gaps can still be filled by archaeological evidence.

The question of trade within England itself is one where archaeology can make a very positive contribution, for in this case we have few documents which can compete with the Customs Accounts for completeness and detail. Some of the larger towns do possess sufficient documentation for trading links to be worked out (see in particular Platt and Coleman-Smith 1975 for Southampton), but these are exceptions. Pottery is once again the main medium of archaeological evidence, and innumerable distribution maps have been drawn up on the basis of pottery found in excavations in medieval towns. In King's Lynn, for example, it could be shown that the axis of the town's trade changed in the thirteenth century from emphasis on its East Anglian and south-east Midland hinterland to a more wide-ranging series of contacts with eastern England as a whole and north-east England in particular.[80] The catchment area for the products of the late medieval kilns at Malvern, Worcestershire, has been worked out on the basis of the distribution of the wares[81] and recent work on the South-East has illustrated complex trading patterns between kiln site and consumer in Sussex and in Kent.[82] Much more work remains to be done before the pattern of internal trade in medieval England can be seen in its entirety and regional studies such as these are the first steps to achieving this end.

As so much energy has been expended by archaeologists in investigating trade routes it is strange that comparatively little interest has been displayed in the means

A   B

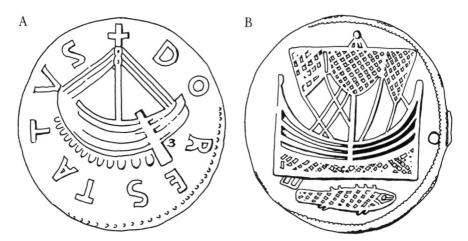

95. Early medieval coins from Dorestad, Netherlands (left) and Haithabu, Germany (right) depicting a hulk and a cog respectively.

of communication employed in carrying goods from place to place. One of the biggest gaps in our knowledge concerns medieval ships, although there are signs that this will be at least partly filled in the near future.[83] The archaeological discovery of medieval ships has been largely fortuitous and the sample from which one can generalise extremely small. Nevertheless, much information about medieval ships can be culled from detailed investigation of documents which tell us about the quantity and bulk of goods carried and hence give some idea of the size of vessels plying the seas around the British Isles.[84] The types of ships in use at the time are also recorded: *navis* (ship), *galia* (galley), *batella* (small boat), *carvela* (caravel), *balingera* (barge), *scapha* (skiff) and *spurancea* (spinnace); there is also the 'general ship', which may be equated with the hulk, and the cog, which seem largely to have made up the fleets which sailed in north European and Atlantic waters.

Hulks and cogs are portrayed on medieval coins and seals.[85] The hulk, which appears to have devloped earlier, was a clinker-built vessel such as that portrayed on a ninth-century coin from Dorestad, Netherlands (fig. 95a), and was in continuous use until the end of the Middle Ages. A twelfth-century hulk has recently been found in Utrecht, Netherlands,[86] and the ship excavated in Bergen is also of the same type.[87] Some seals from medieval English ports, such as Great Yarmouth, Norfolk, show that this type of vessel was not unknown to English merchants.

The cog was developed for use in northern waters at the end of the Viking Age and continued as a common form of vessel until about 1400. It had a flat, carvel-built bottom and steep stem and stern and is well known to us from representations on coins and seals (fig. 95b) and from the almost complete example excavated in the River Weser near Bremen, Germany (fig. 96).[88] Less complete examples have also been excavated in Denmark[89] and in Stockholm, Sweden, where the remains of eleven ships of varying type spanning the thirteenth to sixteenth centuries have recently been discovered.[90] The Stockholm discovery has contributed spectacularly to our knowledge of medieval ships and is relevant to English medieval conditions even though discovered in a Baltic port. By their very nature ships travelled from one country to another, carrying their traditions with them and perhaps influencing native ship-building in those ports where they docked. We know from historical sources that ships built in Gdańsk were purchased there in the fifteenth century and sailed, fully loaded with Polish softwoods, to the ports of eastern England, and that ships were bought together with their cargoes of salt in the Bay of Bourgneuf in western France and sailed home to England. Ships were, indeed, the most international artifacts of the Middle Ages and remind us that, although this book has been devoted to the archaeology of medieval England, the country was by no means isolated from its neighbours in the Middle Ages and that the trends and developments which can be traced there were not isolated phenomena but closely enmeshed with developments in the rest of Europe and beyond.

This book has concentrated on the archaeological evidence for medieval England, with only passing reference to the written sources which have been, and still are, used by historians to write the history of the period. My purpose has been to show

96. The fourteenth-century cog recovered from the bed of the River Weser in Bremen, Germany, and now undergoing conservation in the maritime museum in Bremerhaven.

that archaeology can, in its own right, make an independent contribution to the study of a period which is so well documented, and that medieval archaeology should no longer be regarded as a mere adjunct to historical evidence. Medieval archaeology has at last come of age and can be regarded as an independent discipline; it can make as great a contribution to our knowledge of the Middle Ages in England and abroad as can prehistoric archaeology to our knowledge of those eras before the advent of literate man.

Archaeology is the study of the material remains of the past. More remains of human activity have been preserved from the Middle Ages than from any other age of human existence; should we not, therefore, expect archaeology to be a vital tool in the interpretation of life in England and beyond from the eleventh to the fifteenth centuries?

Notes

INTRODUCTION

1. Barker 1977, 40.
2. Cherry *et al.* 1978.
3. Hodges 1983; Rahtz 1981, 1983.
4. Jope 1972.
5. Northamptonshire: *RCHM* 1979; West Yorkshire: *West Yorkshire* 1981.
6. Hall and Kenward 1982.
7. W. J. Rodwell 1980a.

1. THE COUNTRYSIDE

1. M. W. Beresford, Hurst and Sheail 1980, 36.
2. M. W. Beresford, 1983, fig. 5.
3. M. W. Beresford and Hurst 1971, fig. 13.
4. M. W. Beresford 1954, 217–61.
5. See, for example, *West Yorkshire* 1981.
6. For example, Janssen 1981.
7. Dyer 1982, 19.
8. M. W. Beresford and Hurst 1971, 27.
9. Addyman 1965.
10. M. W. Beresford and Hurst 1971, 5, 35, 68.
11. Douglas and Greenway 1981, 153–6.
12. Allison, Beresford and Hurst 1966, 45.
13. Dyer 1982, 21.
14. Miller and Hatcher 1978, 29; Russell 1948.
15. Lamb 1977, 449–61; Parry 1978.
16. Record Commission 1807.
17. Allison, Beresford and Hurst 1966, 15.
18. M. W. Beresford and Hurst 1971, 11–17.
19. *Med. Archaeol.* 1974, 1976.
20. Wrathmell 1977, 53.
21. Dyer 1982.
22. Wright 1976.
23. Dudley and Minter 1962–3.
24. G. Beresford 1979, 145.
25. C. C. Taylor 1974a, 87–118.
26. M. W. Beresford and St Joseph 1979, 112.
27. M. W. Beresford and Hurst 1971, 47–53; Rowley and Wood 1982, 56–8.
28. Wade-Martins 1980.
29. C. C. Taylor 1975.
30. M. W. Beresford and Hurst 1971, 85–9.
31. C. C. Taylor 1981, 31.
32. J. G. Hurst 1965.
33. Postan 1975, 154.
34. G. Beresford 1975, figs 14 and 15.
35. Field 1965.
36. Hilton and Rahtz 1966, 106.
37. Algar and Musty 1969.
38. Holden 1963; J. G. Hurst and D. G. Hurst 1964.
39. J. T. Smith 1970.
40. Field 1965.
41. Alcock 1981; Charles 1967.
42. Andrews and Milne 1979, 69.
43. G. Beresford 1979.
44. D. G. Hurst and J. G. Hurst 1969, 177.
45. Andrews and Milne 1979, 71, fig. 25.
46. *Med. Archaeol.* 1965.
47. *Med. Archaeol.* 1976.
48. *Med. Archaeol.* 1972.
49. *Med. Archaeol.* 1967.
50. P. Eames 1977.
51. Biddle 1961–2, 111.
52. *Med. Archaeol.* 1974.

53. Wharram Percy: Andrews and Milne 1979, fig. 25; Great Beere: Jope & Threlfall 1958, fig. 26; Goltho and Barton Blount: G. Beresford 1975, figs 18 and 19.
54. Charles 1981; Rahtz *et al.* 1982.
55. Roberts 1977.
56. Barker 1977, 85–7.
57. Dyer 1982, 27–8; Field 1965, 111.
58. Andrews and Milne 1979, 138; M. W. Beresford and Hurst 1976; J. G. Hurst 1972, 1981.
59. Klingelhöfer 1974.
60. See, for example, Miller and Hatcher 1978, and the references cited there.
61. M. W. Beresford and Hurst 1971.
62. Ault 1972; Bowen 1961; Gray 1915; Hilton 1976.
63. Rowley 1981, 1982; C. C. Taylor 1974b.
64. Barker and Lawson 1971.
65. G. R. J. Jones 1983.
66. Aberg 1978, fig. 1.
67. C. C. Taylor 1974a, 87–146.
68. Rahtz 1969.
69. Aberg 1983.
70. Congress of Archaeological Societies 1901.
71. Emery 1962.
72. Aberg 1978, 3.
73. Le Patourel 1973, 1.
74. Aberg 1978, 1.
75. C. C. Taylor 1978, 5.
76. Rigold 1978.
77. *RCHM* 1968, lxi–lxiv; Le Patourel 1973, 3–5.
78. Roberts 1965.
79. Aberg 1983, fig. 6.
80. Barry 1977, 1978, 1981.
81. Le Patourel 1978.
82. Le Patourel and Roberts 1978, 47.
83. G. Beresford 1977a.
84. West 1970.
85. Le Patourel 1978, table II.
86. Stiesdal 1975.
87. Hoek 1981; Schuyf 1980.
88. Verhaeghe 1981.
89. Bur 1981.
90. *Med. Archaeol.* 1976.
91. D. G. Hurst and J. G. Hurst 1967.
92. West 1970.
93. *Med. Archaeol.* 1978, 1980.
94. J. G. Hurst 1961.
95. *Report MSRG* 1980, 22.
96. Addyman 1960.
97. *Med. Archaeol.* 1973.
98. Aberg 1983, 100.
99. *Med. Archaeol.* 1977–9.
100. Le Patourel 1973.
101. Rahtz 1969.
102. G. Beresford 1977a.

2. PARISH CHURCHES

1. Roxan and Morris 1983.
2. L. A. S. Butler 1983.
3. Jesson 1973, 4.
4. H. M. Taylor 1973.
5. Deerhurst: L. A. S. Butler *et al.* 1975; Rahtz 1976a, 1976b; Repton: H. M. Taylor 1977, 1979.
6. Drury and Rodwell 1978; W. J. Rodwell 1976; W. J. Rodwell and K. A. Rodwell 1973.
7. Cramp 1977; *Med. Archaeol.* 1979.
8. K. A. Rodwell and W. J. Rodwell 1976.
9. L. A. S. Butler *et al.* 1975, 346.
10. J. Jones 1976; Rahtz 1976c.
11. W. J. Rodwell 1981, 140.
12. Brothwell 1972.
13. J. G. Hurst 1976a, 39.
14. Dawes and Magilton 1980.
15. W. J. Rodwell 1981, 136.
16. Platt 1981, 22.
17. R. K. Morris 1979, 44.
18. Grimes 1968.
19. Brandel 1918.
20. Wilson 1972.
21. Jesson 1973, 8–16; W. J. Rodwell and K. A. Rodwell 1977.
22. R. K. Morris 1983, 63–76.
23. Darby 1977, 52–6.
24. D. M. Owen 1976, 23.
25. Biddle 1976c, 329.
26. Biddle 1975a, 312–20.
27. Asheldham: Drury and Rodwell 1978; Rivenhall: W. J. Rodwell and K. A. Rodwell 1973; Thetford: *Med. Archaeol.* 1971; Wharram Percy: J. G. Hurst 1976a.
28. Olsen 1976, 15.
29. Nau 1972.
30. Biddle 1975a, fig. 16 (St Pancras), fig. 15 (St Mary Tanner Street).
31. Biddle 1969, 317–23.
32. Keene 1983.
33. St Helen-on-the-Walls: Magilton 1980; St Mary Tanner Street: Biddle 1972, 1975a; St

Paul-in-the-Bail: Colyer and Gilmour 1978; St Pancras: Biddle 1972, 1975a; St Nicholas-in-the-Shambles: A. Thompson 1979; St Mark: M. J. Jones 1981.

34. Colyer and Gilmour 1978, 102.
35. M. J. Jones 1981, 99.
36. Hirst, Walsh and Wright 1983, 7–101.
37. Biddle 1976c, 332.
38. R. K. Morris 1979.
39. Wade-Martins 1980.
40. Biddle 1976a, 65; R. K. Morris 1983, 40–5; R. K. Morris and Roxan 1980.
41. Gracie 1958.
42. *Med. Archaeol.* 1978–82; R. K. Morris 1983, fig. 21.
43. Biddle 1976c.
44. Cunliffe 1964.
45. M. W. Beresford and Hurst 1971, 134.
46. Klingelhöfer 1974.
47. H. M. Taylor and J. Taylor 1965; H. M. Taylor 1972, 1978.
48. W. J. Rodwell 1981, figs 35–7.
49. Hadstock: W. J. Rodwell 1976; St Oswald's Priory: Heighway 1978; Warram Percy: J. G. Hurst 1976a.
50. R. K. Morris 1983, 94–108.
51. W. J. Rodwell and K. A. Rodwell 1981.
52. W. J. Rodwell 1981, fig. 59.
53. *Med. Archaeol.* 1979.
54. *Med. Archaeol.* 1971.

3. MONASTERIES

1. Knowles and Hadcock 1971, 1–5.
2. See R. K. Morris 1979, 43–50 and Gazetteer, for an excellent introductory bibliography to nineteenth-century archtectural works.
3. Rahtz 1973.
4. Faversham: Philp 1968, 1–61; Elstow: *Med. Archaeol.* 1966–72.
5. *Med. Archaeol.* 1978.
6. Mellor and Pearce 1981, 4.
7. Hirst, Walsh and Wright 1983; Rahtz and Hirst 1976.
8. Robinson 1980, 157.
9. Bagley and Rowley 1966, 9–34; C. Butler 1927; Knowles 1940, 3–15.
10. Knowles 1940, 4.
11. Cramp 1976, 206–8.
12. Horn and Born 1979, I, xx.
13. Gwynn and Hadcock 1970, 10–46; Hughes 1966; Hughes and Hamlin 1977; Leask

1977, 1–47; Norman and St Joseph 1969, 90–121.
14. Glastonbury: Radford 1961; 1968; Burgh Castle: Cramp 1976, 212–15.
15. Cramp 1969; 1976, 229–41.
16. Knowles 1940, 32–3.
17. Cramp 1969, 25.
18. Knowles 1940, 31–56.
19. Knowles 1940, 100.
20. Winchester: Biddle 1972, 118–24, fig. 6; Canterbury: A. D. Saunders 1978, fig. 1.
21. Knowles 1948, 163.
22. Knowles 1940, 1948, 1963; Knowles and Hadcock 1971.
23. Cook 1961; Dickinson 1961; Midmer 1979.
24. Dickinson 1950; Donkin 1978; Robinson 1980.
25. Drewett and Stuart 1975.
26. Conant 1966, 82–5, 110–20.
27. Knowles and Hadcock 1971, 97.
28. Midmer 1979, 8.
29. Pontefract: Bellamy 1965; Faversham: Philp 1968, 1–61.
30. Evans 1931.
31. *Med. Archaeol.* 1973.
32. Knowles and Hadcock 1971, 127–8.
33. Douglas and Greenaway 1981, 737–42.
34. Donkin 1969.
35. Hirst, Walsh and Wright 1983, 71.
36. D. E. Owen 1961, 57.
37. D. E. Owen 1961, 57, 82, 85–7.
38. Knowles and Hadcock 1971, 135.
39. Charterhouse: Knowles and Grimes 1954; Mount Grace: *Med. Archaeol.* 1970; pers. comm. L. Keen.
40. Knowles and Hadcock 1971, 168.
41. E. S. Eames 1980, 90.
42. *Med. Archaeol.* 1971–81.
43. *Med. Archaeol.* 1981.
44. *Med. Archaeol.* 1961ff.
45. *Med. Archaeol.* 1975.
46. Tynemouth: *Med. Archaeol.* 1964; Pontefract: Bellamy 1965; Leighton Buzzard: *Med. Archaeol.* 1981; Bicester: Hinton 1969, 28; Faversham: Philp 1968, 27.
47. *Med. Archaeol.* 1965.
48. E. S. Eames 1961.
49. Platt 1969a.
50. Greene and Johnson 1978.
51. *Med. Archaeol.* 1967–70.

52. *Med. Archaeol.* 1970–2.
53. *Med. Archaeol.* 1971–2.
54. *Med. Archaeol.* 1966–7.

4. CASTLES

1. Bloch 1961; Brown 1973; Prestwich 1963.
2. Brown 1976, 21.
3. King 1972, 102.
4. King and Alcock 1969.
5. King 1972; Renn 1959, 1968.
6. Armitage 1912, 88–9.
7. Bennett, Frere and Stow 1982, 73.
8. Colvin 1963, 33–42; Renn 1968, 18–20.
9. Brown 1976; Colvin 1963; J.R. Kenyon 1978; King 1983; Platt 1982.
10. A.D. Saunders 1977.
11. Barker and Higham 1982.
12. Whitlock 1961, 119.
13. Curnow and Thompson 1969.
14. Sulgrave: Davison 1977; Goltho: G. Beresford 1977b, 1982.
15. Whitlock 1955, 432.
16. Faccombe: *Med. Archaeol.* 1977–80; Raunds: R.K. Morris 1983, fig. 21.
17. Davison 1969a.
18. Davison 1967a, 210.
19. Platt 1982, 4.
20. Davison 1972.
21. Davison 1969b.
22. Hope-Taylor 1950.
23. Ascot Doilly: Jope and Threlfall 1959; Aldingbourne: Brewster and Brewster 1969; Farnham: M.W. Thompson 1960; Castle Acre: Coad and Streeten 1982.
24. Barker and Barton 1977.
25. Addyman and Priestley 1977.
26. Barker and Higham 1982.

5. CRAFTS AND INDUSTRIES

1. Harvey 1983, 79.
2. Crossley (ed.) 1981.
3. Keene 1981a, 153.
4. Bridbury 1982; Lloyd 1977; Power 1941.
5. Salzman 1923, 194–224.
6. Postan and Rich 1952, 378–81.
7. Carus-Wilson 1957.
8. Carus-Wilson 1954.
9. Bridbury 1982, 16–26.
10. Ryder 1981, 21.
11. Hildyard 1949, fig. 6.

12. James 1935, f.263.
13. Millar 1932, pl. 138.
14. Postan and Rich 1952, 379.
15. H. Clarke and Carter 1977, fig. 171.
16. Wilson 1976, 271.
17. Geijer 1979, 30–2.
18. Hoffman 1964.
19. Wilson 1976, 271.
20. *Med. Archaeol.* 1970.
21. M.W. Thompson 1967.
22. Hermann 1971, fig. 69.
23. Geijer 1979, 34.
24. M.W. Thompson 1968.
25. Kamińska and Nahlik 1960.
26. Geijer 1979, 34.
27. Carus–Wilson 1969.
28. Wilson 1976, 272–3.
29. Hoffman 1964, 135–45.
30. Crawfoot 1977, 312.
31. *Med. Archaeol.* 1981.
32. Biddle 1970, 306.
33. Biddle 1976c, 435.
34. Biddle 1976c, 438.
35. *Med. Archaeol.* 1975.
36. Biddle 1970, 306; 1972, 108–9; Keene 1979, 157.
37. Goodall 1981, 54.
38. Carus–Wilson 1957, pl. xv.
39. Schofield *et al.* 1981, 11.
40. Baart *et al.* 1977, 110–25.
41. Egan and Endrei 1982.
42. Bristol: *Med. Archaeol.* 1975; Winchester: Biddle 1972, 102–3; Fountains Abbey: *Med. Archaeol.* 1981.
43. H. Clarke and Carter 1977, 410.
44. Hoffenk-de Graaf 1983; M.W. Thompson 1967, 96.
45. Wilson 1976, 272.
46. M.W. Thompson 1967, 96.
47. Vons-Comis 1982, 153.
48. Southampton: Crowfoot 1975; Northampton: Crowfoot 1979.
49. Platt and Coleman-Smith 1975, 49.
50. Vons-Comis 1982, 154.
51. Franzén and Geijer 1968.
52. Kamińska and Nahlik 1960.
53. M.W. Thompson 1967, 97.
54. Foote and Wilson 1970, 55.
55. Crowfoot 1977, 376.
56. Kauffman 1975; Lonsdale and Tarver 1874; Morgan 1982; Newton 1980.
57. Port. Mon. Brass Soc.; Tummers 1980.

58. Liebermann 1903, I, 455.
59. Biddle 1976c, 434.
60. *Med. Archaeol.* 1975.
61. Biddle 1975a, 317.
62. Goodall 1981, 54.
63. Wiklak 1960.
64. MacGregor 1978.
65. Groenman- van Waateringe 1975.
66. Broberg and Hasselmo 1982.
67. O'Riordain 1971, 75.
68. Myrvoll 1983.
69. Høeg *et al.* 1977, 250.
70. Mahany *et al.* 1982, 32–50.
71. Hewitt 1969, 1974.
72. Fletcher 1978; Morgan 1982.
73. Hillam and Morgan 1981; Milne and Milne 1978, 1982.
74. Rigold 1975.
75. O. Rackham *et al.* 1978, fig. 7.
76. Hewitt 1982, 343–8.
77. Walker 1982.
78. Stenton 1957, pl. 51.
79. Salzman 1952, pl. 13.
80. Goodall 1981, 51–5; Huggins and Huggins 1973, fig. 11.
81. Dunning 1939, 135–7.
82. G. Beresford 1975, 45.
83. Long 1975.
84. Southampton: Platt and Coleman-Smith 1975, 228–30; King's Lynn: H. Clarke and Carter 1977, 370–1; Gloucester: Heighway *et al.* 1979, 200; Durham: Carver 1979, 26–7.
85. C. A. Morris 1982.
86. Hall 1982.
87. R. Morgan 1982.
88. Huggins and Huggins 1973, 180–3.
89. Harden 1978, 1–6.
90. Hunter 1981, 143.
91. *Med. Archaeol.* 1958.
92. Harden 1956, 132.
93. Cramp 1970, 1975.
94. MacGregor 1978, 42.
95. Holdsworth 1980, fig. 11, 2.
96. Lundström 1976; 1981, 19.
97. Hunter 1981, 146.
98. Millar 1932, pl. 168.
99. Harden 1978, 11–17.
100. Charleston 1975, 204–11.
101. G. H. Kenyon 1967.
102. Frank 1982, 32.
103. Hunter 1981, 143.
104. Frank 1982, 98–100; G. H. Kenyon 1967, 59–67.
105. Bagot's Park: Crossley 1967; Alfold: Frank 1982, 100.
106. Hunter 1981, 149.
107. Platt 1978, 116–25.
108. Moorhouse 1983.
109. E. S. Eames 1980, passim; Le Patourel 1968, 1976, 1983; Moorhouse 1978, 1981; Streeten 1980, 1982.
110. Musty *et al.* 1969.
111. Bryant and Steane 1969, 1971; Steane and Bryant 1975.
112. Drury and Pratt 1975.
113. Musty 1974.
114. Bryant 1977; *Curr. Archaeol.* 1967.
115. Moorhouse 1981, 102; 1983, 11–12.
116. Thetford: J. G. Hurst 1976b, 314–20; Torksey: Barley 1981; Northampton: Williams 1974.
117. Kilmurry 1980, 198.
118. Clarendon Palace: E. S. Eames 1980, 28; Norton Priory: Greene and Johnson 1978; Meaux Abbey: E. S. Eames 1961.
119. Danbury: Drury and Pratt 1975; Penn: E. S. Eames 1980, 221–3; Hohler 1942.
120. St Albans: Biddle and Kjølbye-Biddle 1980; Bury St Edmunds: Gem and Keen 1981; Winchester: Biddle 1964, 209–10; York: Gem and Keen 1981.
121. E. S. Eames 1968, 1.
122. E. S. Eames 1975.
123. Le Patourel 1979, 76.
124. Musty 1974, fig. 3.
125. Le Patourel 1968, figs 25–7.
126. Moorhouse 1981, 104.
127. Steane and Bryant 1975, 88–91.
128. Mayes forthcoming.
129. Farmer 1979; B. Rackham 1972, pls 12–13.
130. Musty 1974.
131. Corder 1957.
132. J. G. Hurst 1976b, fig. 7.32.
133. Mayes forthcoming; *Med. Archaeol.* 1968.
134. Musty *et al.* 1969, 90.
135. Bryant 1977.
136. E. S. Eames 1980, 17–52.
137. For example, Emden 1977.
138. E. S. Eames 1980, pl. 1.
139. Greene and Johnson 1978, 31.
140. Keen 1979.
141. Norton Priory: Greene 1972; Old Warden Abbey: *Med. Archaeol.* 1975.

142. J.G. Hurst 1962–3.
143. Moorhouse 1983, 109.
144. Crossley 1981, 29.
145. Wilson 1976, 261–6.
146. Cleere 1965, 1976.
147. Crossley 1981.
148. Tylecote 1981.
149. H. Clarke 1979b.
150. Pleiner 1982; Gömöri 1981; M.W. Thompson 1967, 71–82.
151. Tylecote 1962, 175–9.
152. M.W. Beresford and St Joseph 1979, 256–9.
153. Crossley 1981, fig. 29; Straker 1931.
154. Mahany *et al.* 1982, 105–44.
155. Money 1971.
156. *Med. Archaeol.* 1965.
157. Hoover and Hoover 1950.
158. Tylecote 1959.
159. Serning 1979, fig. 7.
160. Crossley 1975.
161. Ketteringham 1976.
162. Huggins and Huggins 1973, 142, 169, fig. 11.
163. McDonnell 1983.
164. *Med. Archaeol.* 1973.
165. Tylecote 1981, 42–5.
166. Huggins and Huggins 1973, 135.
167. Notably Treue and Goldmann 1966.
168. Thalin-Bergman 1979, 109–15.
169. Tylecote 1962, 1976, 1981.
170. M.W. Thompson 1967, 73.
171. Tylecote 1981, 48.
172. G. Beresford 1975, 79–82.

6. TOWNS AND TRADE

1. Hassall 1977; Palliser 1975; Platt 1969b.
2. King's Lynn: D.M. Owen forthcoming; Hull: Ayres *et al.* 1979; Horrox 1978; Southampton: Platt 1973.
3. Pantin 1960; Pantin and Mitchell 1969.
4. Lobel 1969, 1975.
5. London: Grimes 1968; Canterbury: Williams and Frere 1948.
6. Oxford: Jope 1952–3; Southampton: Platt and Coleman-Smith 1975, 126–74; York: Radley 1971.
7. Biddle 1964–75.
8. Mahany *et al.* 1982.
9. H. Clarke and Carter 1977.
10. Schofield *et al.* 1981.
11. Heighway 1972.
12. Biddle and Hudson 1973.
13. Sweden: Andersson and Redin 1980; Finland: Hiekkanen 1981; Denmark: Nielsen and Schiørring 1977; Schiørring 1980.
14. Oslo: Høeg *et al.* 1977; Schia 1979, 1981; Tønsberg: Lindh and Brendalsmo 1982; Trondheim: Lunde 1977.
15. Herteig 1975a.
16. Thompson 1967.
17. Zbierski 1964.
18. Schofield 1983.
19. Wiltshire: Haslam 1976; Avon: Leech 1975; Oxfordshire: K.A. Rodwell 1975; Cornwall: Sheppard 1980.
20. Baker *et al.* 1979.
21. Carver 1980.
22. M.W. Beresford 1967.
23. M.W. Beresford and Finberg 1973: Tait 1936.
24. Reynolds 1977, ix.
25. Biddle 1976b, 100.
26. Ipswich: Dunmore *et al.* 1975, 1976; Southampton: Holdsworth 1980.
27. Biddle 1974.
28. Biddle 1976b; Hill 1978; Reynolds 1977, 34–42.
29. Hill 1981, 133–42.
30. Platt 1976, 21.
31. Reynolds 1977, 44.
32. M.W. Beresford 1967; Butler 1975.
33. Platt 1975.
34. For example, Maitland 1898; Reynolds 1977; Tait 1936.
35. King's Lynn: Hillen 1907, 1911; Canterbury: Urry 1967.
36. Mackerell 1738.
37. D.M. Owen forthcoming.
38. H. Clarke and Carter 1977.
39. *V.C.H. Norfolk* 1906, 130.
40. H.W. Saunders 1939.
41. H. Clarke and Carter 1977, 112–61.
42. H. Clarke and Carter 1977, 411–13.
43. *Med. Archaeol.* 1977.
44. Waltham Abbey: *Med. Archaeol.* 1974; Lincoln: *Med. Archaeol.* 1973; Stafford: *Med. Archaeol.* 1976.
45. Bedford: *Med. Archaeol.* 1972; Durham: *Med. Archaeol.* 1962–3; Shrewsbury: *Med. Archaeol.* 1975.
46. *Med. Archaeol.* 1971.

47. Biddle and Hill 1971.
48. Crummy 1979.
49. Hall 1978, 36.
50. Biddle 1965, 247.
51. Biddle 1976c, 345.
52. Lincoln: R.H. Jones 1980; Shrewsbury: Carver 1983.
53. Herteig 1959, 1968, 1975a, 1975b.
54. Netherlands: Sarfatij 1972; Germany: Eckstein 1981; Vogel 1983.
55. H. Clarke and Carter 1977, 100–12; Parker 1965.
56. Milne and Hobley 1981.
57. Hull: Armstrong 1977; Ayers *et al.* 1979; Norwich: Ayers and Murphy 1983.
58. Hobley and Schofield 1977; Milne and Milne 1978, 1982.
59. Biddle and Hudson 1973.
60. Tatton-Brown 1974, 1975.
61. Marsden 1981.
62. *The London Archaeologist* 4:10, 1983, 274.
63. Hillam and Morgan 1981.
64. Milne 1981, 33.
65. Amsterdam: van Regteren Altena and Zantkuyl 1969; Dordrecht: Sarfatij 1972.
66. H. Clarke and Carter 1977, 424.
67. Milne and Milne 1982, 68.
68. Schofield 1981.
69. H. Clarke 1979a.
70. Barley 1975; Turner 1971.
71. Canterbury: Frere, Stowe and Bennett 1982; Shrewsbury: Barker 1961.
72. T.P. Smith 1970; H. Clarke and Carter 1977, 432–8.
73. Keene 1975.
74. Le Patourel 1983.
75. Gras 1918, 435.
76. Gras 1918, 452.
77. Le Patourel 1983, table 3.1.
78. Davey and Hodges 1983.
79. H. Clarke 1983.
80. H. Clarke 1973.
81. Vince 1977.
82. Streeten 1980, 1982.
83. McGrail 1981; Marsden 1981.
84. Nedkvitne 1976.
85. Brindley 1938; Ellmers 1972, fig. 39; McGrail 1981, figs 17–19.
86. Hoekstra 1975.
87. McGrail 1981, fig. 21.
88. Ellmers 1979.
89. Crumlin-Pedersen 1979.
90. Dahlbäck 1982, 145–81.

Abbreviations

Antiq. Jnl.	*The Antiquaries Journal*
Archaeol. Ael.	*Archaeologia Aeliana*
Archaeol. Jnl.	*The Archaeological Journal*
B.A.R.	British Archaeological Reports
Beds. Archaeol. Jnl.	*Bedfordshire Archaeological Journal*
Berichten R.O.B.	*Berichten van de Rijkdienst voor het Oudheidkundig Bodemonderzoek*
Bulletin Univ. London Inst. Archaeol.	*Bulletin of the University of London Institute of Archaeology*
C.B.A. Res. Rep.	Council for British Archaeology Research Report
Current Archaeol.	*Current Archaeology*
Econ. Hist. Rev.	*Economic History Review*
Essex Archaeol. Hist.	*Essex Archaeology and History*
Int. Jnl. Naut. Archaeol.	*International Journal for Nautical Archaeology and Underwater Exploration*
Jnl. Brit. Archaeol. Assoc.	*Journal of the British Archaeological Association*
Jnl. Northants Mus. and Art Gallery	*Journal of the Northampton Museums and Art Gallery*
London and Middx. Archaeol. Soc.	*London and Middlesex Archaeological Society*
Med. Archaeol.	*Medieval Archaeology*
Port. Mon. Brass Soc.	*Portfolios of the Monumental Brass Society*
Post-med. Archaeol.	*Post-Medieval Archaeology*
Proc. Camb. Antiq. Soc.	*Proceedings of the Cambridgeshire Antiquarian Society*
Proc. Isle Wight Nat. Hist. Archaeol. Soc.	*Proceedings of the Isle of Wight Natural History and Archaeological Society*
Proc. Soms. Archaeol. Nat. Hist. Soc.	*Proceedings of the Somerset Archaeological and Natural History Society*
Proc. Sfk. Inst. Archaeol.	*Proceedings of the Suffolk Institute of Archaeology*

Proc. Wilts. Archaeol. Nat. Hist. Soc.	*Proceedings of the Wiltshire Archaeological and Natural History Society*
Report MSRG	*Annual Report of the Moated Sites Research Group*
Report MVRG	*Annual Report of the Medieval Village Research Group*
Royal Archaeol. Inst. Monograph	Royal Archaeological Institute Monograph Series
Soc. Med. Archaeol. Monograph	Society for Medieval Archaeology Monograph Series
Surrey Archaeol. Soc. Res. Vol.	Surrey Archaeological Society Research Volumes
Sussex Archaeol. Coll.	*Sussex Archaeological Collections*
Trans. Birmingham Archaeol. Soc.	*Transactions of the Birmingham Archaeological Society*
Trans. Bristol Gloucs. Archaeol. Soc.	*Transactions of the Bristol and Gloucester Archaeological Society*
Trans. Leics. Archaeol. Hist. Soc.	*Transactions of the Leicestershire Archaeological and Historical Society*
Trans. Salop. Archaeol. Soc.	*Transactions of the Shropshire Archaeological Society*
Worcs. Archaeol. Soc.	*Worcestershire Archaeological Society*

Bibliography

ABERG, F.A. 1978. 'Introduction', in Aberg (ed.) 1978, 1–4.

ABERG, F.A. (ed.). 1978. *Medieval Moated Sites*. C.B.A. Res. Rep. 17. London.

ABERG, F.A. 1983. 'The Moated Sites Research Group', in Hinton 1983, 97–101.

ABERG, F.A. and A.E. BROWN (eds). 1981. *Medieval Moated Sites in North-West Europe*. B.A.R. International Series 121. Oxford.

ADDYMAN, P.V. 1960. 'Excavations at a moated site at Sapcote', *Trans. Leics. Archaeol. Hist. Soc.* 36, 1–5.

ADDYMAN, P.V. 1965. 'Late Saxon settlements in the St Neots area: I. The Saxon settlement and Norman castle at Eaton Socon, Bedfordshire', *Proc. Camb. Antiq. Soc.* 42, 59–93.

ADDYMAN, P.V. and R.K. MORRIS (eds). 1976. *The Archaeological Study of Churches*. C.B.A. Res. Rep. 13. London.

ADDYMAN, P.V. and J. PRIESTLEY. 1977. 'Baile Hill, York: a report on the Institute's excavations', *Archaeol. Jnl.* 134, 115–56.

ALCOCK, N.W. 1981. *Cruck Construction: An Introduction and Catalogue*. C.B.A. Res. Rep. 42. London.

ALGAR, D. and J. MUSTY. 1969. 'Gomeldon', *Current Archaeol.* 14, 87–91.

ALLISON, K.J., M.W. BERESFORD, and J.G. HURST. 1966. *The Deserted villages of Northamptonshire*. Department of English Local History Occasional Papers 15. Leicester.

ANDERSSON, H. and L. REDIN. 1980. 'Stadsarkeologi i mellansverige', *Rapport Medeltidsstaden* 19.

ANDREWS, D.D. and G. MILNE (eds). 1979. *Wharram. A Study of Settlement on the Yorkshire Wolds I*. Soc. Med. Archaeol. Monograph 8.

ARMITAGE, E.S. 1912. *Early Norman Castles of the British Isles*. London.

ARMSTRONG, P. 1977. 'Excavations in Sewer Lane, Hull, 1974', *East Riding Archaeologist 3;* Hull Old Town Report Series 1.

AULT, W.O. 1972. *Open-Field Farming in Medieval England*. London.

AYERS, B. and P. MURPHY. 1983. 'A waterfront excavation at Whitefriars Street Car Park, Norwich 1979', *East Anglian Archaeology* 17, 1–60.

AYERS, B. *et al.* 1979. 'Chapel Lane Staith, 1978', *East Riding Archaeologist 5;* Hull Old Town Report Series 3.

BAART, J. *et al.* 1977. *Opgravningen in Amsterdam*. Amsterdam.

BAGLEY, J.J. and P.B. ROWLEY. 1966. *A Documentary History of England I (1066–1540)*. Harmondsworth.

BAKER, D. *et al.* 1979. 'Excavations in Bedford 1967–77', *Beds Archaeol. Jnl.* 13.

B A R K E R, P. A. 1961. 'Excavations on the town wall, Roushill, Shrewsbury', *Med. Archaeol.* 5, 181–210.

B A R K E R, P. A. 1977. *Techniques of Archaeological Excavation*. London.

B A R K E R, P. A. and K. J. B A R T O N. 1977. 'Excavations at Hastings Castle', *Archaeol. Jnl.* 134, 80–100.

B A R K E R, P. A. and R. H I G H A M. 1982. *Hen Domen, Montgomery. A Timber Castle on the English–Welsh Border I.* Royal Archaeol. Inst. Monograph.

B A R K E R, P. A. and J. L A W S O N. 1971. 'A pre-Norman field system at Hen Domen', *Med. Archaeol.* 15, 58–72.

B A R L E Y, M. W. 1975. 'Town defences in England and Wales after 1066', in Barley (ed.) 1975, 57–71.

B A R L E Y, M. W. (ed.). 1975. *The Plans and Topography of Medieval Towns*. C.B.A. Res. Rep. 14. London.

B A R L E Y, M. W. (ed.). 1977. *European Towns. Their Archaeology and Early History*. London, New York, San Francisco.

B A R L E Y, M. W. 1981. 'The medieval borough of Torksey: excavations 1963–8', *Antiq. Jnl.* 61, 264–91.

B A R R Y, T. B. 1977. *Medieval Moated Sites of S.E. Ireland*. B.A.R. 35. Oxford.

B A R R Y, T. B. 1978. 'Moated sites in Ireland', in Aberg (ed.) 1978, 57–9.

B A R R Y, T. B. 1981. 'The shifting frontier: medieval moated sites in Counties Cork and Limerick', in Aberg and Brown 1981, 71–85.

B E L L A M Y, C. V. 1965. 'Pontefract Priory excavations 1957–61, *Publ. of the Thoresby Soc.* 49.

B E N N E T T, P., S. S. F R E R E and S. S T O W. 1982. *Excavations at Canterbury Castle*. The Archaeology of Canterbury I.

B E R E S F O R D, G. 1975. *The Medieval Clay-Land Village: Excavations at Goltho and Barton Blount*. Soc. Med. Archaeol. Monograph 6.

B E R E S F O R D, G. 1977a. 'Excavation of a moated house at Wintringham in Huntingdonshire', *Archaeol. Jnl.* 134, 194–286.

B E R E S F O R D, G. 1977b. 'The excavation of the deserted medieval village of Goltho, Lincolnshire', *Chateau Gaillard* 8, 47–68.

B E R E S F O R D, G. 1979. 'Three deserted medieval settlements on Dartmoor: a report on the late E. Marie Minter's excavations', *Med. Archaeol.* 23, 98–158.

B E R E S F O R D, G. 1982. 'Goltho manor, Lincolnshire: the buildings and their surrounding defences', *Proc. Battle Conference* 4, 1–36.

B E R E S F O R D, M. W. 1954. *The Lost Villages of England*. London.

B E R E S F O R D, M. W. 1967. *New Towns of the Middle Ages*. London.

B E R E S F O R D, M. W. 1983. 'The Medieval Village Research Group: the first thirty years 1952–81', in Hinton 1983, 90–6.

B E R E S F O R D, M. W. and H. P. R. F I N B E R G. 1973. *English Medieval Boroughs: a Handlist*. Newton Abbott.

B E R E S F O R D, M. W. and J. G. H U R S T (eds). 1971. *Deserted Medieval Villages*. Guildford and London.

B E R E S F O R D, M. W. and J. G. H U R S T. 1976. 'Wharram Percy: a case study in microtopography', in Sawyer 1976, 52–85.

B E R E S F O R D, M. W., J. G. H U R S T and J. S H E A I L. 1980. 'MVRG: the first thirty years', *Report MVRG* 28, 36–8.

B E R E S F O R D, M. W. and J. K. S. S t J O S E P H. 1979. *Medieval England: An Aerial Survey*, 2nd edition. Cambridge.

B I D D L E, M. 1961–2. 'The deserted medieval village of Seacourt, Berkshire', *Oxoniensia* 26–7, 70–201.

B I D D L E, M. 1964. 'Excavations at Winchester 1962–3', *Antiq. Jnl.* 44, 188–219.

B I D D L E, M. 1965. 'Excavations at Winchester 1964', *Antiq. Jnl.* 45, 230–64.

B I D D L E, M. 1966. 'Excavations at Winchester 1965', *Antiq. Jnl.* 46, 308–32.

Bibliography

BIDDLE, M. 1967. 'Excavations at Winchester 1966', *Antiq. Jnl.* 47, 251–79.

BIDDLE, M. 1968. 'Excavations at Winchester 1967', *Antiq. Jnl.* 48, 250–84.

BIDDLE, M. 1969. 'Excavations at Winchester 1968', *Antiq. Jnl.* 49, 295–329.

BIDDLE, M. 1970. 'Excavations at Winchester 1969', *Antiq. Jnl.* 50, 276–326.

BIDDLE, M. 1972. 'Excavations at Winchester 1970', *Antiq. Jnl.* 52, 93–131.

BIDDLE, M. 1974. 'The development of the Anglo-Saxon town', *Settimane di studio de centro italiano di studi sull'alto medioevo, Spoleto*, 203–30.

BIDDLE, M. 1975a. 'Excavations at Winchester 1971', *Antiq. Jnl.* 55, 295–337.

BIDDLE, M. 1975b. 'Planned towns before 1066', in Barley (ed.) 1975, 19–32.

BIDDLE, M. 1976a. 'A widening horizon', in Addyman and Morris 1976, 65–71.

BIDDLE, M. 1976b. 'Towns' in Wilson (ed.) 1976, 99–150.

BIDDLE, M. (ed.). 1976c. *Winchester in the Early Middle Ages.* Winchester Studies I. Oxford.

BIDDLE, M. and D.HILL. 1971. 'Late Saxon planned towns', *Antiq. Jnl.* 51, 70–85.

BIDDLE, M. and D.HUDSON. 1973. *The Future of London's Past: A Survey of the Archaeological Implications of Planning and Development in the Nation's Capital.* Worcester.

BIDDLE, M. and B.KJØLBYE-BIDDLE. 1980. 'England's premier abbey', *Expedition* 22:2, 17–32.

BLACKMAN, D.J. (ed.). 1973. *Marine Archaeology.* Proceedings of the 23rd Symposium of Colston Research Society, Bristol.

BLOCH, M. 1961. *Feudal Society.* London.

BLOMQVIST, R. and A.MÅRTENSSON. 1965. *Thule Grävningen.* Lund.

BOWEN, H.C. 1961. *Ancient Fields.* London.

BRANDEL, S. 1918. *Kyrkor i Danderyds Skeppslag.* Stockholm.

BREWSTER, T.C.M. and A.BREWSTER. 1969. 'Tote Copse castle, Aldingbourne, Sussex', *Sussex Archaeol. Coll.* 107, 141–79.

BRIDBURY, A.R. 1982. *Medieval English Clothmaking.* London.

BRINDLEY, H.H. 1938. *Impressions and Casts of Seals, Coins, Tokens, Medals and Other Objects of Art Exhibited in the Seal Room, National Maritime Museum.* Greenwich.

BROBERG, B. and M.HASSELMO. 1982. 'Keramik, kammer och skor–variationer i fyndmaterialet i olika regioner'. *Bebyggelsehistorisk Tidskrift* 3, 89–103.

BROTHWELL, D. 1972. 'British palaeodemography and earlier British populations', *World Archaeology* 4, 75–87.

BROWN, R.A. 1973. *The Origins of English Feudalism.* London.

BROWN, R.A. 1976. *English Castles.* 3rd edition. London.

BRUCE-MITFORD, R.L.S. (ed.). 1975. *Recent Archaeological Excavations in Europe.* London.

BRYANT, G.F. 1977. 'Experimental kiln firings at Barton-on-Humber, S. Humberside, 1971', *Med. Archaeol.* 21, 106–123.

BRYANT, G.F. and J.M.STEANE. 1969. 'Excavations at the deserted medieval settlement at Lyveden: a second interim report', *Jnl. Northants Mus. and Art Gallery* 5.

BRYANT, G.F. and J.M.STEANE. 1971. 'Excavations at the deserted medieval settlement at Lyveden: a third interim report', *Jnl. Northants Mus. and Art Gallery* 9.

BUR, M. 1981. 'Research on the medieval fortified house in eastern France: the moated sites of the Champagne', in Aberg and Brown 1981, 87–101.

BURNHAM, B.C. and J.KINGSBURY. (eds.) 1979. *Space, Hierarchy and Society.* B.A.R. International Series 59. Oxford.

BUTLER, C. (ed.). 1927. *S. Benedicti, Regula Monasteriorum.* 2nd edition. Freiburg-im-Breisgau.

BUTLER, L.A.S. 1963. 'Hambleton Moat, Scredington, Lincolnshire', *Jnl. Brit. Archaeol. Assoc.* 3rd series. 26, 51–78.

BUTLER, L.A.S. 1975. 'The evolution of towns: planted towns after 1066,' in Barley (ed.) 1975, 32–48.

BUTLER, L.A.S. 1983. 'Church archaeology and the work of the Council for British Archaeology's Churches Committee', in Hinton 1983, 117–26.

BUTLER, L.A.S. *et al.* 1975. 'Deerhurst 1971–1974', *Antiq. Jnl.* 55, 346–65.

CANTOR, L. (ed.). 1982. *The English Medieval Landscape*. London.

CARUS-WILSON, E.M. 1954. *Medieval Merchant Venturers*. London.

CARUS-WILSON, E.M. 1957. 'The significance of the secular sculptures in the Lane Chapel, Cullompton, Devon', *Med. Archaeol.* 1, 104–17.

CARUS-WILSON, E.M. 1969. 'Haberget: a medieval textile conundrum', *Med. Archaeol.* 13, 148–66.

CARVER, M.O.H. 1979. 'Three Saxo-Norman tenements in Durham City', *Med. Archaeol.* 23, 1–80.

CARVER, M.O.H. (ed.). 1980. 'Medieval Worcester, an archaeological framework', *Worcs. Archaeol. Soc.* 3rd series: 7.

CARVER, M.O.H. (ed.). 1983. 'Two town houses in medieval Shrewsbury', *Trans Salop Archaeol. Soc.* 61.

CHARLES, F.W.B. 1967. *Medieval Cruck-Building and its Derivatives*. Soc. Med. Archaeol. Monograph 2.

CHARLES, F.W.B. 1981. 'Post-construction and the rafter roof', *Vernacular Architecture* 12, 12.03– 12.19.

CHARLESTON, R.J. 1975. 'The glass', in Platt and Coleman-Smith 1975, 204–26.

CHERRY, J.F. *et al.* (eds). 1978. *Sampling in Contemporary British Archaeology*. B.A.R. 50. Oxford.

CLARKE, D.L. (ed.). 1972. *Models in Archaeology*. London.

CLARKE, H. 1973. 'King's Lynn and east coast trade in the middle ages', in Blackman 1973, 277–91.

CLARKE, H. 1979a. 'The archaeology, history and architecture of the medieval ports of the east coast, with special reference to King's Lynn', in McGrail 1979, 155–65.

CLARKE, H. (ed.). 1979b. *Iron and Man in Prehistoric Sweden*. Stockholm.

CLARKE, H. 1983. 'The historical background to North Sea trade *c.*1200–1500, in Davey and Hodges 1983, 17–25.

CLARKE, H. and A. CARTER. 1977. *Excavations in King's Lynn 1963–1970*. Soc. Med. Archaeol. Monograph 7.

CLEERE, H. 1965. 'The iron industry in Roman Britain (AD 43–400)', in Guyan 1965, 91–102.

CLEERE, H. 1976. 'Some operating parameters for Roman ironworks', *Bulletin Univ. London Inst. Archaeol.* 13, 233–46.

COAD, J.G. and A.D.F. STREETEN. 1982. 'Excavations at Castle Acre Norfolk, 1972–77: Country house and castle of the Norman Earls of Surrey', *Archaeol. Jnl.* 139, 138–301.

COLVIN, H.M. (ed.). 1963. *The History of the King's Works* I, London.

COLYER, C. and B. GILMOUR. 1978. 'St Paul-in-the-Bail, Lincoln', *Current Archaeol.* 63, 102–5.

CONANT, K.J. 1966. *Carolingian and Romanesque Architecture*. 2nd edition. Harmondsworth.

CONGRESS OF ARCHAEOLOGICAL SOCIETIES 1901. Congress of Archaeological Societies in union with The Society of Antiquaries of London; provisional scheme for recording ancient defensive earthworks.

COOK, G.H. 1961. *English Monasteries in the Middle Ages*. London.

CORDER, P. 1957. 'The structure of Romano-British pottery kilns', *Archaeol. Jnl.* 114, 10–27.

CRAMP, R.J. 1969. 'Excavations at the Saxon monastic sites of Wearmouth and Jarrow, Co. Durham: an interim report', *Med. Archaeol.* 13, 21–66.

CRAMP, R.J. 1970. 'Decorated window-glass and millefiori from Monkwearmouth', *Antiq. Jnl.* 50, 327–35.

CRAMP, R.J. 1975. 'Window glass from the monastic site of Jarrow', *Jnl. of Glass Studies* 17, 88–96.

CRAMP, R.J. 1976. 'Monastic sites', in Wilson (ed.) 1976, 201–52.

CRAMP, R.J. 1977. 'The Brixworth Archaeological Research Committee', *Jnl. Brit. Archaeol. Assoc.* 130, 52–4.

CROSSLEY, D.W. 1967. 'Glassmaking in Bagot's Park, Staffordshire, in the 16th century', *Post-med. Archaeol.* 1, 44–83.

CROSSLEY, D.W. 1975. *The Bewl Valley Ironworks, Kent, c.1300–1730 AD*. Royal Archaeol. Inst. Monograph.

Bibliography

CROSSLEY, D.W. 1981. 'Medieval iron smelting', in Crossley (ed.) 1981, 29–41.

CROSSLEY, D.W. (ed.). 1981. *Medieval Industry*. C.B.A. Res.Rep.40. London.

CROWFOOT, E. 1975. 'The textiles', in Platt and Coleman-Smith 1975, 334–9.

CROWFOOT, E. 1977, 'Textiles' in H.Clarke and Carter 1977, 374–7.

CROWFOOT, E. 1979. 'The textiles', in Williams 1979, 306–7.

CRUMLIN-PEDERSEN, O. 1979. 'Danish cog finds', in McGrail 1979, 17–34.

CRUMMY, P. 1979. 'The system of measurement used in town planning from the 9th to 13th centuries', *Anglo-Saxon Studies* I. B.A.R. 72, 149–64.

CUNLIFFE, B. (ed.). 1964. *Winchester Excavations 1949–60* I. Winchester.

CURNOW, P.E. and M.W.THOMPSON. 1969. 'Excavations at Richard's Castle, Herefordshire', *Jnl. Brit. Archaeol. Assoc.* 3rd series. 32, 105–37.

CURRENT ARCHAEOL. 1967. 'The Leeds kiln experiment', *Current Archaeol.* 4, 94–7.

DAHLBÄCK, G. (ed.). 1982. *Helgeandsholmen. 1000 År i Stockholms Ström*. Stockholm.

DARBY, H.C. 1977. *Domesday England*. Cambridge.

DAVEY, P. and R.HODGES (eds). 1983. *Ceramics and Trade*. Sheffield.

DAVISON, B.K. 1967. 'The origins of the castle in England', *Archaeol. Jnl.* 124, 202–11.

DAVISON, B.K. 1969a. 'Early earthwork castles: a new model', *Chateau Gaillard* 3, 37–47.

DAVISON, B.K. 1969b. 'Aldingham', *Current Archaeol.* 12, 23–4.

DAVISON, B.K. 1972. 'Castle Neroche: an abandoned Norman fortress in south Somerset', *Proc. Soms. Archaeol. Nat. Hist. Soc.* 116, 16–58.

DAVISON, B.K. 1977. 'Excavations at Sulgrave, Northamptonshire, 1960–76', *Archaeol. Jnl.* 134, 105–14.

DAVISON, B.K. 1979. *Castles*. London.

DAWES, J.D. and J.R.MAGILTON. 1980. *The Cemetery of St Helen-on-the-Walls, Aldwark*. The Archaeology of York 12:2.

DICKINSON, J.C. 1950. *The Origins of the Austin Canons and their Introduction into England*. London.

DICKINSON, J.C. 1961. *Monastic Life in Medieval England*. London.

DONKIN, R.A. 1969. 'A check list of printed works relating to the Cistercian order as a whole and to the houses of the British Isles in particular', *Documentation Cistercienne* 2.

DONKIN, R.A. 1978. *The Cistercians: Studies in the Geography of Medieval England and Wales*. Toronto.

DOUGLAS, D.C. and G.W.GREENAWAY (eds). 1981. *English Historical Documents II 1042–1189*. 2nd edition, London and New York.

DREWETT, P. and I.STUART. 1975. 'Excavations in the Norman gate house, Bury St Edmunds Abbey', *Proc. Sfk. Inst. Archaeol.* 33:3, 241–52.

DRURY, P.J. 1981. 'The production of brick and tile in medieval England', in Crossley (ed.) 1981, 126–42.

DRURY, P.J. and G.D.PRATT. 1975. 'A late 13th and early 14th century tile factory at Danbury, Essex', *Med. Archaeol.* 19, 92–164.

DRURY, P.J. and W.J.RODWELL. 1978. 'Investigations at Asheldham, Essex. An interim report on the church and the historic landscape', *Antiq. Jnl.* 58, 133–51.

DUDLEY, D. and E.M.MINTER. 1962–3. 'The medieval village at Garrow Tor, Bodmin Moor, Cornwall', *Med. Archaeol.* 6–7, 272–94.

DUGDALE, W. 1655–73. *Monasticon Anglicanum*. London.

DUNMORE, S. *et al.* 1975. 'The origin and development of Ipswich', *East Anglian Archaeology* 1, 57–67.

DUNMORE, S. *et al.* 1976. 'Ipswich Archaeological Survey', *East Anglian Archaeology* 3, 135–40.

DUNNING, G.C. 1939. 'A 13th-century midden at Windcliff near Niton', *Proc. Isle Wight Nat. Hist. Archaeol. Soc.* 3, 128–37.

DUNNING, G.C. 1968. 'The trade in medieval pottery around the North Sea', in Renaud 1968, 35–58.

D Y E R , C. 1982. 'Deserted medieval villages in the west midlands', *Econ. Hist. Rev.* 2nd series. 35:1, 19–35.

E A M E S , E.S. 1961. 'A 13th-century tile kiln at North Grange, Meaux, Beverley, Yorkshire', *Med. Archaeol.* 5, 137–68.

E A M E S , E.S. 1968. *Medieval Tiles: a Handbook.* London.

E A M E S , E.S. 1975. 'Decorated tile pavements in English medieval houses', in Renaud 1975, 5–15.

E A M E S , E.S. 1980. *Catalogue of Medieval Lead-Glazed Earthenware Tiles.* London.

E A M E S , P. 1977. *Medieval Furniture.* London.

E C K S T E I N , D. 1981. 'The medieval waterfront of Schleswig', in Milne and Hobley 1981, 96–101.

E G A N , G. and W. E N D R E I . 1982. 'The sealing of cloth in Europe', *Textile History* 13:1, 47–75.

E L L M E R S , D. 1972. *Frühmittelalterliche Handelsschiffahrt in Mittel und Nordeuropa.* Neumünster.

E L L M E R S , D. 1979. 'The cog of Bremen and related boats', in McGrail 1979, 1–15.

E M D E N , A.B. 1977. *Medieval Decorated Tiles in Dorset.* London and Chichester.

E M E R Y , E.V. 1962. 'Moated settlements in England', *Geography* 47, 378–88.

E V A N S , J. 1931. *Monastic Life at Cluny 910–1157.* Oxford.

E V I S O N , V.I. (ed.). 1981. *Angles, Saxons and Jutes.* London.

E V I S O N , V.I. *et al.* (eds). 1974. *Medieval Pottery from Excavations.* London.

F A R M E R , P.G. 1979. *An Introduction to Scarborough Ware and a Reassessment of Knight Jugs.* Privately printed.

F E H R I N G , G.P. 1972. *Unterregenbach.* Stuttgart.

F I E L D , R.K. 1965. 'Worcestershire peasant buildings, household goods and farming equipment in the later middle ages', *Med. Archaeol.* 9, 105–45.

F L E T C H E R , J. (ed.). 1978. *Dendrochronology in Europe: Principles, and Approaches to Archaeology and History.* B.A.R. International Series 51. Oxford.

F O O T E , P. and D.M. W I L S O N . 1970. *The Viking Achievement.* London.

F O W L E R , P.J. (ed.). 1972. *Archaeology and the Landscape.* London.

F R A N K , S. 1982. *Glass and Archaeology.* London and New York.

F R A N Z É N , A.M. and A. G E I J E R . 1968. 'Textile finds from excavations in Swedish towns 1960–66', *Res Mediaevales* 3, 129–34.

F R E R E , S.S., S. S T O W and P. B E N N E T T . 1982. *Excavations on the Roman and Medieval Defences of Canterbury.* The Archaeology of Canterbury II.

G E I J E R , A. 1979. *A History of Textile Art.* London.

G E M , R. and L. K E E N . 1981. 'Late Anglo-Saxon finds from the site of St Edmunds Abbey', *Proc. Sfk. Inst. Archaeol.* 35:1, 1–30.

G Ö M Ö R I , J. (ed.). 1981. *Industrial Archaeology. Kilns and Furnaces.* Veszprém.

G O O D A L L , I.H. 1981. 'The medieval blacksmith and his products', in Crossley (ed.) 1981, 51–62.

G R A C I E , H.S. 1958. 'St Peter's Church Frocester and an underlying Roman building', *Trans. Bristol Gloucs. Archaeol. Soc.* 77, 23–30.

G R A S , N.S.B. 1918. *The Early English Customs System.* Harvard.

G R A Y , H.L. 1915. *English Field Systems.* Harvard.

G R E E N E , J.P. 1972. *Norton Priory Excavations 1972.* Runcorn.

G R E E N E , J.P. and B. J O H N S O N . 1978. 'An experimental tile kiln at Norton Priory, Cheshire', *Medieval Ceramics* 2, 31–42.

G R I M E S , W.F. 1968. *The Excavation of Roman and Medieval London.* London.

G R O E N M A N - V A N W A A T E R I N G E , W. 1975. 'Society … rests on leather', in Renaud 1975, 23–34.

G U Y A N , W.U. (ed.). 1965. *Vita Pro Ferro: Festschrift für Robert Durrer.* Schaffhausen.

G W Y N N , A. and R.N. H A D C O C K . 1970. *Medieval Religious Houses: Ireland.* London.

H A L L , A.R. and H.R. K E N W A R D (eds). 1982. *Environmental Archaeology in the Urban Context.* C.B.A. Res. Rep. 43. London.

H A L L , R.A. 1978. 'The topography of Anglo-Scandinavian York', in Hall (ed.) 1978, 31–6.

H A L L , R.A. (ed.). 1978. *Viking Age York and the North.* C.B.A. Res. Rep. 27. London.

H A L L , R.A. 1982. '10th-century woodworking in Coppergate, York', in McGrail 1982, 231–44.

Bibliography

HARDEN, D.B. 1956. 'Glass vessels in Britain and Ireland, AD 400–1000', in Harden (ed.) 1956, 132–67.

HARDEN, D.B. (ed.). 1956. *Dark Age Britain*. London.

HARDEN, D.B. 1978. 'Anglo-Saxon and later medieval glass in Britain: some recent developments', *Med. Archaeol.* 22, 1–24.

HARTE, N.B. and K.G.PONTING (eds). 1983. *Cloth and Clothing in Medieval Europe*. London.

HARVEY, P.D.A. 1983. 'English archaeology after the conquest: a historian's view', in Hinton 1983, 74–82.

HASSALL, T.G. 1977. 'Urban archaeology in England, 1975', in Barley (ed.) 1977, 3–18.

HASLAM, J. 1976. *Wiltshire Towns: the Archaeological Potential*. Devizes.

HEIGHWAY, C.M. (ed.). 1972. *The Erosion of History: Archaeology and Planning in Towns*. London.

HEIGHWAY, C.M. 1978. 'Excavations at Gloucester, fourth interim report: St Oswald's Priory 1975–6', *Antiq. Jnl.* 58, 103–32.

HEIGHWAY, C.M. *et al.* 1979. 'Excavations at 1 Westgate Street, Gloucester 1975', *Med. Archaeol.* 23, 159–213.

HERRMANN, J. 1971. *Zwischen Hradschin und Vineta, frühe Kulturen der Westslawen*. Berlin.

HERTEIG, A. 1959. 'The excavation of Bryggen, the old Hanseatic wharf in Bergen', *Med. Archaeol.* 3, 177–86.

HERTEIG, A. 1968. 'The Hansa town of Bergen and its commercial relations, seen in the light of excavations at Bryggen', in Renaud 1968, 73–9.

HERTEIG, A. 1975a. 'The excavation of Bryggen, Bergen, Norway', in Bruce-Mitford 1975, 65–89.

HERTEIG, A. 1975b. 'Bryggen, the medieval wharves of Bergen', *Archaeological Contributions to the Early History of Urban Communities in Norway*. Instituttet for Sammenlignende Kulturforskning. Series A. 27, 49–89.

HEWITT, C.A. 1969. *The Development of Carpentry 1200–1700*. Newton Abbot.

HEWITT, C.A. 1974. *Church Carpentry*. London and Chichester.

HEWITT, C.A. 1982. 'Toolmarks on surviving works from the Saxon, Norman and later medieval periods', in McGrail 1982, 339–48.

HIEKKANEN, M. 1981. 'Borgå (fi. Porvoo)', *Rapport Medeltidsstaden* 1, Helsinki.

HILDYARD, E.J.W. 1949. 'Further excavations at Cambokeels in Weardale', *Archaeol. Ael.* 4th series. 27, 177–206.

HILL, D. 1978. 'Trends in the development of towns during the reign of Ethelred II', in Hill (ed.) 1978, 213–26.

HILL, D. (ed.). 1978. *Ethelred the Unready*. B.A.R. 59. Oxford.

HILL, D. 1981. *An Atlas of Anglo-Saxon England*. Oxford.

HILLAM, J. and R.A.MORGAN. 1981. 'What value is dendrochronology to waterfront archaeology?', in Milne and Hobley 1981, 39–46.

HILLEN, H.J. 1907, 1911. *History of the Borough of King's Lynn* I–II. Norwich.

HILTON, R.H. (ed.). 1976. *Peasants, Knights and Heretics*. Cambridge.

HILTON, R.H. and P.A.RAHTZ. 1966. 'Upton, Gloucestershire, 1959–1964', *Trans. Bristol Gloucs. Archaeol. Soc.* 85, 70–146.

HINTON, D.A. 1969. 'Excavation at Bicester Priory 1968, *Oxoniensia* 34, 21–8.

HINTON, D.A. (ed.). 1983. *25 Years of Medieval Archaeology*. Sheffield.

HIRST, S.M., D.A.WALSH and S.M.WRIGHT. 1983. *Bordesley Abbey II*. B.A.R. 111. Oxford.

HOBLEY, B. and J.SCHOFIELD. 1977. 'Excavations in the City of London, first interim report, 1974–1975', *Antiq. Jnl.* 57, 31–66.

HODGES, R. 1983. 'New approaches to medieval archaeology, part 2', in Hinton 1983, 24–32.

HØEG, H.I. *et al.* 1977. *De Arkeologiske Utgravningen i Gamlebyen, Oslo* I. Oslo, Bergen and Tromsø.

HOEK, C. 1981. 'Moated sites in the county of Holland', in Aberg and Brown 1981, 173–96.

HOEKSTRA, T. 1975. 'Note on ancient ships found in Utrecht', *Int. Jnl. Naut. Archaeol.* 4, 390–1.

HOFENK-DE GRAAF, J.H. 1983. 'The chemistry of red dyestuffs in medieval and early modern Europe', in Harte and Ponting 1983, 71–9.

HOFFMANN, M. 1964. *The Warp-Weighted Loom*. Studia Norvegica 14.

HOHLER, C. 1942. 'Medieval pavingtiles in Buckinghamshire', *Records of Buckinghamshire* 14:1, 1–49; 14:2, 99–131.

HOLDEN, E.W. 1963. 'Excavations at the deserted medieval village of Hangleton, Part I', *Sussex Archaeol. Coll.* 101, 54–181.

HOLDSWORTH, P. 1980. *Excavations at Melbourne Street, Southampton, 1971–76*. C.B.A. Res. Rep. 33.

HOPE-TAYLOR, B. 1950. 'The excavation of a motte at Abinger, Surrey', *Archaeol. Jnl.* 107, 15–43.

HOOVER, H.C. and L.H. HOOVER (eds). 1950. *De Re Metallica*. New York.

HORN, W. and E. BORN. 1979. *The Plan of St Gall; a Study of the Architecture and Economy of and Life in a Paradigmatic Carolingian Monastery*. Berkeley.

HORROX, R. 1978. *The Changing Plan of Hull 1290–1650*. Kingston upon Hull.

HOSKINS, W.G. 1955. *The Making of the English Landscape*. London.

HUGGINS, P.J. and R.M. HUGGINS. 1973. 'Excavations of a monastic forge and Saxo-Norman enclosure, Waltham Abbey, Essex 1972–73', *Essex Archaeol. Hist.* 5, 127–84.

HUGHES, K. 1966. *The Church in Early Irish Society*. London.

HUGHES, K. and A. HAMLIN. 1977. *The Modern Traveller to the Early Irish Church*. London.

HUNTER, J.R. 1981. 'The medieval glass industry', in Crossley (ed.) 1981, 143–50.

HURST, D.G. and J.G. HURST. 1967. 'Excavation of two moated sites: Milton, Hampshire and Ashwell, Hertfordshire'; *Jnl. Brit. Archaeol. Assoc.* 3rd series. 30, 48–86.

HURST, D.G. and J.G. HURST. 1969. 'Excavations at the medieval village of Wythemail', *Med. Archaeol.* 13, 167–203.

HURST, J.G. 1961. 'The kitchen area of Northolt Manor, Middlesex', *Med. Archaeol.* 5, 211–99.

HURST, J.G. 1962–3. 'White Castle and the dating of medieval pottery', *Med. Archaeol.* 6–7, 135–55.

HURST, J.G. 1965. 'The medieval peasant house', in Small 1965, 190–6.

HURST, J.G. 1972. 'The changing medieval village in England', in Ucko 1972, 531–40.

HURST, J.G. 1976a. 'Wharram Percy: St Martin's Church', in Addyman and Morris 1976, 36–9.

HURST, J.G. 1976b. 'The pottery', in Wilson (ed.) 1976, 283–348.

HURST, J.G. 1981. 'Wharram: Roman to medieval', in Evison 1981, 241–54.

HURST, J.G. and D.G. HURST. 1964. 'Excavations at the deserted medieval village of Hangleton, Part II', *Sussex Archaeol. Coll.* 102, 94–142.

JAMES, M.R. 1935. *The Canterbury Psalter*. Canterbury.

JANSSEN, W. 1981. 'Research on medieval settlement sites of the Rhineland', *Report MVRG* 29, 36–40.

JESSON, M. 1973. *The Archaeology of Churches, a Report from the Churches Committee of the C.B.A.* London.

JONES, G.R.J. 1983. 'The pre-Norman field system and its implications for early territorial organization', in Mayes and Butler 1983, 70–2.

JONES, J. 1976. *How to Record Graveyards*. C.B.A./Rescue Handbook. London.

JONES, M.J. (ed.). 1981. 'Excavations at Lincoln. Third interim report: sites outside the walled city', *Antiq. Jnl.* 61, 83–114.

JONES, R.H. 1980. *Medieval House at Flaxengate, Lincoln*. The Archaeology of Lincoln XI:1. Lincoln.

JOPE, E.M. 1952–3. 'Late Saxon pits under Oxford castle mound: excavations 1952', *Oxoniensia* 17–18, 77–81.

JOPE, E.M. 1972. 'Models in medieval studies', in D.L. Clarke 1972, 963–90.

JOPE, E.M. and R.I. THRELFALL. 1958. 'Excavation of a medieval settlement at Beere, North Tawton, Devon', *Med. Archaeol.* 2, 112–40.

JOPE, E.M. and R.I.THRELFALL. 1959. 'The 12th-century castle at Ascot Doilly, Oxfordshire', *Antiq. Jnl.* 39, 219–73.

JØRGENSEN, L.B. and K.TIDOW (eds). 1982. *Textilsymposium Neumünster, Archäologische Textilfunde.* Neumünster.

KAMIŃSKA, J. and A.NAHLIK. 1960. 'Etudes sur l'industrie textile du Haut Moyen Age en Pologne', *Archaeologia Polona* 3, 89–119.

KAUFFMANN, C.M. 1975. *Romanesque Manuscripts 1066–1190.* London.

KEEN, L. 1979. 'The 14th-century tile pavements in Prior Crauden's Chapel and in the south transept', *Medieval Art and Architecture at Ely Cathedral.* Brit. Archaeol. Assoc. Conference Transactions II, 47–57.

KEENE, D.J. 1975. 'Surburban growth', in Barley (ed.) 1975, 71–82.

KEENE, D.J. 1979. 'Medieval Winchester: its spatial organization', in Burnham and Kingsbury 1979, 149–59.

KEENE, D.J. 1981a. 'Some concluding reflections', in Crossley (ed.) 1981, 151–3.

KEENE, D.J. 1981b. 'Research priorities for urban archaeology', in Schofield *et al.* 1981, v–ix.

KEENE, D.J. 1983. 'Urban Research Committee Working Party on Urban Churches: notes on the survey of urban churches', in R.K.Morris 1983, 109–12.

KENYON, G.H. 1967. *The Glass Industry of the Weald.* Leicester.

KENYON, J.R. 1978. *Castles, Town Defences and Artillery Fortifications in Britain: a Bibliography 1947–74.* C.B.A.Res.Rep.25. London.

KETTERINGHAM, L.L. 1976. *Alsted: the Excavation of a 13th–14th Century Sub-manor with its Ironworks in Netherne Wood, Merstham, Surrey.* Surrey Archaeol. Soc. Res. Vol. 2.

KILMURRY, K. 1980. *The Pottery Industry of Stamford, Lincs. c.AD 850–1250.* B.A.R. 84. Oxford.

KING, D.J.C. 1972. 'The field archaeology of mottes in England and Wales', *Chateau Gaillard* 5, 101–13.

KING, D.J.C. 1983. *Castellarium Anglicanum: An Index and Bibliography of the Castles of England, Wales, and the Islands.* New York.

KING, D.J.C. and L.ALCOCK. 1969. 'Ringworks of England and Wales', *Chateau Gaillard* 3, 90–127.

KLINGELHÖFER, E.C. 1974. *Broadfield Deserted Medieval Village.* B.A.R. 2. Oxford.

KNOWLES, D. 1940. *The Monastic Order in England.* Cambridge.

KNOWLES, D. 1948. *The Religious Orders in England.* Cambridge.

KNOWLES, D. 1963. *The Historian and Character.* Cambridge.

KNOWLES, D. and W.F.GRIMES. 1954. *Charterhouse.* London.

KNOWLES, D. and R.N.HADCOCK. 1971. *Medieval Religious Houses, England and Wales.* 2nd edition. London.

LAMB, H.H. 1977. *Climate. Present, Past and Future.* London.

LEACH, P.E. (ed.). 1982. *Archaeology in Kent to AD 1500.* C.B.A.Res.Rep.48. London.

LEASK, H.G. 1977. *Irish Churches and Monastic Buildings.* 2nd edition. Dundalk.

LEECH, R. 1975. *Small Medieval Towns in Avon: Archaeology and Planning.* Committee for Rescue Archaeology in Avon, Gloucestershire and Somerset, Survey 1.

LE PATOUREL, H.E.J. 1968. 'Documentary evidence and the medieval pottery industry', *Med. Archaeol.* 12, 101–26.

LE PATOUREL, H.E.J. 1973. *The Moated Sites of Yorkshire.* Soc. Med. Archaeol. Monograph 5.

LE PATOUREL, H.E.J. 1976. 'Pottery as evidence for social and economic change', in Sawyer 1976, 86–96.

LE PATOUREL, H.E.J. 1978. 'Documentary evidence', in Aberg (ed.) 1978, 21–8.

LE PATOUREL, H.E.J. 1979. 'Medieval pottery', in Andrews and Milne 1979, 74–6.

LE PATOUREL, H.E.J. 1981. 'Moated sites in their European context', in Aberg and Brown 1981, 1–18.

LE PATOUREL, H.E.J. 1983. 'Documentary evidence for the pottery trade in north-west Europe', in Davey and Hodges 1983, 27–35.

LE PATOUREL, H.E.J. and B.K.ROBERTS. 1978. 'The significance of moated sites', in Aberg (ed.) 1978, 46–55.

LIEBERMANN, F. 1903. *Die Gesetze der Angelsachsen*. Halle.

LIMBREY, S. and J.G.EVANS. (eds).1975. *The Impact of Man on the Landscape*. C.B.A. Res. Rep. 21. London.

LINDH, J. and J.BRENDALSMO. 1982. *Funn fra en Utgravning*. Tønsberg.

LLOYD, T.H. 1977. *The English Wool Trade in the Middle Ages,* Cambridge.

LOBEL, M.D. (ed.). 1969. *Historic Towns: Maps and Plans of Towns and Cities in the British Isles* I. Oxford.

LOBEL, M.D. (ed.). 1975. *The Atlas of Historic Towns*. London.

LONG, C.D. 1975. 'Excavations in the medieval city of Trondheim, Norway', *Med. Archaeol.* 19, 1–32.

LONSDALE, H.W. and E.J.TARVER. 1874. *Illustrations of Medieval Costume*. London.

LUNDE, Ø. 1977. *Trondheims Fortid i Bygrunnen. Middelalderbyens Topografi på Grunnlag av det Arkeologiske Materialet inntil 1970*. Riksantikvarens Skrifter 2.

LUNDSTRÖM, A. 1976. 'Bead making in Scandinavia in the early middle ages', *Early Medieval Studies* 9, Antikvariskt Arkiv 61. Stockholm.

LUNDSTRÖM, A. 1981. 'Survey of the glass from Helgö', in Lundström and Clarke 1981, 1–38.

LUNDSTRÖM, A. and H.CLARKE (eds). 1981. *Excavations at Helgö* 7. Stockholm.

MCDONNELL, G. 1983. 'Tap slags and hearth bottoms', *Current Archaeol.* 86, 81–3.

MCGRAIL, S. (ed.). 1979. *Medieval Ships and Harbours in Northern Europe*. B.A.R. International Series 66. Oxford.

MCGRAIL, S. 1981. 'Medieval boats, ships and landing places', in Milne and Hobley 1981, 17–23.

MCGRAIL, S. (ed.). 1982. *Woodworking Techniques before AD 1500*. B.A.R. International Series 129. Oxford.

MACGREGOR, A. 1978. 'Industry and commerce in Anglo-Scandinavian York', in Hall (ed.) 1978, 37–57.

MACKERELL, B. 1738. *The History and Antiquities of the Flourishing Corporation of King's Lynn in the County of Norfolk*. London.

MAGILTON, J.R. 1980. *The Church of St Helen-on-the-Walls, Aldwark*. The Archaeology of York 10:1.

MAHANY, C. *et al*. 1982. *Excavations in Stamford, Lincolnshire 1963–1969*. Soc. Med. Archaeol. Monograph 9.

MAITLAND, F.W. 1898. *Township and Borough*. Cambridge.

MARSDEN, P. 1981. 'Early shipping and the waterfronts of London', in Milne and Hobley 1981, 10–16.

MAYES, P. and L.A.S.BUTLER. 1983. *Sandal Castle Excavations 1964–1973*. Wakefield.

MAYES, P., forthcoming. *Pottery Kilns at Chilvers Coton, Nuneaton, Warwickshire*. Soc. Med. Archaeol. Monograph 10.

MELLOR, J.E. and T.PEARCE. 1981. *The Austin Friars, Leicester*. C.B.A.Res.Rep.35.

MIDMER, R. 1979. *English Medieval Monasteries 1066–1540*. London.

MILLAR, E.G. 1932. *The Luttrell Psalter*. London.

MILLER, E. and J.HATCHER. 1978. *Medieval England. Rural Society and Economic Change 1086–1348*. London and New York.

MILNE, G. 1981. 'Medieval riverfront reclamation in London', in Milne and Hobley 1981, 32–8.

MILNE, G. and B.HOBLEY (eds). 1981. *Waterfront Archaeology in Britain and Northern Europe*. C.B.A.Res.Rep.41.

MILNE, G. and C.MILNE. 1978. 'Excavations on the Thames waterfront at Trig Lane, London, 1974–76', *Med. Archaeol.* 22, 84–104.

MILNE, G. and C.MILNE. 1982. *Medieval Waterfront Development at Trig Lane, London*. London and Middx. Archaeol. Soc. Special Paper 5.

Bibliography

MONEY, J.H. 1971. 'Medieval iron-workings in Minepit Wood, Rotherfield, Sussex', *Med. Archaeol.* 15, 86−111.

MOORHOUSE, S. 1978. 'Documentary evidence for the uses of medieval pottery', *Medieval Ceramics* 2, 3−21.

MOORHOUSE, S. 1981. 'The medieval pottery industry and its markets', in Crossley (ed.) 1981, 96−125.

MOORHOUSE, S. 1983. 'The Medieval Pottery Research Group', in Hinton 1983, 102−16.

MORGAN, N.J. 1982. *Early Gothic Manuscripts (I)*. Oxford.

MORGAN, R. 1982. 'Tree-ring studies on urban waterlogged wood: problems and possibilities', in Hall and Kenward 1982, 31−9.

MORRIS, C.A. 1982. 'Aspects of Anglo-Saxon and Anglo-Scandinavian lathe-turning', in McGrail 1982, 245−61.

MORRIS, R.K. 1979. *Cathedrals and Abbeys of England and Wales*. London.

MORRIS, R.K. 1983. *The Church in British Archaeology*. C.B.A.Res.Rep.47. London.

MORRIS, R.K. and J.ROXAN. 1980. 'Churches on Roman buildings', in W.J.Rodwell 1980b, 211−42.

MUSTY, J. 1974. 'Medieval pottery kilns', in Evison *et al.* 1974, 41−65.

MUSTY, J. *et al.* 1969. 'The medieval pottery kilns at Laverstock near Salisbury, Wiltshire', *Archaeologia* 102, 83−150.

MYRVOLL, S. 1983. 'The town of Skien, Norway − development from market place to medieval town in the 12th and 13th century', *Lübecker Schriften zur Archäologie und Kulturgesehichte* 7, 271−5.

NAU, E. 1972. 'Münzen', in Fehring 1972, 170−83.

NEDKVITNE, A. 1976. 'Handelsjøfarten mellan Norge og England i højmiddelalderen', *Sjøfartshistorisk Årbok*, 7−254.

NEWTON, S.M. 1980. *Fashion in the Age of the Black Prince*. Woodbridge.

NIELSEN, I. and O.SCHIØRRING. 1977. 'Vejledning til Projektets registreringssystem og -kort', *Projekt Middelalderbyen Meddelelser* I.

NORMAN, E.R. and J.K.S.St JOSEPH. 1969. *The Early Development of Irish Society*. Cambridge.

OLSEN, O. 1976. 'The legal situation in Denmark', in Addyman and Morris 1976, 14−15.

O'RIORDAIN, B. 1971. 'Excavations at High Street and Winetavern Street, Dublin', *Med. Archaeol.* 15, 73−85.

OWEN, D.E. 1961. 'Kirkstall Abbey excavations: 8th report', *Publ. of the Thoresby Soc.* 48, 56−77.

OWEN, D.M. 1976. 'Documentary sources for the building history of churches in the middle ages', in Addyman and Morris 1976, 21−27.

OWEN, D.M., forthcoming. *The Making of King's Lynn 3: Medieval King's Lynn, a Documentary Survey*. British Academy.

PALLISER, D.M. 1975. 'Sources for urban topography: documents, buildings and archaeology', in Barley (ed.) 1975, 1−7.

PANTIN, W.A. (ed.). 1960. *Survey of Oxford I*. Oxford Historical Society, new series 14.

PANTIN, W.A. and W.T.MITCHELL. 1969. *Survey of Oxford II*. Oxford Historical Society, new series 20.

PARKER, H. 1965. 'A medieval wharf in Thoresby College courtyard, King's Lynn', *Med. Archaeol.* 9, 94−104.

PARRY, M.L. 1978. *Climatic Change, Agriculture and Settlement*. Folkestone and Hamden.

PEACOCK, D.P.S. (ed.). 1977. *Pottery and Early Commerce*. London.

PHILP, B. 1968. *Excavations at Faversham 1965*. Kent Archaeol. Res. Group's Council Report 1, 1−61.

PLATT, C.P.S. 1969a. *The Monastic Grange in Medieval England*. London.

PLATT, C.P.S. 1969b. *Medieval Archaeology in England: A Guide to the Historical Sources*. Shalfleet, Isle of Wight.

PLATT, C.P.S. 1973. *Medieval Southampton. The Port and Trading Community AD 1000–1600.* London.

PLATT, C.P.S. 1975. 'The evolution of towns: natural growth', in Barley (ed.) 1975, 48–56.

PLATT, C.P.S. 1976. *The English Medieval Town.* London.

PLATT, C.P.S. 1978. *Medieval England.* London.

PLATT, C.P.S. 1981. *The Parish Churches of Medieval England.* London.

PLATT, C.P.S. 1982. *The Castle in Medieval England and Wales.* London.

PLATT, C.P.S. and R.COLEMAN-SMITH. 1975. *Excavations in Medieval Southampton 1953–1969.* Leicester.

PLEINER, R. 1982. 'Die Schmiedtecknik', in Richter 1982, 298–300.

POSTAN, M.M. 1975. *The Medieval Economy and Society.* Harmondsworth.

POSTAN, M.M. and E.E.RICH (eds). 1952. *Trade and Industry in the Middle Ages. Cambridge Economic History of Europe* II.

POWER, E. 1941. *The Wool Trade in English Medieval History.* Oxford.

PRESTWICH, J.O. 1963. 'Anglo-Norman feudalism and the problem of continuity', *Past and Present* 26, 39–57.

RACKHAM, B. 1972. *English Medieval Pottery.* 2nd edition. London.

RACKHAM, O. *et al.* 1978. 'The thirteenth-century roof and floor of Blackfriars Priory at Gloucester', *Med. Archaeol.* 22, 105–22.

RADFORD, C.A.R. 1961. 'Excavations at Glastonbury Abbey 1951–4, *Somerset and Dorset Notes and Queries* 27, 21–4, 68–73, 165–9.

RADFORD, C.A.R. 1968. 'Excavations at Glastonbury Abbey, 1962', *Somerset and Dorset Notes and Queries* 28, 114–17.

RADLEY, J. 1971. 'Economic aspects of Anglo-Danish York', *Med. Archaeol.* 15, 37–57.

RAHTZ, P.A. 1969. *Excavations at King John's Hunting Lodge, Writtle, Essex, 1955–57.* Soc. Med. Archaeol. Monograph 3.

RAHTZ, P.A. 1973. 'Monasteries as settlements', *Scottish Archaeological Forum* 5, 123–35.

RAHTZ, P.A. 1976a. *Deerhurst 1971–73.* C.B.A.Res.Rep. 15. London.

RAHTZ, P.A. 1976b. 'Research directions at Deerhurst', in Addyman and Morris 1976, 60–3.

RAHTZ, P.A. 1976c. 'The archaeology of the churchyard', in Addyman and Morris 1976, 41–5.

RAHTZ, P.A. 1981. *The New Medieval Archaeology.* York.

RAHTZ, P.A. 1983. 'New approaches to medieval archaeology, part 1', in Hinton 1983, 12–23.

RAHTZ, P.A. and S.M.HIRST. 1976. *Bordesley Abbey.* B.A.R. 23. Oxford.

RAHTZ, P.A. *et al.* 1982. 'Architectural reconstruction of timber buildings from archaeological evidence', *Vernacular Architecture* 13, 13.39–13.47.

RECORD COMMISSION 1807. *Nonarum Inquisitiones in Curia Scaccarii, temp. regis Edwardi III.*

RENAUD, J.G.N. (ed.). 1968. *Rotterdam Papers. A Contribution to Medieval Archaeology* I. Rotterdam.

RENAUD, J.G.N. (ed.). 1975. *Rotterdam Papers. A Contribution to Medieval Archaeology* II. Rotterdam.

RENN, D.F. 1959. 'Mottes: a classification', *Antiquity* 33, 106–12.

RENN, D.F. 1968. *Norman Castles in Britain.* London.

REYNOLDS, S. 1977. *An Introduction to the History of English Medieval Towns.* Oxford.

RICHTER, M. 1982. *Hradištko u Davle.* Monumenta Archaeologica 20. Prague.

RIGOLD, S.E. 1975. 'Structural aspects of medieval timber bridges', *Med. Archaeol.* 19, 48–91.

RIGOLD, S.E. 1978. 'Structures within English moated sites', in Aberg (ed.) 1978, 29–36.

ROBERTS, B.K. 1965. 'Moated sites in midland England', *Trans. Birmingham Archaeol. Soc.* 80, 26–36.

ROBERTS, B.K. 1977. *Rural Settlement in Britain.* London.

ROBINSON, D.M. 1980. *The Geography of Augustinian Settlement.* B.A.R. 80. Oxford.

RODWELL, K.A. (ed.). 1975. *Historic Towns in Oxfordshire: A Survey of the New County.* Oxfordshire Archaeol. Unit Survey 3.

RODWELL, K.A. and W.J.RODWELL. 1976. 'The investigation of churches in use: a problem in rescue archaeology', in Addyman and Morris 1976, 45–54.

RODWELL, W.J. 1975. 'Archaeology and the church', *Antiquity* 49, 33–42.

RODWELL, W.J. 1976. 'The archaeological investigation of Hadstock church, Essex', *Antiq. Jnl.* 56, 55–71.

RODWELL, W.J. 1980a. *Wells Cathedral. Excavations and Discoveries.* Wells.

RODWELL, W.J. (ed.). 1980b. *Temples, Churches and Religion: Recent Research in Roman Britain.* B.A.R. 77. Oxford.

RODWELL, W.J. 1981. *The Archaeology of the English Church.* London.

RODWELL, W.J. and K.A.RODWELL. 1973. 'Excavations at Rivenhall church, Essex', *Antiq. Jnl.* 53, 219–31.

RODWELL, W.J. and K.A.RODWELL. 1977. *Historic Churches – A Wasting Asset.* C.B.A.Res.Rep. 19. London.

RODWELL, W.J. and K.A.RODWELL. 1981. 'Barton-on-Humber', *Current Archaeol.* 7, 208–15.

ROWLEY, T. (ed.). 1981. *The Origins of Open Field Agriculture.* London.

ROWLEY, T. 1982. 'Medieval field systems', in Cantor 1982, 25–55.

ROWLEY, T. and J.WOOD. 1982. *Deserted Villages.* Aylesbury.

ROXAN, J. and R.K.MORRIS. 1983. 'Church archaeology in Britain, 1955–80', in R.K.Morris 1983, 94–108.

R.C.H.M. NORTHAMPTONSHIRE 1979. *An Inventory of the Historical Monuments in the County of Northampton* I–III. London.

R.C.H.M. WEST CAMBRIDGESHIRE 1968. *An Inventory of the Monuments in the County of Cambridge* I. London.

RUSSELL, J.C. 1948. *British Medieval Population.* Albuquerque.

RYDER, M.L. 1981. 'Medieval sheep and their wool types', in Crossley (ed.) 1981, 16–28.

SALZMAN, L.F. 1923. *English Industries of the Middle Ages.* Oxford.

SALZMAN, L.F. 1952. *Building in England down to 1540.* Oxford.

SARFATIJ, H. 1972. 'Dordrecht: opgravningen in Hollands oudste stad', *Spiegel Historiael* 7, 620–7, 659–67.

SARFATIJ, H. 1973. 'Digging in Dutch towns: twenty-five years of research by the ROB in medieval town centres', *Berichten R.O.B.* 23, 367–420.

SAUNDERS, A.D. 1977. 'Five castle excavations: introduction', *Archaeol. Jnl.* 134, 1–10.

SAUNDERS, A.D. 1978. 'Excavations in the church of St Augustine's Abbey, Canterbury 1955–58', *Med. Archaeol.* 22, 25–63.

SAUNDERS, H.W. 1939. 'The first register of Norwich Cathedral Priory', *Norfolk Record Society* 11.

SAWYER, P.H. (ed.). 1976. *English Medieval Settlement.* London.

SCHIA, E. (ed.). 1979. *De Arkeologiske Utgravningen i Gamlebyen Oslo* II. Oslo.

SCHIA, E. (ed.). 1981. *Fra Christianias Bygrunn.* Riksantikvarens Skrifter 4.

SCHIØRRING, O. (ed.). 1980. *Ti Byer.* Projekt Middelalderbyen, Århus.

SCHOFIELD, J.A. 1981. 'Medieval waterfront buildings in the City of London', in Milne and Hobley 1981, 24–31.

SCHOFIELD, J.A. 1983. 'The Council for British Archaeology's Urban Research Committee, 1970–81', in Hinton 1983, 83–9.

SCHOFIELD, J.A. and T.DYSON. 1980. *Archaeology of the City of London.* London.

SCHOFIELD, J.A. *et al.* (eds). 1981. *Recent Archaeological Research in English Towns.* C.B.A. London.

SCHUYF, J. 1980. 'Moated sites in the Netherlands', *Report MSRG* 7, 33–9.

SERNING, I. 1979. 'Prehistoric iron production', in H.Clarke 1979b, 50–98.

SHEPPARD, P. 1980. *The Historic Towns of Cornwall: An Archaeological Survey.* Cornwall Committee for Rescue Archaeology.

SMALL, A. (ed.). 1965. *The Fourth Viking Congress, 1961.* Aberdeen University Studies 149.

SMITH, J.T. 1970. 'The evolution of the English peasant house in the late 17th century', *Jnl. Brit. Archaeol. Assoc.* 3rd series. 33, 122–47.

SMITH, T.P. 1970. 'The medieval town defences of King's Lynn', *Jnl. Brit. Archaeol. Assoc.* 3rd series. 33, 57–88.

SPEED, J. 1676. *The Theatre of the Empire of Great Britain.* London.

STAMPER, P. 1980. 'Barton Blount: climatic or economic change: an addendum', *Report MSRG* 7, 43–6.

STEANE, J.M. 1967. 'Excavations at Lyveden 1965–1967', *Jnl. Northants Mus. and Art Gallery* 2.

STEANE, J.M. and G.F.BRYANT. 1975. 'Excavations at the deserted medieval settlement at Lyveden', *Jnl. Northants Mus. and Art Gallery* 12, 2–160.

STENTON, F. (ed.). 1957. *The Bayeux Tapestry.* London.

STIESDAL, H. 1975. 'Moats in Denmark', *Report MSRG* 2, 13–14.

STRAKER, E. 1931. *Wealden Iron.* London.

STREETEN, A.D.F. 1980. 'Potters, kilns and markets in medieval Sussex: a preliminary study', *Sussex Archaeol. Coll.* 118, 105–18.

STREETEN, A.D.F. 1982. 'Potters, kilns and markets in medieval Kent: a preliminary study', in Leach 1982, 87–95.

TAIT, J. 1936. *The Medieval English Borough.* Manchester.

TATTON-BROWN, T. 1974. 'Excavations at the Custom House site, City of London, 1973', *Trans. London and Middx. Archaeol. Soc.* 25, 117–219.

TATTON-BROWN, T. 1975. 'Excavations at the Custom House site, City of London, 1973: part 2', *Trans. London and Middx. Archaeol. Soc.* 26, 103–70.

TAYLOR, C.C. 1972. 'Medieval moats in Cambridgeshire', in Fowler 1972, 237–48.

TAYLOR, C.C. 1974a. *Fieldwork in Medieval Archaeology.* London.

TAYLOR, C.C. 1974b. *Fields in the English Landscape.* London.

TAYLOR, C.C. 1975. 'Aspects of village mobility in medieval and later times', in Limbrey and Evans 1975, 126–34.

TAYLOR, C.C. 1978. 'Moated sites: their definition, form, and classification', in Aberg (ed.) 1978, 5–13.

TAYLOR, C.C. 1981. 'The role of fieldwork in medieval settlement studies', *Report MVRG* 29, 29–31.

TAYLOR, H.M. 1972. 'Structural criticism: a plea for more systematic study of Anglo-Saxon buildings', *Anglo-Saxon England* 1, 259–72.

TAYLOR, H.M. 1973. 'Archaeological investigation of churches in Great Britain', *Antiq. Jnl.* 53, 13–15.

TAYLOR, H.M. 1977. *Repton Studies 1: The Anglo-Saxon Crypt.* Privately printed.

TAYLOR, H.M. 1978. *Anglo-Saxon Architecture* III. Cambridge.

TAYLOR, H.M. 1979. *Repton Studies 2: The Anglo-Saxon Crypt and Church.* Privately printed.

TAYLOR, H.M. and J.TAYLOR. 1965. *Anglo-Saxon Architecture* I–II. Cambridge.

THÄLIN-BERGMAN, L. 1979. 'Blacksmithing in prehistoric Sweden', in H.Clarke 1979b, 99–133.

THOMPSON, A. 1979. 'St Nicholas in the Shambles', *Current Archaeol.* 65, 176–9.

THOMPSON, M.W. 1960. 'Recent excavations in the keep of Farnham castle, Surrey', *Med. Archaeol.* 4, 81–94.

THOMPSON, M.W. 1967. *Novgorod the Great.* London.

THOMPSON, M.W. 1968. 'The horizontal loom at Novgorod', *Med. Archaeol.* 12, 146–7.

TREUE, W. and K.GOLDMANN. 1966. *Das Hausbuch der Mendelschen Zwölfbrüderstiftung zu Nürnberg.* Munich.

TUMMERS, H.A. 1980. *Early Secular Effigies in England.* Leiden.

TURNER, H.L. 1971. *Town Defences in England and Wales, 900–1500.* London.

TYLECOTE, R.F. 1959. 'An early medieval iron-smelting site in Weardale', *Jnl. Iron and Steel Institute* 192, 26–34.

TYLECOTE, R.F. 1962. *Metallurgy in Archaeology.* London.

Bibliography

TYLECOTE, R.F. 1976. *A History of Metallurgy*. London.

TYLECOTE, R.F. 1981. 'The medieval smith and his methods', in Crossley (ed.) 1981, 42–50.

UCKO, P.J. (ed.). 1972. *Man, Settlement and Urbanism*. London.

URRY, W. 1967. *Canterbury under the Angevin Kings*. London.

VAN REGTEREN ALTENA, H.H. and H.J.ZANTKUYL. 1969. 'A medieval house site in Amsterdam', *Berichten R.O.B.* 30, 233–66.

VERHAEGHE, F. 1981. 'Medieval moated sites in coastal Flanders', in Aberg and Brown 1981, 127–71.

V.C.H. *NORFOLK* 1906. *Victoria History of the Counties of England, Norfolk* II. London.

VINCE, A. 1977. 'The medieval and post-medieval ceramic industry of the Malvern region: the study of a ware and its distribution', in Peacock 1977, 257–305.

VOGEL, V. 1983. *Ausgrabungen in Schleswig. Berichte und Studien I*. Neumünster.

VONS-COMIS, S.Y. 1982. 'Medieval textile finds from the Netherlands', in Jørgensen and Tidow 1982, 151–62.

WADE-MARTINS, P. 1980. 'Village sites in Launditch Hundred', *East Anglian Archaeology* 10.

WALKER, P. 1982. 'The tools available to the medieval woodworker', in McGrail 1982, 349–56.

WEST, S.E. 1970. 'Brome, Suffolk. The excavation of a moated site, 1967', *Jnl. Brit. Archaeol. Assoc.* 3rd series. 33, 89–121.

WEST YORKSHIRE 1981. *West Yorkshire: An Archaeological Survey to AD 1500*. Wakefield.

WHITLOCK, D. (ed.). 1955. *English Historical Documents* I. London.

WHITLOCK, D. (ed.). 1961. *Anglo-Saxon Chronicle*. London.

WIKLAK, H. 1960. 'The footwear of Gdańsk in the 10th–13th centuries', *Gdańsk Wczesnośredniowieczny* 3, 102–4.

WILLIAMS, A. and S.S.FRERE. 1948. 'Canterbury excavations, Christmas 1945 and Easter 1946', *Archaeol. Cantiana* 61, 1–45.

WILLIAMS, J.H. 1974. 'A Saxo-Norman kiln group from Northampton', *Northants. Archaeol.* 9, 45–56.

WILLIAMS, J.H. 1979. *St Peter's Street, Northampton*. Northampton.

WILSON, D.M. 1972. Review of *Danmarks Kirker, Århus amt*, in *Med. Archaeol.* 17, 204–5.

WILSON, D.M. 1976. 'Craft and industry', in Wilson (ed.) 1976, 253–82.

WILSON, D.M. (ed.). 1976. *The Archaeology of Anglo-Saxon England*. London.

WRATHMELL, S. 1977. 'Desertion, shrinkage and depopulation', *Report MVRG* 25, 52–4.

WRIGHT, S.M. 1976. 'Barton Blount: climatic or economic change?', *Med. Archaeol.* 20, 148–52.

ZBIERSKI, A. 1964. 'Port Gdański na tle miasta W X–XIII wieku', *Gdańsk Wczesnośredniowieczny* 5.

Acknowledgements

The author and publishers wish to thank the following for permission to reproduce the photographs:

Bayeux Museum 50; Bodleian Library, Oxford 41; British Library, London 63, 68, 69, 82; British Museum 32, 34, 42, 74, 78, back cover; Buckinghamshire Record Society 6; Carlisle Archaeological Unit 81; Committee for Aerial Photography, University of Cambridge 4, 7, 17, 18; Crown Copyright 44, 45, 47, 52; Deutsches Schiffahrtsmuseum, Bremerhaven 96; King's Lynn Archaeological Survey 75; Museum of London 66 (photo John Freeman Group), 91; Medieval Village Research Group 30; Norfolk Archaeological Unit 2; Stadtbibliothek Nürnberg 80; Phaidon Press Ltd 59; Rijksdienst voor het Oudheidkundig Bodemonderzoek, Amersfoort 89; W. J. Rodwell 33; University College London, Department of Medieval Archaeology 40; Weald and Downland Museum, Chichester 15.

Figs 1, 3, 23, 24, 43, 46, 49, 51, 53, 54, 64, 67 and 87 are the copyright of the author.
The line drawings in the text are by Peter E. Leach; the front cover illustration was drawn by Anne Searight.

Index

The references are to page numbers, except for the figures in italic, which refer to illustrations